Making Sense of War

Strategy for the 21st Century

Strategy is commonly referred to as the art of war, as the way in which military force is used to achieve political objectives. *Making Sense of War: Strategy for the 21st Century* provides a comprehensive and clear analysis of the complex business of waging war. Written in lucid prose, the book gives readers a thorough understanding of the key concepts in strategic thought, concepts that have endured since the Athenian general Thucydides and the Chinese philosopher/warrior Sun Tzu first wrote about strategy some 2500 years ago. It also examines the influence on strategic choice and military strategy of political, legal, and technological change.

Making Sense of War explains the nature and significance of such strategic choices as compellence and coercion, and such strategic principles as identifying and attacking the centre of gravity, seizing and holding ground, firepower and manoeuvre, and the knockout blow. It discusses the constraints and opportunities facing military commanders in the 21st century, and demonstrates that the formulation of military strategy will continue to be perhaps the single most important responsibility for senior security officials.

The book discusses strategy at every level of competition, employing a thematic approach and using historical examples from 500 BCE to the present. It offers original insights into the imperatives of military success in the era of asymmetric warfare, but remains readable for a wide range of readers.

Alan Stephens is a senior lecturer at the University of New South Wales Australian Defence Force Academy. Previous appointments include principal adviser to the Australian Federal Parliament's Joint Foreign Affairs and Defence Committee, official historian for the RAAF, contributing editor to *Asia-Pacific Defence Reporter*, military history commentator on ABC television, and RAAF pilot.

Nicola Baker is a lecturer on Strategic Studies at the University of New South Wales Australian Defence Force Academy. She has worked as a consultant to various Australian defence organisations and written on a range of military and strategic issues.

Making Sense of War

Strategy for the 21st Century

Alan Stephens and Nicola Baker

CAMBRIDGE
UNIVERSITY PRESS

CAMBRIDGE UNIVERSITY PRESS
Cambridge, New York, Melbourne, Madrid, Cape Town,
Singapore, São Paulo, Delhi, Tokyo, Mexico City

Cambridge University Press
The Edinburgh Building, Cambridge CB2 8RU, UK

Published in the United States of America by
Cambridge University Press, New York

www.cambridge.org
Information on this title: www.cambridge.org/9780521676649

First published 2006

A catalogue record for this publication is available from the British Library

National Library of Australia Cataloguing in Publication data

Stephens, Alan, 1944–.
Making sense of war: Strategy for the 21ˢᵗ Century
Bibliography
Includes index.
ISBN-13 978-0-52167-664-9 paperback
ISBN-10 0-52167-664-9 paperback
1. Strategy. 2. Military policy. 3. War. I. Baker, Nicola, 1956-. II. Title. 355.02

ISBN 978-0-521-67664-9 Paperback

Contents

Abbreviations

ATF	Australian Task Force
CENTO	Central Treaty Organisation
CIA	Central Intelligence Agency (US)
DCA	defensive counter-air
ECOMOG	Economic Community of West African States Monitoring Group
EBP	effects-based planning
ECOWAS	Economic Community of West African States
IAF	Israeli Air Force
ICBM	inter-continental ballistic missile
INTERFET	International Force for East Timor
ISTAR	intelligence, surveillance, target acquisition, reconnaissance
MAD	mutual assured destruction
MOOTW	military operations other than war
NATO	North Atlantic Treaty Organisation
NCW	network-centric warfare
NSC	National Security Council
ONUC	Operation des Nations Unies au Congo
OODA	observation-orientation-decision-action
PGMs	precision-guided munitions
PLO	Palestine Liberation Organisation
PSO	Peace Support Operations
QRF	Quick Reaction Force

RAF	Royal Air Force
ROE	rules of engagement
SACEUR	Supreme Allied Commander, Europe
SEATO	Southeast Asia Treaty Organisation
UNAMET	United Nations Mission in East Timor
UNAMSIL	United Nations Mission in Sierra Leone
UNFICYP	United Nations Force in Cyprus
UNITA	National Union for Total Independence of Angola
UNITAF	Unified Task Force
UNOMOC	United Nations Operation Mission in the Democratic Republic of the Congo
UNOSOM	United Nations Operation in Somalia
UNPROFOR	United Nations Protection Force

Preface

CHAPTERS one to six were written by Alan Stephens and chapters seven to ten by Nicola Baker. Both authors contributed to the Introduction and chapter eleven.

For their valuable comments on parts or all of the draft the authors wish to thank Robert Ayson, John Harvey, Christina Stephens, Craig Stockings, and Graham Walker.

Introduction

AT THE BEGINNING of the twenty-first century many long-standing strategic beliefs and practices appear to be under serious challenge, to the extent that some commentators have even declared 'the end of strategy'.[1]

There can be little doubt that the international environment is experiencing momentous change. The phenomenon of globalisation seems to be sweeping away national boundaries; the communications and information revolution is redefining who relates to whom, how, when and where, again on a global basis; and the 'market' may be superseding the 'nation' as the basis of statehood. Those secular pressures are undermining the nation-state but ironically contributing to a resurgence in the innately exclusive and often antagonistic phenomenon of nationalism. A new element of uncertainty and insecurity has been introduced by al-Qa'ida's stunning attack on New York City and Washington on September 11, 2001 and the rise more generally of the incidence of suicide bombing.

Simultaneously, the potential for the large-scale, theatre-level wars between nations that have shaped both the nature of conflict and the structure of defence forces for centuries seems to be diminishing. The Korean Peninsula, the Taiwan Straits, and Israel and the Middle East remain dangerous flashpoints, but major inter-state wars have generally been on the decline. Following a Cold War that ended with a whimper not a bang, the number of armed conflicts around the world between 1991 and 2003 decreased by more than 40 per cent, international crises declined by 70 per cent, and expenditure on international arms transfers fell by 33 per cent.[2] Europe's remarkable shift towards economic unity and political stability since World War II has been particularly significant, its recent progress tending to make us forget that, prior to 1945, it was the cockpit for most of the world's critical inter-state tensions.

Where major conflict does still occur, it often takes the shape of civil war. The extreme human rights abuses often associated with these wars present the community of states with a moral and legal dilemma: should they intervene to prevent suffering or should the sovereign rights of states – a key element of international law – remain paramount? Inter-state conflicts, which are now usually less brutal, present a related challenge, namely, how to reconcile a limited military commitment with the achievement of long-term political objectives. As General Rupert Smith has noted, a significant consequence of the failure to resolve these issues is that even when a military action has been concluded, the confrontation will continue; that is, competitors are likely to be in a 'condition of continuous conflict'.[3]

The early twenty-first century is also characterised by a diverse range of military capabilities and strategies. At one extreme is the United States of America, with its advanced technology, enormously expensive weapon systems, complex networks of people and machines, and doctrines of overwhelming force and paralysis, while at the other extreme are states which have no armed forces at all. In-between states have a wide range of capabilities, and some of those and some sub-state and trans-national groups have developed inventive ways to confound their high-technology opponents.

The first-world approach has produced the kinds of armies, navies and air forces that during the 1990s and the early years of the twenty-first century were overwhelmingly effective in defeating their conventional opponents in the Middle East. But the utility of massive conventional force appears to be becoming increasingly questionable for reasons that this book will explore.

At the start of the twenty-first century it is clear that a thorough understanding of the utility of force and a sound appreciation of strategic possibilities and constraints will be required if politicians are to navigate the changing security environment and military commanders are to match their operations to political objectives. Much of the literature on strategy and war has been too compartmentalised to provide a useful survey of ideas and practice or offer suggestions for the way forward. Some authors have concentrated on the approaches of particular theorists like Sun Tzu or Clausewitz, or on military commanders like Alexander, Napoleon, or Mao Tse-tung. Others have focused on combat power in the different environments of land, sea, air, the potential of the various services, and the merit of individual concepts such as the indirect approach or the knock-out blow. Despite the obvious current blurring of operational boundaries, much of the contemporary writing on strategy continues to assume that war can be analytically and practically divided into different levels and types of conflict and understood in isolation.

A more integrated, explanatory and prescriptive analysis is warranted and this book has been written with that objective in mind. Our approach has been to examine the subject through themes rather than single issues or eras, and through the influence of powerful agents of transformation as diverse as technology and social attitudes.

Strategy is best described as the bridge between policy and operations; that is, as a plan for the employment of military forces in pursuit of political objectives. Military force can be utilised in a variety of ways: to exert influence in the interests of stability and security, to deter attack, and to prosecute wars. The slogan 'shape-deter-respond' describes these approaches not as alternatives but as a necessary continuum to be implemented in sequence. This sequence reflects the long-standing strategic judgment that it is better to achieve objectives by shaping – by gaining and exploiting influence – than by relying on the more uncertain notion of deterrence; but that if shaping fails, it is better to deter than have to move into the decidedly uncertain arena of responding. In this book, we describe strategy and discuss its potential and limitations at all three stages.

A good strategy should always fit securely into the enduring ends-ways-means construct, in which 'ends' identifies the political objective, or, in current terminology, the effect we wish to create; 'ways' defines the method we choose to pursue that effect; and 'means' describes the tools available to implement that way. It follows that if either the means or the ways is inconsistent with the desired ends, then the strategic approach will be unsound, regardless of the available firepower, technology, doctrine, and organisational arrangements.

It is no use winning battles if they do not contribute in some way to the achievement of political objectives; conversely, some military defeats can make a contribution to eventual political victory. Depending on the circumstances, a particular outcome might be regarded as a win by some, as a loss by others. For example, in 480 BCE a small Spartan-led alliance of Greeks defending the mountain pass at Thermopylae against a massive Persian army was eventually defeated. However, the time won by the defenders enabled their countrymen further afield to prepare for war, and was crucial to the Greeks' ultimate victory. In the greater scheme of things, the Spartans' loss was the first step towards this goal.

Strategy is best appreciated by an understanding of its enduring themes and significant shifts, and through familiarity with its classical texts and the ideas of its most influential theorists and practitioners. That has been our aim in casting a wide historical net, in addition to enlivening abstract theory by way of tangible illustration. *Making Sense of War* has made extensive use of specific historical examples to illustrate general strategic issues. In some chapters our approach is thematic or ahistorical, in others we focus on the evolution of ideas and practices.

Chapters one and two on 'How to win' and 'Stove-piped strategy' are concerned primarily with theory, in the first instance by establishing the nature of strategy and discussing the essential logic of the ends-ways-means construct; and in the second by reviewing the major theories that have underpinned traditional Western approaches to war. Chapters three and four address the transition from theory to practice by examining traditional approaches to warfighting and tracing the translation of strategy into action through the fundamental expressions of manoeuvre and the application of force.

That translation is continued in chapters five and six, but in a more applied form. The mechanism of 'shaping' is discussed, describing the idealised concept of winning without fighting through the manipulation of influence; while the concept of 'strategic paralysis' examines the possibility of winning with minimum costs by stunning an adversary into inaction. The idea of defining desired outcomes in terms of effects rather than physical destruction, damage or conquest is an important addition to strategic thinking analysed in chapter six.

It is axiomatic that if we are to make good strategy, we must understand the nature of war, especially its political dimension. Chapters seven to nine are concerned with this essential window into strategic thought, particularly as it relates to the twenty-first century. Because of the emphasis on the present, these chapters inevitably refer frequently to the US experience. As the world's only military superpower during the 1990s and into the start of the twenty-first century, the United States has exerted an extraordinary influence on contemporary international relations in general, and on patterns of strategic behaviour in particular.

When states are contemplating war – before they make a decision to commit or finalise their military strategy – they must consider a whole range of political, diplomatic, social, economic and other factors. Chapter seven examines these issues, and some of the problems they pose for war planners and chapter eight extends the discussion to the evolving legal and enduring prudential constraints on strategy and war. Chapter nine explores the vexed issue of civil–military relations and the impact that debates over this issue have had on strategic flexibility and international security. Chapter ten examines the special challenges of armed humanitarian interventions and the lessons drawn from these types of deployments for the conduct of all future wars. Finally, chapter eleven discusses the nature of twenty-first century threats and distinguishes between what is likely to endure in strategy and what may have to change.

1

How to win
The nature of strategy

'STRATEGY' IS ONE OF those words that is used so freely and within such a wide variety of contexts that its meaning might seem confused. There was nothing confused about its original Greek form, *strategos*, which simply meant the art of leading an army. Today, however, so-called strategies are claimed for an enormous range of activities. Businesses have strategies to sell their products; sporting teams have strategies to overwhelm their opponents; individuals have strategies for saving money, managing their social lives, sorting their music collections; and so on. Uncertainty can also arise from the somewhat casual way in which military actions and weapons systems are often called strategic, regardless of the circumstances in which they are being applied. Air forces provide a case in point. For years any target which was distant from an attacking aircraft's homebase almost automatically attracted the label 'strategic'. Any bomber raid against an enemy's homeland was strategic, regardless of the target or the mission's objective, and an aircraft with four engines and capable of carrying a heavy bombload was always a strategic bomber. Conversely, smaller aircraft carrying lighter loads over shorter distances were routinely described as tactical, as were their missions, regardless of their objective. Yet from 1965 to 1972 during the US war in Indochina, 'tactical' single-engine F-105 fighter/bombers were used for 'strategic' missions in North Vietnam and 'strategic' multi-engine B-52 bombers were used for 'tactical' strikes in South Vietnam. Similarly, during the opening phases of the 1991 Gulf War, army 'battlefield' helicopters were used for long-range 'strategic' strikes. Those examples would suggest that 'strategic' should be defined, not by the target, platform, weapon or distance flown, but by the objective of the mission – by the effect being sought. They also illustrate the semantic confusion that has often accompanied the use of the noun strategy and the adjective strategic.

The notion that a military action should be defined by its intended outcome or, indeed, by its post-facto effect, gained widespread acceptance after the 1991 Gulf War, and is discussed in detail in chapter six. Despite that acceptance, the general use of the word 'strategic' remains casual. In particular, combat capabilities that are able to operate at long range or which can deploy rapidly, such as special forces, submarines, and heavy bomber and transport aircraft, still tend to attract the description strategic, while their shorter-range, slower counterparts are still described as tactical.

There is far less ambiguity over the use of the noun 'tactic', which is applied almost universally by defence forces to describe specific actions that have been developed in response to specific circumstances. In the main, those actions are related to the various ways in which combat forces might manoeuvre and apply firepower. For example, an infantry section will have learnt and practised scores of tactics dealing with offensive and defensive manoeuvre, laying down mutually supporting patterns of fire, setting up or reacting to ambushes, and so on; and fighter pilots and naval formations will have done the same in relation to the most commonly experienced combat contingencies in the air and at sea respectively.

This clear distinction between strategy and tactic is indirectly reflected in the recognition history has given to military commanders. The people whom history has acknowledged as great generals – men such as Alexander, Caesar, Napoleon, and Lee – have been viewed primarily as strategists: as people capable of developing successful over-arching concepts (strategies) for the conduct of wars and campaigns, without necessarily having to direct those strategies; that is, without having to translate them into tactics on the battlefield (while noting that many great generals have excelled in both strategy and tactics). We might infer from that observation that strategic thinking is a more abstract and intellectually demanding process than is the application of tactics, an inference which in turn perhaps partly explains the continuing ambiguity attached to the use of 'strategic'.

It is characteristic of the bureaucratic disposition of the political, diplomatic and military institutions with whose activities this book is frequently concerned that many of them have tried to precisely define levels of strategy, partly as a means of setting the limits of authority within their respective organisations. Thus, the highest level has been titled 'grand strategy' and is nominally the preserve of the most senior arm of government or institutional leadership. A grand strategy should, in theory at least, succinctly describe the key objective towards which all resources – human, diplomatic, economic, scientific, informational, social, industrial, military, perhaps even artistic, and so on – are directed in the national interest.

Within this construct of definitions, grand strategy is underpinned by a number of complementary or subordinate strategies which explicitly address such issues as economics, diplomacy, and military operations, noting that an extensive range of options can exist for each one of these and other potential ways of pursuing objectives. A military strategy, for example, might broadly endorse any one of a number of alternative approaches to protecting national sovereignty, such as deterrence, massive retaliation, terrorism, people's war, and pre-emptive strike. Because competing strategies are by definition interactive, grand and military strategies can be time-limited and, depending on circumstances, they can and do change, as shown by the allies' shifting objectives during World War II.

During the early stages of the war against Germany, the allies' relative military weakness and the Nazis' stunning battlefield successes left Great Britain and its few supporters with little option other than to try to survive. From September 1939 through to the Battle of Britain a year later, all that Britain's leaders could realistically aspire to achieve was to hang on, which they did. In other words, survival was the grand strategy, even if it was not officially defined as such, and all military actions should have been directed towards that end, as in fact most were. Hitler's invasion of the USSR in June 1941 forced the Soviets to join the allied cause, and Japan's attack on Pearl Harbor six months later brought the United States into the war. Both strikes proved disastrous for the axis. Japan's attempted knock-out blow failed to force the Americans to retreat into isolationism, as the Imperial war cabinet had hoped; and Hitler's dream of establishing a Slavic empire foundered in the brutal winter and dreadful fighting at Stalingrad, Kursk and other epic battles on the Eastern Front.

By the middle of 1943 the military/industrial balance had started to change and it was reasonably clear that the allies would eventually win, even though a great deal of sacrifice and hardship would still be required. Also by this time the full extent of the depravity of the German and Japanese regimes had become apparent, which prompted a fundamental change in the allied grand strategy. Now, the allies declared that nothing less than the unconditional surrender of their enemies would be acceptable. There were other objectives the allies might have settled on, such as: a conditional surrender under which the axis could have retained certain political rights; a negotiated settlement along, say, the territorial boundaries as they existed at the time; and so on. The allies' supreme objective, however, had become the complete destruction of the Nazi and Imperial Japanese political and belief systems, which meant that unconditional victory could be their only logical grand strategy.

There was a direct linkage between that grand strategy and its subordinate military strategy, as should always be the case. Because the allies believed Germany represented a more immediate threat to civilised states than did Japan, they decided they should beat Hitler first, a judgment which greatly influenced priorities for the conduct of campaigns, the choice of theatres of operations, and the allocation of warfighting resources. And there were subsets within the 'beat Hitler first' strategy, such as the decision to mount a major campaign in North Africa late in 1942 because the allies were not strong enough to land in strength in Europe at the time. When the Nazis capitulated in May 1945 the allies' strategic situation changed and so too did their grand strategic objectives, as they turned their full attention against Japan.

THE ART OF WINNING

Trying to place a commonly accepted meaning on words is important for the obvious reason of establishing understanding. On the other hand, attempts to construct immutable definitions can place boundaries around commonsense and entrench inflexible thinking, which in turn can inhibit progress. Rather than trying to impose descriptions that might not only be confusing but also self-limiting, it is often more constructive simply to acknowledge that a particular word will be used broadly and to accept a practical, uncomplicated interpretation.

Regardless of whether our interest is retail business, diplomatic negotiations, or war, the fact that we believe we need a strategy implies involvement in competition of some kind. And it is by accepting the notion of 'competition' that the most useful interpretation of strategy emerges. In its purest, most straightforward expression, strategy is the art of winning. It is a theory of victory; it is how to win.

The key to using this meaning is to have a clear understanding of what is, and what is not, meant by 'winning'. Like everything else in life, winning is relative. Consequently, once again, an open-minded interpretation of the concept is likely to be most useful as it will generate options and facilitate flexible thinking.

Almost invariably, if we believe we need a strategy either to shape or to respond to a particular set of events, our objective should be to achieve as much as possible from the available resources at the lowest affordable cost. This is a critical judgment because it implies that an end result perceived by one individual as a loss can be perceived by another as a win. The example of the Spartans at Thermopylae in 480 BCE has already been mentioned. In other words, depending on the point of view, a winning outcome might fall anywhere along a continuum of possibilities ranging from unconditional victory to acceptable defeat. The experience of the US-led alliance in Indochina between 1962 and 1975 further illustrates the point. By almost every military measure that alliance defeated its North Vietnamese and Vietcong enemies, inflicting huge human and material losses. But because of the politics of the situation all the North Vietnamese and Vietcong had to do to win was to not lose ('victory denial'). Their success in applying that strategy eventually precipitated the US withdrawal from Vietnam in 1973, which in turn was the precursor to the collapse of its puppet South Vietnamese government in 1975.

People employ strategies for victory at every level of conflict. The definition of strategy as being 'how to win' applies just as much to a hand-to-hand fight between two infantrymen as it does to the grand strategy endorsed by a government in pursuit of the ultimate resolution of a clash of national wills. The difference between those two examples is in the effect their outcome is likely to have on the overall conflict. Individual combat is a matter of life or death for those involved, but in modern war it is unlikely to have much effect, if any, on the greater scheme of things. Conversely, according to Biblical legend, when the Israeli shepherd boy David killed the Philistine giant Goliath in single combat, the entire Philistine army yielded the field of battle.

Which leads to the notion of 'strategic outcome'. A strategic outcome is one that has a profound effect on the event at issue. It is likely to be sudden, and will dramatically alter the state of affairs, the balance of power, who controls what, and so on. A strategic outcome represents the ideal end-state of any action, regardless of its size. In the extreme it may have the potential to achieve the objective in one decisive stroke, as in the case of David's well-aimed blow. The use by the United States of atomic weapons to end the war with Japan is another obvious if controversial example, but one of an entirely different magnitude. Depending on the circumstances, the application of force may not even be needed: simply deploying military units can generate a strategic effect via deterrence. During the early phases of the UN-sanctioned operation to liberate East Timor in 1999–2000, for example, there were concerns that extremist elements of the Indonesian government and army might escalate their armed opposition to dangerous levels. The deployment of Australian Defence Force F-111 bombers to a base in northern Australia within range of Timor and key Indonesian targets, and of submarines to the Timor Sea, sent a message of intent that reportedly was understood in Jakarta and which, together with complementary non-military coercive measures, made it easier for wise heads to prevail.

The point should be stressed: in the pursuit of a strategic outcome, the concept of operations and the means employed are details. What matters is the effect that a particular action generates. The methods used by the terrorist organisations Hamas and Islamic Jihad in their efforts to drive Israeli forces of occupation out of Palestinian-mandated territories provide a useful if grotesque illustration. Lacking the kinds of military capabilities commonly associated with strategic operations, such as highly trained professional defence forces and advanced technology, those groups adopted the systematic use of suicide bombers as their primary warlike activity, with the expectation of achieving their ends by creating terror throughout Israel. It is noteworthy that this method was formalised only after the leaders of Hamas and Islamic Jihad realised that the previously random acts of suicide bombers were in fact creating a strategic effect, partly through terror and partly through their exposure on the global media. That a single person with only several kilograms of explosive taped to their body could, in the prevailing circumstances, both represent a *strategy* and be a *strategic* weapon says a great deal about the nature of those words.

The mere existence of a strategy need not imply that its authors wish to pursue an immediate strategic outcome. On the contrary, as noted above, depending on the circumstances, an honourable defeat may satisfy the objective. Nor are the great majority of military actions, ranging from skirmishes between a handful of riflemen through to theatre-level campaigns involving tens of thousands of people and machines, likely to produce a strategic effect by themselves. But ideally every one of those actions should be relevant to the overall strategic objective.

In order to generate a strategic outcome, it is imperative that strategists identify both their own and their enemy's centre/s of gravity. Defined by the great nineteenth-century Prussian soldier and philosopher Carl von Clausewitz as 'a centre of power and movement . . . on which everything depends', there is no more powerful concept in strategic thinking than centre of gravity.[1] The suggestion that every protagonist will have one or more centres of gravity implies an essential focus for every strategic analysis and action, regardless of the level of conflict. Strategists and protagonists must be continually prepared to attack their enemy's centres and to defend their own.

Precisely what constitutes a centre of gravity is, of course, the crucial question. Is it the army? The leadership? The economy? Civilian morale? Does it vary between nations, cultures, eras? History is replete with examples of campaigns that failed because the wrong centres of gravity were attacked and protected, and with those that succeeded because one set of competing strategists got its centre-of-gravity analysis more or less right. The concept is so important that it will constantly recur throughout this book.

ENDS, WAYS, AND MEANS

The essence of any strategy, varying from, say, a small advertising campaign to a theatre-level military campaign, is the relationship between ends, ways, and means, in which 'ends' is the objective, such as total victory, conditional victory, stalemate, or victory denial; 'ways' is the form through which a strategy is pursued, such as a military campaign, diplomacy, or economic sanctions; and 'means' is the resources available, for example, people, weapons, international influence and money. If the ends-ways-means relationship is not logical, practical, and clearly established from the outset, then the entire campaign is likely to be at risk, or at the least seriously flawed. It is here that one of the best-known aphorisms in military strategy comes into play, namely, Clausewitz's conclusion that 'war is a mere continuation of policy by other means'. Clausewitz's seminal point is that ultimately war is a political act, and therefore every aspect of its conduct, including the development of strategy, must reflect the political dimension and must be designed to support the political objective. All activities undertaken in the pursuit of a strategy should be measured against that truism.

Translating that ideal into practice has not always been straightforward, especially in the modern era when it has become less common for a single individual to represent both the state and the military. Within liberal democracies, legislation invariably establishes the authority of representative civilian governments over the military, but it remains the case that in some states defence forces have enormous political power. Furthermore, elected representatives with vested interests, such as a large defence community or infrastructure in their home state, might promote parochial defence interests; while there can often be significant differences between the security policies promoted by a nation's defence department and by its state department, with the United States providing the obvious example. An argument might be made that the model which best observed Clausewitz's dictum was the one established in the USSR after the Bolsheviks gained power in 1917, when political commissars who directly represented the Communist Party's policy position were attached to all military units, to oversee decision-making and to ensure conformity with national (as defined by the Party) objectives. While that system was frequently dysfunctional during World War II, when the political and ideological demands of the commissars could conflict with battlefield realities, the ruthless manner in which it was enforced ensured an exceptional degree of policy unity.

The element of the ends-ways-means nexus most responsive to Clausewitz's maxim is the ends. Before embarking on any campaign – that is, before attempting to put any strategy into practice – the desired political ends should be determined. In other words there should be a clear understanding of what, in the prevailing circumstances, is meant by winning. This is the crux of Clausewitz's stricture. The mere achievement of an apparently satisfactory military result may be of little consequence if it does not support the ultimate political objective; or if, more probably, the desired ends have not been clearly identified. Few better examples can be found than US President George H. Bush's experience following Operation Desert Storm during the 1991 Gulf War.

The international coalition led by the United States against Iraq's Saddam Hussein achieved a remarkably quick and conclusive military victory, routing the ostensibly powerful Iraqi armed forces in only forty-three days with relatively few friendly casualties. Bush and his Administration had, however, thought little beyond the military operation. It was one thing to drive the Iraqi invaders out of occupied Kuwait, but the political question remained: what then?

In the event, when the coalition's commanding General, Norman Schwarzkopf, attended a hastily arranged meeting with his Iraqi counterparts to draft an instrument of surrender, he had almost no guidance from Bush regarding the required political ends. What was the envisaged post-war political form of defeated Iraq? How would that affect the balance of power in the Middle East? How would the numerous dissident groups in Iraq respond to Saddam's defeat? What did the coalition want to do with Saddam? How would other influential players react to US actions? Working in a political vacuum, Schwarzkopf was understandably uncertain and, as it happened, in the longer term, not surprisingly, unsuccessful. Within weeks of the war's conclusion Saddam Hussein was again dominating Iraq, and within a year was again perceived as a major threat to international security. Indeed, despite his army's humiliation in 1991, by the mid-1990s Saddam could with some justification claim to have won a political victory of sorts over the United States.

An even more unexpected outcome followed the second US-led war in Iraq in 2003. Having decided this time that Saddam Hussein's regime had to be forcibly removed, coalition military forces directed by the Administration of President George W. Bush (George H. Bush's son) took only weeks to crush the political and military apparatus of Saddam's ruling Ba'athist Party. Largely ignorant of Iraqi culture and social mores, this second Bush Administration had expected that military victory would be accompanied by a spontaneous outbreak of democracy and the installation of an Iraqi government favourable to Western interests. Instead, what followed was a campaign of attacks against US forces and urban terrorism, as many Iraqis who might have detested Saddam nevertheless resented even more the presence of Western invaders.

One of the reasons for President George H. Bush's vacillation in 1991 was his concern that if he forced Saddam and his minority Sunni supporters out of office, the balance of power in Iraq would shift to the majority Shi'ites, who might introduce a theocratic governance similar to that in neighbouring Iran, and which was hostile to US interests. Ironically, following his son's military victory but political failure, that is precisely what happened when the free elections that were held in Iraq early in 2005 returned a dominant Shi'ite government that increasingly began to reflect conservative Islamic values. Furthermore, it might also prove to be the case that the second US invasion of Iraq hastened Iran's efforts to acquire nuclear weapons, as protection against becoming a similar target of US military intervention in the future. And it is possible that the invasion convinced otherwise moderate Palestinians to vote the extremist Hamas party into power in January 2006.

The unsatisfactory end-states arrived at by both Bush father and son in their respective campaigns against Saddam Hussein also serve to illustrate the critical factors of context and time which must be taken into account when any desired end is defined. In each instance, the short-term objective of dealing with Saddam militarily was realised, but the implicit question of what to do about his legacy and the broader political situation in the Middle East in the longer term was not.

The example cited previously of the allies' grand strategy during World War II provides an equally informative case study, but in a positive sense. Plainly the long-term effect that the allies needed to create was to defeat the axis powers, but until about 1943 that was not militarily feasible; consequently, as noted, the desired effect was simply to survive. The implications of that decision were momentous. Among other things, they implied the abandonment, if necessary, of major allies and territories in the Pacific region, in order to achieve the immediate and over-riding objective of surviving in the primary theatre of Europe. That decision was seen as ruthless by some, but there is no doubt that within the context of the war it was the correct strategic objective for the time.

Suffice to say that if the desired ends of any proposed course of action are not clearly understood, realistic, timely, and situated within context, then the executing strategy will be either incomplete or likely to fail. The ineluctable relationship between ends and strategy was perfectly understood by one of the twentieth century's greatest soldier-statesmen, General George C. Marshall, who believed that if the objectives were correctly defined, then even a lieutenant – in other words almost anyone – could write the strategy.

'Ways' defines how a particular strategy is to be implemented; how, in broad terms, the ends are to be pursued. In World War II the allies and the axis both overwhelmingly relied on the application of military force as their way of trying to achieve their objective of unconditional victory, with other potential ways such as diplomatic negotiation and economic pressure playing comparatively minor roles. During the Cold War, by contrast, it was through the threat of force, expressed via the linked doctrines of mutual assured destruction and deterrence, that the United States and the Soviets both sought to contain each other's global influence and to avoid a nuclear holocaust. Incidentally, the fact that the representatives of warring ideologies not only shared a strategic objective but also cooperated towards that end, while continuing to engage in open hostility across a range of other military, economic and social fronts, would seem to confirm the suggestion that intellectual flexibility is a prime characteristic of strategic thinking.

Finally, the means are the resources needed to implement the chosen way in pursuit of the desired ends. The over-riding principle here is not to let one's ambition exceed one's grasp; that is, if the means to an end do not exist then the end is unrealistic. Matching ends to means is an art in itself. Notwithstanding the caution regarding over-ambitious ends, the fact remains that even ostensibly poor nations and organisations are likely to have a large array of means at their disposal. Suicide bombers have already been mentioned as a potent strategic weapon; other commonly available measures might include diplomatic pressure, the manipulation of international opinion, and exploiting a comparative advantage in a vital resource such as oil, timber, geography, or intellectual capital.

China and the United States provide instructive contrasting approaches to making the most of one's inherent military means. It should come as no surprise that from World War II through to the 1990s economically poor but population-rich China planned to rely on its vast pool of manpower as its means to drive any protagonists into a war characterised by mass, close-up fighting, and attrition. The United States' means, by contrast, have come to epitomise the Western way of war, in which a powerful economy and a broadly based education system have underwritten a reliance on overwhelming technological superiority and highly trained individuals, which in turn has facilitated the ability to fight with knowledge and precision, at a distance.

The fact that, in the past decade or so, China has begun to restructure its military forces to reflect its growing prosperity and rapidly improving technological base demonstrates that, like grand strategy, military means such as people, tanks, ships, aircraft, and computers can and do change. And when means change significantly, it is reasonable to expect that, sooner or later, the basic concepts through which strategists envisage using those means will also change. In the case of China, that would suggest a shift from an emphasis on old-fashioned attrition warfare towards a more contemporary model of conflict, such as that employed by the United States, a shift which, as it happens, seems to be reflected in recent Chinese military doctrine.

Troops in uniform and machines of war are only the most visible components of any set of military means. Logistics failure has brought just as many generals undone as has defeat on the battlefield. Napoleon Bonaparte's famous dictum that an army marches on its stomach remains valid, but today would also have to mention fuel, oil, ammunition, and spare parts for a vast and complex array of weapons systems. Even the tactically outstanding German General Erwin Rommel could not overcome the shortage of fuel for his mechanised units that in the end contributed as much to his eventual defeat in the North African desert in 1941 to 1943 as did the endeavours of the allies. And to take a more contemporary example, it is not by chance that most nations have been unable to develop and sustain an effective air force: the essential technological and scientific research elements of the means are generally too difficult to achieve and too expensive to sustain.

***

It is a military axiom that time spent on reconnaissance is never wasted. That maxim could be paraphrased for strategists. The time any decision-maker, from a president to a commanding general to a private soldier, spends on two critical strategic considerations will never be wasted. First, they must clearly understand what, in the prevailing circumstances, they mean by winning. And second, they must ensure that their desired ends are realistic, clearly defined, and consistent with political objectives; that the ways chosen to pursue those ends are feasible; and that the available means are suitable and sustainable. The importance of establishing and maintaining a logical relationship between winning and ends, ways and means cannot be overstated.

2

Stove-piped strategy
The schools of strategic thought

T HE STUDY OF strategic thinking traditionally has been conducted by dividing the topic by environment or nature into a number of schools of thought, the most common of which are the continental, maritime, air, nuclear, guerilla, and terrorist. One consequence of this has been a tendency for strategy to evolve within the mutually exclusive environmental stove-pipes of land, sea and air. But because advanced nations now almost invariably conduct warfare – and therefore the development of strategies and the planning of operations – with joint forces, which are intended to function as an integrated whole rather than as three distinct environmental entities, this approach has become somewhat artificial. The different mediums in which armies, navies and air forces operate may induce their leaders to adopt different tactics and to develop distinctive cultures, but ultimately all of those means must be applied through a common strategy to achieve the desired outcome.

Nevertheless, placing boundaries around a subject as complex as strategy is a useful way of keeping the material under control and assisting understanding. Furthermore, the fact is that until air forces started to appear in the early twentieth century, armies and navies generally conducted their operations separately; that is, genuine joint warfare scarcely existed. And the rise of terrorism as a preferred method of coercion has meant that, of the six schools, it at least can still be identified as a discrete method of operations, albeit one proscribed by international law. Consequently it is both useful and historically valid to examine key elements of the various schools separately, before discussing them from an integrated perspective that better reflects contemporary strategic practice.

CONTINENTAL STRATEGY

Because land operations have been the predominant form of warfare, the continental school of strategy has been the main focus of attention since the greatest military historian, the Athenian General Thucydides, wrote the original recorded account of a major conflict, *The Peloponnesian War*, during the fifth century BCE.[1] Thucydides' masterful first-hand report of the terrible conflict between the Athenians and the Spartans holds as many lessons today as it did 2500 years ago. His protagonists might have fought with swords and javelins rather than space-based systems and electronics, but his observations on the nature and morality of war, and on power politics, have not been surpassed.

While Thucydides was concerned primarily with the nature of human conflict, many other continental strategists have addressed themselves largely to the *form* of their business. In particular, they have examined at great length two central intellectual and practical challenges: how best to apply the available force against the enemy; and how best to close with the enemy to gain maximum advantage or to minimise any disadvantage inherent in the physical setting and the capabilities of one's own forces. This approach has been encapsulated in the aphorism 'firepower and manoeuvre'. Like Thucydides' observations, the importance of firepower and manoeuvre – or more accurately firepower and the manipulation of force – remains undiminished. It is fundamental to all of the so-called schools of strategic thought. Even a suicide bomber has to manoeuvre into position and then decide when to apply his firepower.

Most of the central aspects of solving the firepower and manoeuvre equation have become so well known as to be clichés, but this does not lessen either their continuing relevance or the achievement of those who first codified general solutions. For example, as far as manoeuvring or getting into position is concerned, practices such as deception, camouflage, surprise, timeliness, and so on, may all seem blindingly obvious, but that has not always been the case. Nor are those apparently self-evident practices invariably observed in the modern era, as demonstrated by the disastrous experience of the large Serbian land force that carelessly massed in open terrain during the war between the North Atlantic Treaty Organisation (NATO) and the former Republic of Yugoslavia in 1999, and was decimated by NATO strike aircraft. Similarly, the application of firepower usually follows well-established precedent regardless of the size of the forces involved: weapons should be matched to targets; it is usually preferable to fire along (enfilade) rather than across enemy lines; rates of fire should correspond to the level of threat; firepower can be used to facilitate manoeuvre; and so on. Some of the better-known continental strategists have made their reputations essentially by advocating specific models of firepower and manoeuvre. That this might incline some commentators to regard those individuals as tacticians rather than as strategists merely confirms the semantics associated with the word 'strategy', and should not be allowed to divert attention. Captain Basil Liddell Hart is the author of a large body of work on warfare, but he is often identified above all else as the codifier, first, of blitzkrieg, and second, of the indirect approach. The extent to which Liddell Hart can be credited with the emergence of blitzkrieg is debatable, but that does not matter here. What does matter is that by advocating techniques that closely coordinated the individual capabilities of armour, infantry and attack aircraft into a dynamic and fast-moving force, the authors of blitzkrieg developed a new and potent form of firepower and manoeuvre whose whole was considerably greater than the sum of its parts. In the right circumstances, such as the open fields of Poland, the Low Countries and France at the start of World War II, blitzkrieg as a general warfighting practice was for several years seemingly irresistible

If there are questions regarding the origins of blitzkrieg there is none regarding the indirect approach. Liddell Hart never claimed to have devised the concept, but he became its leading advocate through what is perhaps his best-known book, simply titled *Strategy*.[2] The indirect approach, too, appeared simple – once it had been brought to notice. The idea is, if possible, always to approach the enemy from an unexpected direction and in an unexpected manner. Alexander the

Great was one of the concept's first known practitioners, sometimes closing with enemy formations at an oblique angle, then suddenly swinging the line of his own forces around at the last moment either to outflank the opposition or to strike at its weakest point, or both.[3] In modern times one of the more spectacular examples of an indirect approach was provided by the theatrical US commander, General Douglas MacArthur, early in the Korean War. With his main force almost driven off the southern tip of the Korean Peninsula by rampaging communist troops, on 15 September 1950 MacArthur mounted an adventurous amphibious landing at Inchon, some 240 kilometres to the North Koreans' rear on the west coast. Now outflanked and with their supply lines cut, the enemy were forced to retreat up the peninsula as quickly as they had advanced down it.

One other case study of continental firepower and manoeuvre warrants attention for the insight it offers into the notion of strategy. The context this time is manoeuvre, and the commander at question is the architect of Germany's mobilisation plan for the start of World War I, Count Alfred von Schlieffen. Chief of the German General Staff from 1891 to 1906, von Schlieffen died in 1913 but his plan, somewhat modified, was implemented by his successor, General Helmuth von Moltke the younger. The Schlieffen/Moltke objective was to conduct a flanking attack against French forces through Belgium and the Netherlands, a plan which involved moving hundreds of thousands of men and their material to the frontline west of Germany in what would be, for the era, a remarkably short time. Only a small army would be held back in Germany to confront another potential opponent, the Russians to the east. Schlieffen's plan was a minor masterpiece of organisational precision and its author is widely recognised as a notable continental strategist. But that recognition perhaps rests on questionable foundations.

The general mobilisation of the German Army was authorised by Kaiser Wilhelm on 1 August 1914, a date which, as it happened, preceded his declaration of war against France by two days. Under Schlieffen and then Moltke, the general staff had spent years planning for this moment. Their organisation was astonishing. Two million men were mobilised and equipped, units were formed, and an enormous force was moved towards the Franco–Belgian border on hundreds of trains in accordance with a railway timetable of extraordinary complexity and precision. Regrettably for General von Moltke, after ordering the mobilisation but before declaring war, the Kaiser had a change of heart and decided that his armies should invade Russia to the east instead of France to the west. Moltke, aghast, would have none of that, telling the Kaiser that the complexity and internal momentum of his plan meant that, once put into effect, it could not be reversed. In a sense, therefore, World War I started in France rather than Russia because the German military commander could not or would not control the manoeuvre of his forces.

The initial deployment of the German Army proved irresistible, not only to the Kaiser but also to the French Army. In a remarkable achievement, the pre-planned phase of the Schlieffen Plan saw almost 1.5 million German troops moved to the front against Belgium and France within seventeen days. But Moltke then proved incapable of directing his troops. Communications were difficult and, remote from the front, Moltke often had little idea where his forces were. Out of touch and confused, he was unable to fully implement complementary manoeuvres intended to outflank the French Army. A fatal disconnection between one of his means (his communications) and a vital component of his way (the movement plan) had been exposed. After only six weeks of war Moltke was relieved of his responsibilities.

We might ask: were Schlieffen and Moltke strategists, tacticians, or merely glorified railway timetable clerks? And do such questions matter? The answer to the latter question at least is, yes, they do.

With the benefit of hindsight, the obvious disjunction in Schlieffen's and Moltke's thinking between ends, ways and means might suggest that they were at best tacticians – doers rather than thinkers – whose grasp exceeded their capabilities. Regardless of whether someone is hastily calculating a spur-of-the-moment response to an ambush by a small band of guerillas, or is preparing a massive invasion plan, he will only be dealing in strategy if his idea of how to win satisfies the logic of the ends-ways-means relationship.

Von Moltke's unhappy experience, caused at least in part by his preoccupation with process (*how* we do things) at the expense of purpose (*why* we do things), brings to mind the contribution of another noted continental strategist, the nineteenth-century Swiss General

Antoine-Henri Jomini.[4] Jomini's thinking was strongly influenced by his first-hand experience of the Napoleonic wars and presents a number of useful, if not necessarily universally applicable, observations. The nature of the manpower-intensive Napoleonic campaigns which Jomini observed understandably led him to emphasise the importance of massing with superior numbers, of taking the offensive, of attacking enemy vulnerabilities, and of seeking victory through one decisive battle as opposed to numerous minor battles. He also placed great emphasis on organisation and logistics; on what he called 'lines of operations'. Jomini believed that an army which had an interior line of operations – that is, a position between separated enemy forces – enjoyed a major advantage. So strong was his conviction that he was moved to assert inviolable principles of war derived from the concept.

It is through this preoccupation with form rather than purpose that the parallel with Moltke becomes evident. Jomini's dogmatic insistence that his principles of military organisation were immune from even the most dramatic technological developments is the main reason his relevance as a strategist has continued to decline with the passage of time.

MARITIME STRATEGY

The best-known writers on maritime power, the American Alfred Thayer Mahan and the Englishman Sir Julian Corbett, exerted a powerful influence on strategic thinking at the time their ideas held currency, Mahan just before the turn of the twentieth century and Corbett during its early decades.

Writing at the height of the competition between imperial powers for empires and wealth derived from colonial exploitation, and using the singular example of Britain as his primary guide, Mahan argued with some validity that sea power held the key to international dominance and, therefore, to economic prosperity. Complementary concepts such as the need to maintain control of the sea and the disproportionate effect derived from concentrating force and winning one decisive battle can be seen as reasonable extensions of his central argument.

Mahan's position was defensible at the time, and it remains true today that maritime trade is a major contributor to most developed economies. But his over-riding strategic notion – that there is an ineluctable link between sea power and national power – has not withstood the demise of overt imperialism, the march of technologies such as high-speed international communications and money transfers, and air transport, the rise of a new economy in which instantly transferable goods like intellectual property have assumed a superseding role, and the increasing globalisation of economies (which in a sense is a corollary of the demise of imperialism). In short, notwithstanding the continuing relevance of economic warfare as a general strategic concept, time has exposed Mahan's ideas as excessively parochial.

Corbett's thinking was more attuned than his predecessor's to the politics of conflict, and displayed among other things a superior appreciation of the interdependence of the individual environmental forms of military power, although his indifference to air power, despite the evidence of World War I, represents a major failure. In addition to demonstrating what was a relatively early understanding of the emergence of genuinely joint operations, at least between land and sea forces, Corbett made a number of thoughtful comments on some of the more abstract applications of coercion. Foremost among these was the emphasis he placed on the 'fleet-in-being', a concept which argued in favour of avoiding decisive actions in order to preserve one's fleet. A somewhat curious-sounding proposition at first glance, the idea is in fact subtle, especially for a navy whose fleet is apparently inferior to its enemy's. Rather than risking all on the decisive battle favoured by Mahan, Corbett argued that by preserving the fleet's integrity, and perhaps creating uncertainty about its location and precise strength, a commander could generate the classic strategic effect of deterrence, enhanced in this instance by a degree of flexibility in manoeuvre largely absent from comparatively slow-moving armies.

AIR POWER THEORY

Alone among the traditional schools of strategic thought, air power doctrine has from the outset had as its objective the rapid achievement of a strategic effect. The Italian Army General Giulio Douhet has been air power's most forceful advocate, to the extent that many regard him as more zealot or prophet than strategist, a judgment not without some validity.[5] Nevertheless, Douhet was correct in his conviction that the quickest and most effective way to win is to generate a strategic effect at the very beginning of hostilities. For Douhet, the way to that end was via a knock-out blow delivered against the enemy's true centre of gravity, which he defined as the ruling élite, the population, and the organs of government. The means through which that way would be pursued was air power, which would bypass purportedly strategically unimportant enemy armies and navies on its way to the enemy homeland to conduct stunning strikes with high explosives, incendiaries and gas. The end would justify the means as victory would be rapid and complete, thus avoiding the appalling stalemate and slaughter of the trenches that Douhet had witnessed in World War I.

Douhet deserves credit for the scope of his vision, but censure for his almost blind faith in technology on the one hand and his disregard for it on the other. Remarkably, for someone who was a science and engineering graduate, Douhet's use of technology as the foundation of his theories was excessively favourable when it suited him but superficial when it did not. For example, his assertions that bomber aircraft would almost invariably reach their targets, and that they would then drop their weapons with exemplary accuracy, could scarcely have been more misplaced, as the early years of World War II were to reveal. Nor did he pay anywhere near enough attention to the full range of the possible psychological effects of air bombardment, the assumed dire consequences of which were fundamental to his theory. There is an element of determinism to his thinking that is at odds with the nature of war, which must always respond to the march of science but which ultimately is an art.

Following the nuclear attacks on Hiroshima and Nagasaki in August 1945 that ended the war in the Pacific, many politicians and analysts believed that the very nature of national security had been permanently changed; that the atomic bombs had 'broken the continuity of military art' and that 'no strategy [was] worth the paper it [was] written on'. Events were to show that this was not the case, and in the ensuing decades many of the fundamentals of strategic thinking, as discussed in this book, have remained largely constant. At the same time, the 'bomb' dramatically expanded the dimension of a range of concepts because of its unparalleled capacity for destruction.

NUCLEAR THEORY

According to the eminent strategist Bernard Brodie, the United States' use of atomic weapons against Japan vindicated Douhet's advocacy of a knock-out blow delivered from the air.[6] But Douhet's interpretation of the knock-out blow never envisaged the shocking scale of death and destruction caused by the weapons dropped on Hiroshima and Nagasaki, and the evolution of nuclear strategies which followed the development of the 'bomb' proved to be a far more complex affair than was indicated by Brodie's early conclusion, especially once the USSR had successfully tested its own atomic weapon in 1949 and the process had become interactive between the United States and the Soviets. The problem was trying to fit a previously unimaginable level of destructive force into a rational strategic construct.

Massive retaliation was one of the earliest nuclear strategies, but its obvious inflexibility and implicit apocalyptic end-state were causes for strategic alarm rather than comfort. Efforts by US academics to devise a less extreme policy led to the promotion of such ideas as graduated deterrence, flexible response, and gradual escalation, the latter also known as incrementalism or risk strategy. The thinking here was that nuclear force would be applied in a calibrated, as opposed to an unrestrained, way.

But if massive retaliation was unfeasible, graduated deterrence, flexible response and gradual escalation were intellectually untenable. All three concepts implied the ability to manage the employment of nuclear weapons, so the central question became: could nuclear war be controlled?; and the answer from too many analysts was 'No'.[7] The suggestion that leaders would respond to a nuclear attack in a measured, carefully calibrated way was simply unsustainable. Confronting possible national annihilation, those leaders might find it difficult to resist the temptation to minimise their own losses by getting in first with a massive strike of their own. It is noteworthy that there seems to have been little interest in the USSR in these ostensibly more sophisticated concepts, with the viscerally deeply suspicious and, therefore, nervous, Soviet leadership subscribing throughout the Cold War to the notion of a single, massive, preferably pre-emptive nuclear attack.

The most credible nuclear strategy turned out to be mutual deterrence, a notion which eventually came to be known by the apt acronym of MAD, for mutual assured destruction. Within the surreal world of nuclear strategy, MAD in fact represented a logic of sorts by acknowledging that defence against the nuclear threat was impotent, and that only deterrence in kind could act as a counter. A fair case can be made that the concept of MAD was intellectually credible, and that for fifty years it underpinned the relative strategic stalemate that existed between the United States and the USSR, even though the two superpowers regularly came into indirect conventional military confrontation via various client states.

Inherent in any successful application of deterrence is the assumption that both protagonists are rational. This assumption applies with far greater force to the nuclear model than to the conventional weapons model. It is noteworthy that MAD thus far has apparently worked only because rational, state-based protagonists have been involved, originally the United States versus the USSR, and subsequently India versus Pakistan. Like other strategies before it, MAD may become redundant, in its case when irrational states or organisations acquire nuclear weapons, as they surely will.

Before discussing the final two schools of strategic thought, guerilla warfare and terrorism, brief mention should be made of some of the terminology which grew out of nuclear strategy, to illustrate the use of language as politics. Specifically, the euphemisms 'counter-force' to describe nuclear attacks against military formations and installations, and 'counter-value' for attacks on cities and civilians, are worrying even by the bizarre standards which sometimes characterise the intellectual dimension of warfare. The same observation can be made in relation to the use of 'denial' for attacks on military forces, 'punishment' for attacks on cities, and 'decapitation' for killing the enemy leadership. Euphemisms can be a rich part of language, but strategists should understand exactly what they are saying when they substitute such impersonal terms for such brutal, albeit presumably necessary, actions.

GUERILLA WARFARE

Guerilla, partisan or irregular operations have been a preferred mode of warfare of the weak against the strong for thousands of years. The practice draws on the ideas of the Chinese General Sun Tzu, and emphasises deception and surprise, and tactics such as short, sharp attacks against enemy vulnerabilities followed by rapid withdrawal. An epigram written by one of guerilla warfare's leading exponents, the twentieth-century Chinese revolutionary Mao Tse-tung, famously summarised the method: 'The enemy advances, we retreat; the enemy camps, we harass; the enemy tires, we attack; the enemy retreats, we pursue'. In what has been a classic guerilla tactic, Mao's armies exploited China's vast spaces to create time for themselves, the belief being that the longer the campaign lasted, the more likely they were to succeed. Time and space have generally been weapons that favour insurgents.

Mao translated theory into practice during the civil war in China between his communists and Chiang Kai-shek's nationalists from the 1920s through to the communists' final victory on the mainland in 1949. A feature of Mao's campaign, later diligently copied by other revolutionaries, was the observance of three distinct phases: win control of the countryside (strategic defence); isolate the cities (strategic stalemate); and, finally, capture the cities (strategic offensive). In the process of moving through those phases the revolutionary army would gradually shift from guerilla warfare to conventional warfare, a change with major implications for the structure of the fighting forces, with small, mobile, flexible units gradually being replaced by the conventional tactics and force structures of massed infantry formations supported by armour and artillery, and perhaps even air power, for the third and decisive phase.

As practised by Mao, guerilla warfare was more correctly known as 'people's war', the distinction arising from the circumstances prevailing in China in the first half of the twentieth century. Any armed force can employ guerilla tactics, and those tactics might simply be part of a larger campaign whose objective is, say, to remove the ruling élite while retaining the same form of governance. By contrast, people's war seeks to achieve revolutionary change in the state's political, ideological and economic apparatus. Perhaps ironically, the American War of Independence from 1775 to 1783 in which free American settlers successfully revolted against British rule fits the latter description. People's war was particularly suited to the period of Chinese history in which it was employed, the model's only subsequent notable successes being the victories won by Vietnamese revolutionaries against the French between 1946 and 1954 and then the United States and its allies from 1962 to 1975.

The observation that a strategic model can be time- and place-specific is an important one. Context is everything, and strategy is no exception. The small-scale revolutionary approach that worked for Fidel Castro and Che Guevara in Cuba in 1956 to 1959, for example, failed dismally in Bolivia only eight years later, ending when the faux-romantic figure of Che was executed in squalid circumstances by local authorities. By the same token, generally applicable characteristics might be identified within specific case studies. Thus, the protracted and psychological aspects of Mao's model, which were also critical in Cuba and Vietnam, remain evident in modern warfare, not least within the so-called asymmetric strategies used by Palestinians against Israelis in the occupied territories, and globally by a number of Islamic jihadist movements.

TERRORISM

Terrorism involves the systematic generation of fear as a means of coercion. Its use might be intended to achieve a specific objective, such as acquiring information or punishing certain groups or individuals, or to create a general level of dread and, therefore, to induce cooperation from the unwilling. By definition terrorism violates both the law of armed conflict and civil law. It is often linked to guerilla warfare, and is often used by irregular forces as their primary way of asserting control. For example, the methodical assassination of community leaders who do not support the particular cause has been a common practice for centuries. But we should note that terrorism has been a component of all kinds of strategies, including continental, maritime and air. Some commentators categorise as terrorism military actions from World War II, such as the Japanese Army's brutal treatment of civilians, the allies' bombing of German and Italian cities, and the sinking of civilian ships by German and Japanese submarine crews. At the least, there would seem to be a case to answer.

Nevertheless, in recent years the practice has been made distinctive through its growing use by otherwise marginalised groups as a way of pursuing a strategic effect. Facilitated by the ease and speed of global travel and communications, easy access to increasingly open societies, and the compelling psychological impact of mass media, terrorism offers a way for the weak to strike at the very heart of their stronger adversaries.

Terrorism is unique among the schools of strategic thought because it is aimed directly against civilians, that is, against non-combatants, among whom it is intended to create fear and uncertainty. A corollary of that definition is that any action against a member of a defence force who is on operational duty technically cannot be classified as terrorism. Plainly there will be areas of apparent contradiction should that meaning be applied too rigidly: for example, are we indulging in semantics when we describe the systematic torture, mutilation, or other extreme mistreatment of captured soldiers as war crimes rather than as terrorism? Or to use the opposite case, is the bombing of cities by uniformed aircrew a legitimate operation, or a war crime, or terrorism?

The cliché that one man's terrorist is another man's freedom fighter contains more than a grain of truth. Any number of elected governments have had their origins in organisations that openly endorsed or covertly applied terrorism as a way of overthrowing a regime, some of the more notable including Israel's first government in 1948, the African National Congress in South Africa in 1994, and Hamas in Palestine in 2006. Additional moral complexity is brought to this issue through the fact that, in recent decades, military operations mounted by the elected governments of Israel and the United States have killed thousand of civilians, probably more than the sum total of all of the various terrorist attacks such as September 11, 2001, Bali 2002, Madrid 2004, and London and Amman 2005, and those carried out by scores of individual suicide bombers, primarily against Western targets. It is important to appreciate the existence of such intellectually grey zones, and to be aware that the strict definition of terrorism applies only when civilians are the target.

Hijacked aircraft, machine-gun attacks in shopping centres, suicide bombers, car bombs and the like have all proven grimly effective in generating massive publicity and sometimes causing serious economic and social damage, for relatively cheap outlays by the perpetrators. Al-Qa'ida's terrorist attack on the World Trade Center in New York on September 11, 2001, rewrote the textbook on strategic effect.

There are also instances of institutional or state terrorism, in which the ruling élite has systematically cultivated fear as a way of controlling its own population. So severe, for example, was the repression deliberately applied by Joseph Stalin in the USSR in the late 1930s that the period is known in Soviet history as 'The Great Terror'. States may also choose to conduct international terrorism indirectly by harbouring perpetrators, or by supplying funds, training and weapons.

STRATEGIC GENIUS: SUN-TZU, CLAUSEWITZ, AND MACHIAVELLI

Most strategists who are identified with a particular environmental school of thought reveal a degree of parochialism; that is, their thinking understandably tends to be firmly located within their era and experience. No such criticism can be made of the two greatest scholars of continental strategy, the philosopher-generals Sun Tzu and Carl von Clausewitz. Unlike almost all other writers on strategy, Sun Tzu and Clausewitz analysed the challenge of how to win in terms that retain a general relevance, largely because their focus was on the character of war – on human will and strategy – rather than on machines and tactics. Sun Tzu's position is obvious from the very outset through the title of his enduring classic, *The Art of War*; while a central feature of Clausewitz's equally masterful opus, *On War*, is his commentary on the great commander, on the strategist who has a 'genius for war'.

Sun Tzu lived in China some time between 403 to 221 BCE.[8] As might be expected of someone who was a practitioner as well as a theorist of warfare, his thoughts on the subject were by no means confined to the abstract, presenting a great deal of wise advice on such practical matters as terrain, weather, logistics, economics, manoeuvre, and the application of force. Many operational practices that today are regarded as maxims for all kinds of conflicts were first identified and codified in *The Art of War*, including guidance on deception, when to advance and when to withdraw, when to attack and when to defend, the disposition of forces, discipline, and intelligence.

The elegant clarity with which those kinds of insights are presented in itself places Sun Tzu's work at the forefront of his field. But even commentary of that quality pales by comparison with his observations on the *character* of war – on the issues a true strategist must consider when determining how to win. Throughout Sun Tzu's book the central importance of the political and psychological facets of conflict are accorded the highest priority. More than 2000 years before Clausewitz's work achieved broad recognition as the primary source on the human dimension of strategy and war, Sun Tzu had revealed many of the central elements of both. Among his numerous compelling observations two are matchless: 'Know the enemy and know yourself'; and 'To subdue the enemy without fighting is the acme of skill'. Strategists contemplating the ends-ways-means construct at any intensity of conflict could not wish for more illuminating wisdom.

Which is not in any way to diminish the contribution of the Prussian Clausewitz (1780–1831), whose mastery of detail, comprehension of human behaviour both within organisations and when under the stress of combat, and peerless logic, have made him the most influential strategist of all time.[9] There are elements of Clausewitz's analysis which reflect his background as a participant in the particular circumstances that defined the Napoleonic wars, notably his enthusiasm for the 'exultation of the offensive', his belief that defence is stronger than offence (while noting that one nevertheless must attack to defeat the enemy), and his advocacy of mass and the great or decisive battle. Technological advances have since made all of those observations questionable at best. But other judgments have retained their brilliance.

Three in particular define Clausewitz's strategic genius. The first is his understanding that war ultimately is a clash of wills in which the objective is not the destruction of the enemy's physical courage, but his moral courage. The second is his formalisation of the notion of the centre of gravity as the pivot against which decisive force should be applied or, in the case of our own centres, be resolutely defended. And the third is his caution that the conduct of war will invariably be affected by 'fog' and 'friction', the former meaning confusion about what is happening, the latter that things will go wrong no matter how well we have prepared. Both insights are acknowledged in modern planning by the aphorism that no campaign plan survives first contact with the enemy.

Among other things, the concept of friction encompasses the possibility that actions we purposely take can generate unintended or unwanted outcomes, which in turn may lead to a situation worse than the one we originally confronted. The observation applies to any field of human endeavour, not just warfare. When, for example, Soviet President Mikhail Gorbachev tried to revive the stagnant USSR in 1987 through a program of modest political, economic and cultural restructuring known as *perestroika*, his intention was to preserve the Soviet Union by fine-tuning its socialist system; instead, his reforms opened a floodgate of pent-up frustration, energies and ideas that within six years had destroyed it. Unintended consequences do not come much more profound than that, and short of severe repression it is difficult to see how Gorbachev and his colleagues could have stopped what they had unwittingly started. In less momentous situations, we need continually to monitor the effects we have generated for unintended consequences and, if necessary, modify our actions, and perhaps our expectations, accordingly. Strategy is invariably competitive and interactive.

Centre of gravity and fog and friction are immensely important contributions to strategic thinking. But Clausewitz's counsel on war as an art goes much further than that. Mention has already been made in chapter one of his most famous axiom, that war is a continuation of policy or politics by other means. Two other observations on the nature of war stand out. The first is his belief that successful practitioners of any of life's special vocations require 'peculiar qualifications of understanding and soul'. Mere technical competence will never be sufficient, although it is likely to be a by-product of Clausewitz's psychological and intellectual demands: what is needed is a 'genius for war'. Among other things, the successful military strategist will possess physical and moral courage, a 'fine and penetrating mind', resolution, and calmness under pressure. Many individuals will display some of those qualities, but because war is not only a merciless arbiter but also is invariably subject to the 'province of chance', in no other profession are all of the elements of genius so necessary.

The second observation is that, above all else, war is a clash of wills. Killing the enemy and physically destroying weapons, buildings, the civil infrastructure, and so on, are in themselves meaningless acts of violence if they do not ultimately lead to the breaking of the enemy's will. In Clausewitz's words, violence is the means and the enemy's forced submission to our will is the objective. If Sun Tzu had had the opportunity to read Clausewitz, he might have qualified his eminent successor by noting that in many circumstances the *threat* of violence may be sufficient in itself to coerce an opponent and, therefore, to change his behaviour. While the caveat is valid, it does not diminish the force of the Prussian's exegesis on the essential nature of conflict and strategy.

No commentary on the clash of wills and the nature of strategists would be complete without reference to that consummate observer of political behaviour, the fifteenth- sixteenth-century Florentine diplomat and administrator, Niccolo Machiavelli. Adviser to the Medici and the Borgias among others, Machiavelli stands unrivalled as an interpreter of power politics.[10] The advice he offered would-be rulers and commanders in his small book *The Prince* has seen him stereotyped as history's ultimate ruthless opportunist, as a 'subtle and amoral pragmatist' for whom the ends always justify the means. The judgment is unfair. Machiavelli reported the world as he saw it, and drew his conclusions accordingly. That he was more interested in realpolitik than, say, redemption, does not necessarily make him personally immoral; it simply reflects his dispassionate interest in why some people win and others lose.

Too many men, Machiavelli wrote, see things as they would like them to be, not as they are, 'and so are ruined'. A would-be prince (for which also read president, general, captain) must be a realist, a fact of life which prompted one of Machiavelli's most famous observations: 'It is much more secure to be feared, than to be loved . . . [the prince who wants to win] must rely upon what he and not others can control . . . he need only strive to avoid being hated'.[11] Psychological domination, through deception if necessary, is fundamental to success: 'It will be well for [a prince] to seem and, actually, to be merciful, faithful, humane, frank, and religious. But he should preserve a disposition which will make a reversal of conduct possible in case the need arises.' Reflecting Sun Tzu's belief that 'all warfare is based on deception', Machiavelli argued that a flexible mind is especially important for generals and strategists, for while it may be 'hateful' to practise fraud in life generally, in the conduct of war it is 'praiseworthy and glorious'. Several hundred years later, his recommendation was couched in more practical terms by the brilliant and unpredictable Confederate commander, General T. J. 'Stonewall' Jackson, whose strategic philosophy was to 'always mystify, mislead and surprise the enemy'.

Just in case anyone had missed the point, Machiavelli translated the psychology of 'might is right' across to the physical domain by reminding his readers that 'all armed prophets have conquered and unarmed ones failed', a bleak conclusion that was to be echoed four hundred years later by Mao Tse-tung, who famously asserted that all political power comes from the barrel of a gun.

We do not have to agree with Machiavelli or conform with his observations on leadership, but any strategist who is interested in understanding how to win will ignore the Florentine's timeless analysis of power politics, competition, and human nature at his peril.

INTEGRATED STRATEGY

At the beginning of the twenty-first century, modern defence services are properly preoccupied with the application of joint force, as opposed to single-service air force, army, navy, or marines force. The idea of using the different environmental elements to complement each other is scarcely new, having been around at least since the first time land forces were embarked on ships to act as maritime-borne soldiers. But while marines have been an important component of sea power for thousands of years, it was not until the emergence of air power during World War I that joint warfare started to achieve the pre-eminence it now enjoys. Today it is highly improbable that an advanced defence force would plan any predominantly land- or sea-based campaign without some reliance on air power. Nor is it credible that a predominantly air campaign, such as the allies' combined bomber offensive against Germany in World War II or Operation Allied Force against the former Republic of Yugoslavia in 1999, could be conducted without the assistance at some level of soldiers and sailors. Indeed, the experience of Operation Iraqi Freedom in 2003 indicated that, rather than simply joint warfare, in which air, land and sea elements complement each other but still tend to fight separate, albeit coordinated, campaigns, advanced defence forces increasingly will fight *integrated* campaigns, in which the environmental elements will be combined as a single formation.

The point here is that the continuing rise of joint and integrated military power as a means will affect the way in which strategy is perceived. As organisations we hitherto have known as armies, air forces and navies increasingly work closer together, and as their enabling technologies similarly draw their means closer together (noting, for example, the emphasis now placed by surface forces on helicopters for manoeuvre and firepower, on a diverse range of rockets for indirect fire support, and on unmanned aerial vehicles for information), the traditional schools of strategic thought are likely to share a far greater degree of common ground. In particular, if geostrategic circumstances are favourable, all three are likely to regard the pursuit of a rapid strategic effect as their first-choice objective, an end which previously was realistic only within Douhet's air power construct, and which was technologically unfeasible for armies and navies, a constraint which helps explain the somewhat sequential and therefore narrow strategic perspectives of the Jominis, the Schlieffens and the Mahans. By contrast, the insights of the greatest thinkers on surface warfare, Sun Tzu and Clausewitz, are likely to flourish in the evolving integrated strategic environment.

Regardless of the circumstances, the true strategist will always take four factors into account when analysing a situation and before deciding on a course of action. The first is that strategy is concerned with how to win; the second is that winning is a relative concept; the third is that strategy should not be constrained by environmental boundaries; and the fourth is that if the objective is legal, moral and realistic, and if the means match the ends, then the strategy is likely to look after itself.

3 Traditional warfighting concepts and practices
What strategy has been

THE DISTINGUISHED MILITARY HISTORIAN Sir Michael Howard once pointed out that 'theory must constantly pass the test of reality'. Howard's wise caution applies equally to strategy. A strategy that has not been applied and tested in conflict might be regarded as theoretical, as unproven against the benchmark of operations. This chapter is concerned with applying the test of reality, with measuring theory against practice, and it will do so by examining the ways in which military forces traditionally have tried to win – that is, by examining what strategy has been.

Reduced to its basics, warfighting comprises two elements: a test of strength, and a clash of wills. The ultimate objective of any military confrontation, regardless of its scale, is to break the enemy's will to fight: to achieve a measure of dominance over his thinking such that he concludes the costs of continued resistance will exceed those of submission; or that he simply loses the spirit to resist. Ideally this outcome would be attained without a shot being fired, through the psychology of coercion, an approach which can take many forms, including physical intimidation, economic measures, diplomatic pressure, and adverse publicity. Countless prospective blood-letting has been prevented by the dynamics of deterrence.

However, because we do not live in an ideal world, psychological coercion might not always be an acceptable option for one or both protagonists. Or, for reasons that sometimes seem impenetrable to others, one side might be determined to pursue military action, regardless of the circumstances. The war between the

United Kingdom and Argentina over the Falkland Islands in 1982, for example, has been likened to two bald men fighting over a comb, such was the questionable logic of the conflict; nevertheless, once the Argentine occupation of the islands became known, it was soon obvious that British Prime Minister Margaret Thatcher would take whatever military measures were necessary to dislodge the invaders.

Once fighting has started, sooner or later one side is likely to come to the realisation that if the hostilities continue it is likely to lose more than it will gain, which is exactly what happened for the Argentineans in the Falklands. At that stage, if the losing side's decision-makers are rational, they will begin to sue for a cessation of open hostilities. Not all decision-makers are rational, of course, and it simply may not be possible to 'get inside the mind' of, say, a fanatical opponent who is determined to fight to the death for his cause. Allied soldiers in the Pacific theatre in World War II were shocked when they discovered that, for many of their Japanese enemies, surrender was not an option. Or to take a grand strategic example, by late 1944 it was clear that Germany was going to lose World War II, and that Hitler's refusal to capitulate could only lead to still greater destruction of his already physically and morally devastated nation, which is precisely what happened.

Alternatively, it may be the intention of one side to annihilate the other regardless of any other considerations, even, perhaps, their opponents' express wish to end hostilities, an attitude which reflects a depressing aspect of human nature but which has been a consistent feature of our behaviour. Bluntly put, we know that we will have permanently got inside the mind of someone whom we have killed. The history of warfare is replete with instances of the take-no-prisoners attitude, a merciless mindset from which few, if any, races, cultures or religions can claim exclusion.

COMPELLENCE AND COERCION

It is the perceived imperative to influence the thinking and, therefore, the behaviour of others that has provided the impetus for the development of military strategy.

Regardless of the circumstances in which a strategy is conceived, it will either have to *compel* or *coerce*, or apply a combination of both, if it is to achieve its objective. Generally speaking, compellence is associated with the manifest *application* of force, and coercion with the *threat* of physical violence or of some other disagreeable pressure.* A number of associated concepts explain a good deal about each of those expressions. For compellence, they include the decisive battle, the knock-out blow, unconditional victory, the presumed necessity to seize and hold ground, and the balance between the offence and the defence; while for coercion, they include deterrence ('winning without fighting'), and risk, which between them incorporate the subsets of gradual escalation, incrementalism, and mutual assured destruction. Underpinning every strategy, regardless of whether it emphasises compellence or coercion, or a combination of both, is perhaps the most vital consideration in any strategic determination, the notion of the centre of gravity.

There can be a fine dividing line between an action one observer sees as compellence and another sees as coercion. Overlapping characteristics and the somewhat abstract nature of the topic combine to make labelling an inexact business at best. But it is precisely those characteristics that make the practice of categorising useful, because without it our attempts to manage the subject matter and to understand the major issues can become confused. As long as we appreciate its limitations, labelling can be a useful aid to comprehension. With that caution in mind, the remainder of this chapter discusses the key concepts derived from the routinely expressed human desires to compel and to coerce.

THE DECISIVE BATTLE

The notion of the decisive or great battle provides the starting point for discussing compellence, first, because it represents a long-standing strategic conviction, and second, because it establishes a useful framework of associated warfighting maxims and practices within which

---

* To say that the use of the words 'compellence' and 'coercion' within the discipline of strategic studies has sometimes been opaque would be an understatement. One early source which examines the distinction (and with which this book differs) is Thomas C. Schelling, *Arms and Influence* (New Haven: Yale University Press, 1966).

a broader discussion can take place. Since strategy is the art of how to win, a decisive battle, by definition, must bring the protagonists directly to their objective: the victor is likely to achieve his immediate military ends within a short time. Even better for the winner, until about the nineteenth century, a decisive battle frequently promised political as well as military victory, because the head of the state was often also the head of the army. Clausewitz was a strong advocate of the great battle, believing that the destruction of the enemy's army was the 'leading principle of war', and that only 'great and general battles' can produce momentous results.[1] It is immeasurably preferable, he argued, to achieve one overwhelming victory than to plan for a series of minor and perhaps strategically inconclusive successes, a viewpoint subsequently endorsed in relation to naval warfare by his sea-power counterpart, Alfred Thayer Mahan.

Prior to the emergence of the modern nation-state system, absolute rulers like pharaohs, kings, emperors, tsars and tribal chieftains tended to embody within their persons the instruments of national power such as armies, navies, treasuries, religion and the law. Consequently, because the head of state was also likely to be the commander of the army, the defeat of that army might mean the collapse of the realm. Napoleon's final defeat by Wellington at Waterloo in 1815 perhaps provides the classic example, to the extent that to say someone has met his Waterloo is now an aphorism for a lost cause in any field of endeavour. Representative examples of other battles that seem to have simultaneously changed the course of wars and the fate of nations include the Greek fleet's defeat of Xerxes' Persians at Salamis in 480 BCE, William of Normandy's invasion of Britain at Hastings in 1066, the Japanese Combined Imperial Fleet's destruction of the Russian Baltic Fleet near Tsushima in 1905, and the Royal Air Force's victory over the Luftwaffe in mid-1940. There are many other instances of apparently decisive battles.

If a leader were confident that victory in an impending, potentially decisive battle was likely, and if such a victory would satisfy his definition of winning, then the action would be consistent with his strategic objectives. If, however, his immediate ambitions were set at a more modest level, perhaps even as low as not losing, then the prospect of having to fight a decisive battle would seem strategically unsound. A ruler whose authority rested in large part on his army was usually keenly aware of the likely dire consequences should that army cease to exist. Furthermore, while the concept of the great battle may have had considerable force from antiquity up to about the period of the Napoleonic wars, in more recent times it seems problematic. The issue is politics, and the essential connection between ends, ways and means.

The gradual separation of the powers of the state from the person of the ruler has been a feature of world affairs since 1215, when rebellious English noblemen forced King John to relinquish certain rights of the absolute monarch, a concession formalised in the Magna Carta. The process has been slow and it remains far from complete, as evidenced by the many dictators who have held power in the twentieth and twenty-first centuries: Joseph Stalin, Adolf Hitler, the Shah of Iran, Fidel Castro, Nikolai Ceaucescu, Saddam Hussein, Ferdinand Marcos, Robert Mugabe, and many more. Nevertheless the trend is clear, and the likelihood that a so-called decisive military battle might lead to a conclusive political victory, which was feasible but by no means certain when Clausewitz lived, has become increasingly remote.

As noted, Clausewitz's endorsement of the great battle as a key strategic concept rested in large part on his conclusion that the destruction of the enemy army was the leading principle of war, because the army de facto embodied the national will. No more powerful illustration of the fallacy of this generalisation as it might apply to the modern world exists than the Tet Offensive mounted by Vietnamese communist armies in early 1968. Named after the Vietnamese New Year period with which it coincided, the offensive saw North Vietnamese and Vietcong forces launch a massive series of coordinated attacks against most major South Vietnamese cities. After being initially caught off-guard, the US-led opposition fought back and inflicted terrible casualties on their enemies. The Vietcong in particular were decimated, to the extent that some commentators believe they never recovered before the war ended seven years later.

In strict military terms the United States and its allies undoubtedly won a major victory. However, the sheer intensity and brazenness of the communists' strategy – the effects of which were watched nightly on television by millions of Americans – sent shock waves through the United States. Savaged in battle and with a major component of their army devastated, the communists nevertheless scored a stunning political victory from which US policy in Indochina never recovered.

President George W. Bush's invasion of Iraq in March 2003 provides a no less illuminating insight into the relationship between the decisive battle as the way, and the political component of the ends. Few more overwhelming military campaigns have been fought than the six-week rout of Saddam Hussein's army by a US-led coalition. So brief and one-sided was the engagement, which centred on a dramatic dash from Basra to Baghdad by the coalition's ground and air forces, that to all intents and purposes it can be regarded as a single battle. In military terms it was utterly decisive, prompting President Bush to claim in May that 'major combat operations in Iraq have ended'. Yet over the ensuing months the security situation in Iraq deteriorated alarmingly as insurgents reverted to guerilla tactics that made a mockery of Bush's assertion. As was the case with the Tet Offensive, the disconnection between the militarily decisive battle and the desired political ends was comprehensive.

Vietnam in 1968 and Iraq in 2003 repeated a profound military and political dynamic that has been evident at the least since the Franco–Prussian War of 1870 to 1871. And that is, defeating a nation's armed forces no longer necessarily equates to achieving a political victory. As Michael Howard has pointed out, even when the entire French regular army was captured following the siege of Metz in October 1870, the conflict continued for another five months as a people's or guerilla war.[2] In other words, regardless of the outcome of any so-called decisive battle, a nation is beaten only when its population capitulates.

Finally, there is the practical difficulty of identifying in advance whether an imminent engagement might or might not be decisive. The point is not facetious. It was all very well for Alexander to crush Darius at Guagamela in 331 BCE and thereby assume control of his kingdom; for William to defeat Harold at Hastings in 1066 and do the same; for Wellington to defeat Napoleon at Waterloo in 1815 and effectively put an end to the French dictator's First Empire; for the Japanese to rout the Russians at Tsushima in 1905 and for the first time assert the superiority of the Asiatic over the European; and so on. The fact remains that such examples are the exception rather than the rule. Furthermore, many battles have been fought which commanders believed beforehand would be decisive, or which historians initially described as decisive, but which were subsequently revealed to have been of little strategic or even military utility, just as there have been many battles which were not regarded as decisive at the time but which were later recognised as such.

Even before the fighting began, the Royal Air Force's heroic defence of the United Kingdom in the northern autumn of 1940 was being characterised as the impending Battle of Britain, and in the years since then it almost invariably has been described as one of history's decisive military engagements, as an epic victory won by the RAF against the odds and by the narrowest of margins, which prevented the Nazi invasion of the United Kingdom and thereby saved liberal democracy in Europe. Yet careful scholarship has shown that the odds were never that long, and that the RAF was stronger at the end of the battle than it was at the beginning.[3] Moreover, even if the RAF had faltered, the Nazis would still have had to face the might of the largely intact Royal Navy had they tried to cross the English Channel, a challenge far beyond the comparatively modest means of the *Kriegsmarine*.

On the other side of the coin, the consequences of the battles of the Coral Sea and Midway in mid-1942 were not entirely appreciated for a considerable time. Effectively the same action but conducted over a month and a distance of some 4000 kilometres, those battles smashed Japanese naval air power. From then on, Japan's grand strategy for territorial conquest in the Pacific was unachievable and its ultimate defeat likely. But it took many months before that outcome became apparent to the allies. In other words, the US Navy had won a decisive battle with profound political implications without fully realising it.

None of the foregoing is to suggest that there is no such thing as a decisive battle or that the concept has no place in strategic thinking. But it is to suggest that the linkage between the concept and any desired political ends is more complex and tenuous than is sometimes believed; additionally, it can be very difficult to determine in advance precisely how an engagement that is perceived as potentially decisive will contribute to our assessment of what we need to do to win. If this conclusion seems obvious to many readers, it has not been so to many generals.

The notion of the decisive battle brings with it a number of associated warfighting theories and maxims. Three are especially noteworthy: the idea of the knock-out blow, with its implication of technology as strategy; the perceived imperative – at least within armies – to seize and hold ground; and the objective of unconditional victory.

THE KNOCK-OUT BLOW

Decisive victories of the kinds achieved by Alexander, William and Wellington, which effectively dismantled the enemy's governing structure, might reasonably be described as knock-out blows. The idea, if not the exact terminology, has always had currency. Classical history routinely records instances in which victorious armies immediately translated military triumph into political form. Thus, Thucydides reported the destruction of the Melian polity in 416 BCE. Following the battle between the grossly mismatched opponents ('this [will be] no fair fight' the Athenians had warned their opponents), the Melians were forced to surrender unconditionally. The Athenians then put to death all the men of military age and sold the women and children as slaves.[4] By any measure it was a knock-out blow of merciless proportions.

Central to the notion has been the capacity to strike rapidly against an enemy's perceived centres of gravity, such as his governing structure, major population centres, and sources of food and wealth, which in turn implies the ability to conduct very long-range operations. Suitable transportation and mobile strike-forces have been the key, which was why powerful navies which could appear unexpectedly at great distances from their homebases were for centuries the most potent expression of the knock-out blow. A fair case can be argued that the Athenians' greatest asset during the Peloponnesian War in the fifth century BCE was their mighty navy, with its innate ability to outflank and to strike unexpectedly. And as shipbuilding technology improved, great empires – Portuguese, Dutch, Spanish, British – were based in large part on the capability of their navies to apply force directly at the right place, sometimes on the far side of the globe.

The constraints of geography have always made it more difficult for armies to pursue a knock-out blow, without making it impossible. Great flanking campaigns, such as those mounted by the allies at Gallipoli in April 1915 and in North Africa in November 1942, have been mounted partly in the hope of creating a crucial breakthrough, if not necessarily bringing a quick end to the war. But those kinds of operations typically demand an enormous logistics effort – the North Africa landings involved some 436 ships – which almost by definition denies speed of action.

Some commentators have asserted an alternative land model in the form of the deep battle doctrine developed by Soviet Marshal M. N. Tukhachevsky when he was attempting to reform and modernise the Red Army in the 1930s. Drawing on the work of his contemporary V. Triandifilov, Tukhachevsky's doctrine envisaged coordinated formations of infantry, cavalry, aircraft and mechanised units attacking the entire depth of the enemy defences simultaneously. Rapid, successive operations in depth against the enemy's fighting forces, and his support bases and lines of communications, would deny the enemy the opportunity to regroup and recover. Tukhachevsky was a brilliant innovator, but his purpose here was not so much to achieve a knock-out blow as to harness emerging technologies such as tanks, aircraft, and two-way radios to new thinking, as a means of re-establishing an offensive war of manoeuvre as the dominant factor in combined unit (infantry, armour, artillery, air) tactics. Among other things, Tukhachevsky was seeking to overcome the relative immobility that trench warfare and mass killing weapons like artillery and machine guns had imposed on battlefields since the time of the American Civil War.

It was no coincidence that a number of German officers who closely analysed Tukhachevsky's ideas subsequently were among the architects of blitzkrieg. When the Nazis applied that doctrine to overwhelming effect in Poland, the Low Countries and France during the early months of World War II, the result was not a knock-out blow but a series of breakthrough battles, in which sequential victories eventually led to the desired end. For all of blitzkrieg's early successes, it nevertheless remained a linear process, which in turn implied that any attempted knock-out blow was likely to be hostage to geography. As it happened, that proved to be precisely the case when the German high command tried to repeat the process in the USSR a year later, in mid-1941. Despite an initial series of stunning victories and breath-taking progress towards the perceived Soviet centre of gravity and the focus of Hitler's intended knock-out blow, Moscow, German forces ultimately simply could not sustain the momentum needed to carry them all the way from the border to the Soviet capital, falling some sixty kilometres short. And once the Nazis had been stopped, the Red Army's sheer weight of numbers, ruthless acceptance of casualties, and Russia's brutal winter, reprised the crushing defensive power that in 1812 had destroyed the French dictator Napoleon.

Notwithstanding its long history, the concept of the knock-out blow had to wait until the rise of air power in the twentieth century to experience its strongest expression. Two factors contributed in equal parts to the doctrine's enhanced currency: first, the wish shared by statesmen, civilians and soldiers never again to experience the slaughter of the trenches that had characterised World War I; and second, the unique qualities of the aeroplane, especially its capacity for high-speed, long-range manoeuvre, which seemed to give the doctrine technological credibility. The technology of flight extended the battlefield to an extent never envisaged by Clausewitz and the strategists who preceded him, by seeming to expose previously immune vital targets deep within the enemy's homeland. Total warfare could now be waged immediately against an entire nation, the objective being the rapid destruction of the national will. Contiguous armies and navies would simply be ignored by overflying bombers on their way to attack true strategic targets.

At the risk of over-simplification, the main point which statesmen, strategists and military leaders drew from air-power theories was the belief that civilian morale would be fragile and national infrastructures vulnerable in the face of irresistible strikes from the sky. During the years between World War I and World War II the idea of air power played a dominant role in international affairs and predisposed politicians and airmen in the United Kingdom and the United States in particular towards strategic bombing as a potentially war-winning force. More than that, the belief in a rapid knock-out blow from the air appeared to offer an alternative to the squalid slaughter in the trenches, a perception which, in the peculiar logic of warfare, was comparatively humane.

In their efforts to translate theory into practice, air-force planners developed sophisticated operational techniques and targeting theories, with staff members from the US Army's Air Corps Tactical School, for example, promoting the idea of large, fast, self-defending bombers flying in formation deep into enemy territory to make knock-out blows against 'national organic systems'. Targets would be 'carefully selected as keystone industries on which the enemy's whole economic structure depended'.[5]

Years after the event, the extent to which the allies' bomber offensives against Germany and Japan achieved their objective remains contentious. While the offensives ultimately brought the axis war economies to their knees, they did so, not with a rapid knock-out blow, but with campaigns of attrition which, ironically, most resembled an aerial version of the trench warfare they were supposed to make redundant. And although the offensives made everyday life wretched for civilians in both target countries, national morale was never fully broken. It might be claimed that at the very end of the war the atomic bombs dropped on Hiroshima and Nagasaki fully realised the concept of the knock-out blow, an argument that was made by one of the twentieth-century's leading strategic thinkers, the American Bernard Brodie.[6] Perhaps; but the appalling death and destruction those attacks caused was inconsistent with the knock-out blow's conceptual origins as an alternative to mass slaughter, and is at odds with contemporary laws of armed conflict.

Nor did the heaviest bombing campaign in history, the air offensive conducted by the United States in Indochina from 1965 to 1972, achieve anything like a quick, clear-cut outcome, even though its final throw of the dice, Operation Linebacker II in December 1972, was brief and brutally effective. Swifter, more focused results were achieved from the air offensives conducted by US-led forces in the wars in Iraq (1991 and 2003), the former Republic of Yugoslavia (1995 and 1999), and Afghanistan (2001 and 2002), but none would merit the descriptor knock-out blow.

During those and other air campaigns, planners have had to take many complex factors into consideration, but none has been more challenging than targeting. The central question from World War I onwards invariably has been: in order to create the desired strategic effect, which targets should be attacked, and how? The histories of World War II and Vietnam reveal that in those conflicts the question was never properly resolved, yet the campaigns continued, in the one case for almost six years, in the other for even longer.

We might wonder whether the architects of those putative knock-out blow campaigns were seeking to compel or to coerce their opponents, whether they fully appreciated the distinction, and whether they matched their means and ways to their desired ends. Obviously the atomic attacks against Japan were intended to compel, which they did, but, as noted previously, this can scarcely serve as a model for future planning. Coercion campaigns have been even less certain, as illustrated by the Combined Bomber Offensive from 1943 to 1945, which with its initial focus on the German population's morale was intended to be coercive, but which through its eventual destruction of cities and industries should be categorised as compellence. Subsequent US campaigns in Vietnam from 1965 to 1972 and Iraq in 2003 demonstrated in starkly different ways that the pursuit of a knock-out blow through coercion can be exceedingly complex and difficult.

During the United States' bombing offensive against North Vietnam, targeting confusion was exacerbated by cultural confusion, with US planners tending to impose their first-world values onto the enemy's third-world social and economic system. Any attempted knock-out blow by definition must be aimed at high-value targets, and plainly that was not the case here. The problem was compounded when, in a curious transfer of strategic concepts, campaign planners searching for alternatives tried to adapt the nuclear strategy of gradual escalation to their use of conventional weapons.

Also known as risk strategy, gradual escalation as attempted against North Vietnam used high-explosive bombs instead of nuclear weapons, and was applied against an opponent who had no capacity whatsoever to retaliate in kind. The intention was to subject North Vietnam to carefully managed, gradually increasing levels of risk, with risk being defined by the intensity of the attacks and the amount of pain North Vietnam was prepared to accept. Should a particular series of attacks fail to coerce North Vietnam's leaders into modifying their unacceptable behaviour, the level of pain would be ratcheted up, and so on.

The rationale behind this theory had been explained in a different context by the American nuclear strategist Thomas Schelling, who argued that, in order to be effective, coercive violence must be anticipated (the parallel with terrorism is noteworthy).[7] Thus, according to the logic of the strategy, at some stage the communists would anticipate that the level of pain – the risk – they were taking would exceed any gains they might make. That was the theory, anyway. In practice, the incremental/risk strategy attempted against North Vietnam achieved mixed results and, like its predecessors, the bombing campaign remains a contentious subject.

Three decades later, the air campaign that was part of the militarily successful US-led invasion of Iraq in 2003 formalised a new approach to the search for a knock-out blow, through its discrete program of decapitation attacks against the Iraqi leadership.

Decapitation in various forms has always been a feature of warfare, having been most commonly expressed through attempts to kill opposing leaders and their inner circle. Superficially appealing because of its intimation of a quick and permanent resolution of the clash of wills, political assassination has in fact been a dubious proposition. In Russia in the late nineteenth century, for example, scores of tsarist officials were assassinated by members of a naïve student-based revolutionary movement, the Narodniks, to little effect, as replacements were quickly found and state-directed repression was intensified. Similarly, by late 2005, four years after the terrorist attacks on New York City and the Pentagon, some 75 per cent of al-Qa'ida's senior leadership at the time of the operation reportedly had been captured or killed, yet terrorism continued to flourish. Apparently more than thirty new terrorist groups had emerged and over 100 000 new combatants had joined the jihadists' cause.

Redefining the challenge has resulted in some limited success in recent years. The description of leadership has been expanded to include command-and-control systems, support groups, and personal wealth, with two objectives: first, to stop leaders from directing their armed units and communicating with their citizens; and second, to break their will. Using that model, decapitation operations conducted against Saddam Hussein in 1991 and 2003, and against Slobodan Milosevic in 1999, contributed to the success of the broader campaigns. But decapitation was unable to precipitate regime collapse by itself. Campaign directors found it difficult to achieve the degree of operational surprise usually needed to locate and kill leaders who are constantly on the move; enemy communications systems had built-in redundancy and were hard to disrupt; concern over possible collateral damage constrained some targeting strategies; and any psychological effects of strikes against the ruling regime seemed slow to emerge and were hard to assess. In short, decapitation did not deliver a knock-out blow.

With its reliance on advanced technologies that few nations possess, the concept of the knock-out blow contains more than a hint of technological determinism. It is tempting to conclude that the Western powers, especially the United States and the United Kingdom, have pursued the knock-out blow, not because they have necessarily believed it to be conceptually credible, but simply because they could. In other words, they have been substituting technology for strategy. None of that is to deny the concept's manifest theoretical appeal and apparent potential, but it does question the relationship that has existed between technology and a mature expression of the ideas needed to translate hardware into an intellectually sustainable strategy.

Substituting technology for ideas can be seductive. To start with, the process can relieve uncertain planners of the sometimes worrisome task of thinking. And all other things being equal, the side with the technological edge in warfare is likely to prevail. Examples abound of battle-winning technologies which one side had and the other did not, from the horse, to the crossbow, to gunpowder, to the machine gun, to night-vision goggles, and so on. The human spirit may be a warrior's fundamental weapon, but it is unlikely to prevail during, say, a frontal assault by riflemen into a storm of machine-gun fire. Additionally, it is much easier to buy guns, aircraft, ships, computers and the like than it is to develop individual skills and foster superior ideas. But technology can never be sufficient in itself. For example, history has seen few better-equipped yet more inept military forces than those of the Shah of Iran in the 1970s and Saddam Hussein in the 1990s. Regardless of its form – firepower, information, platforms, whatever – technology alone can never answer the challenge of strategy.

A carefully harmonised combination of technology and ideas may have given rise to a muted version of the knock-out blow in recent decades, in the form of so-called strategic raids, in which a decisive effect is sought through a precise, clearly circumscribed, time-limited operation. Examples might include Israel's 1976 Entebbe raid and 1981 strike against the Iraqi nuclear reactor at Osirak, the United States' 1986 attack against Libya's President Moammur Gaddafi, and al-Qa'ida's 2001 air strikes against New York City and Washington.

Notwithstanding the concerns mentioned above, the concept of the strategic raid might also have a place for decapitation operations, with the United States' attempts to assassinate Saddam Hussein, his sons and other members of the Ba'athist hierarchy with air strikes during Operation Iraqi Freedom in 2003 perhaps serving as a prototype. The Israelis have certainly pursued the concept vigorously, most notably with the killing of Hamas leader Sheik Ahmed Yassin by a helicopter gunship in March 2004. Yassin's death seemed to serve Israel's interests in the short term at least, as it reportedly prompted other Hamas principals to go into hiding and to stop using traceable communications such as cellular telephones, thereby limiting their ability to manage terrorist operations. There is also evidence from conventional warfare that units that lose 25 per cent or more of their leadership within a finite period become ineffective.

There are arguments for and against decapitation. On the one hand, Israeli officials argue that assassinating enemy leaders undermines terrorist organisations and reduces the possibility that their own citizens will be blown up by suicide bombers. Furthermore, the use of small numbers of precision weapons and the targeting of specific individuals both punishes those believed to be primarily responsible for acts of aggression and minimises collateral damage. And when the target is someone like Saddam Hussein, decapitation seems to offer the promise of a strategic outcome. On the other hand, assassination carries serious legal and ethical implications, especially when a formal state of war does not exist between the protagonists. Nor is it clear that decapitation is ultimately effective. Killing people like Sheik Yassin might well derail an organisation's schemes in the short term, but new leaders usually emerge and may be as bad or worse than their predecessors. Thus far there is little evidence to show that decapitation leads to long-term solutions.

Following the kidnapping and murder of eleven Israeli athletes by Islamic extremists at the 1972 Olympic Games in Munich, a revenge campaign was conducted by Israel's secret service, Mossad. Over the next few years, individuals believed to have been associated with the crime were tracked down and clinically assassinated. According to a then-member of Mossad, the future Prime Minister Ehud Barak (who was personally involved in some assassinations), Israel's intention was 'to strike [against] terror . . . [to] break the will of those who remain alive'. Based on that objective and the incidence of anti-Israeli terrorism since then, Mossad's campaign could only be judged a failure.

It is not clear whether decapitation represents an instance of technology driving ideas – of doing something because we can, not because we should – or whether it is a legitimate and viable operational concept. That concern should not, however, be allowed to divert attention from the potential for precision raids against lawfully determined enemy centres of gravity to achieve rapid strategic effects.

SEIZE AND HOLD GROUND

With its promise of a swift, decisive and, therefore, relatively humane outcome, the theory of the knock-out blow represents an idealised expression of the decisive battle. The contrast with the second notable warfighting doctrine arising from the notion of the decisive battle – the time-honoured army compulsion to seize and hold ground – could scarcely be more pronounced. The impulse to seize and hold ground as a tactical warfighting reality, and as a strategic given, is as old as warfare itself; indeed, for land forces, it has been not so much a doctrine as an article of faith, whose rationale is apparently so obvious as to require no explanation.

Few tactical factors are more important to a soldier than the lie of the land. High ground is usually preferable to low ground; ground hidden from observation is safer than open ground; only by dominating ground can a population be controlled and lines of communication sustained; the capture of a particular location might in the right circumstances achieve a strategic effect in itself; and so on. And there is the self-evident truth that human beings depend utterly on land for their existence. We nevertheless need to understand that, as is the case with many seemingly sacrosanct strategic beliefs, attempts to translate ambitions into outcomes can generate a range of unexpected and deceptively complex issues. In this instance, the most important are related to strategic objective, mass, and attrition.

Because armies primarily move on a two-dimensional surface, they have customarily campaigned by working their way through a linear sequence of objectives, some of which may have no strategic value. It would, of course, be simplistic to suggest that every attempt to seize and hold ground should invariably satisfy a superior strategic logic. There could be a wide range of opportunistic but nonetheless compelling reasons for wanting to occupy a certain piece of land that may of itself be irrelevant to the objectives of the overall campaign, but which promises short-term advantage, such as offering a superior position from which to launch the next manoeuvre, or providing access to shelter or food. It is a fact of life that continental operations almost invariably must remain responsive to the realities of geography, regardless of any other consideration. Put simply, what this means is that in order to arrive at, say, ultimate objective 'D', land forces, unlike sea and air forces, will first have to occupy, however briefly, waypoints 'A', 'B' and 'C'. Progress through those points and across the intervening terrain is commonly characterised by extended campaigns involving a great deal of manoeuvre and numerous engagements, and may eventually culminate in a climactic finale – in an ostensibly decisive battle.

When Alexander the Great set out in 334 BCE to expand his empire, he very reasonably started at the beginning, at the border of his Macedonian homeland, and worked his way progressively eastwards through Asia Minor, Persia, and India. Similarly, when the allies began the liberation of Europe in 1944 they came ashore at Normandy, one of the closest landing points to their base in England, and fought their way across France and the Low Countries to their ultimate objective of Germany. Unlike their air and sea counterparts, the allied armies had little option other than to progress sequentially.

Exceptions can be found, primarily when outflanking manoeuvres are attempted, often with airborne parachute landings or amphibious assaults, to insert forces rapidly behind existing enemy frontlines or to establish a new frontline. Douglas MacArthur's landing at the rear of the North Korean Army near Inchon in September 1950 provided a spectacular example of the former, while his 'island hopping' campaign in the Southwest Pacific Area in World War II, when some enemy strongholds which stood along the line of his advance from Australia to Japan were simply bypassed, represented an equally effective instance of the latter. Such examples are, however, the exception rather than the rule. The history of land campaigns is predominantly one of sequential operations.

At the same time, like every other strategic notion, the perceived need to take and hold ground should be questioned, not simply accepted. When the ends-ways-means relationship is being established before an action is initiated, then regardless of whether that action is going to be a major campaign or a potentially decisive battle or an isolated firefight, the fundamental nature of war should never be forgotten. Ultimately war is a clash of wills and, like any other military operation, the mere taking of ground need not of itself represent an end or a desired effect, just as it will not necessarily break an enemy's spirit. Ends should never be confused with ways.

The emphasis modern armies continue to place on seizing and holding ground as an end in itself – as automatically representing a strategic objective – can perhaps be attributed to a redundant obedience to Clausewitz. But circumstances have changed since the Prussian formulated his treatise. When Clausewitz analysed strategy in the early nineteenth century it was reasonable to argue, as he did, that the destruction of the enemy's army was the highest objective of warfare, because in that era the army often embodied the national will. From that, it followed that the most effective model of combat would be one predicated on the annihilation of soldiers and their machines. This was a model in which the enemy's subjugation to our will was to be involuntary (compellence – he has no choice) rather than imposed (coercion – he has the option to concede), and it favoured the conduct of sequential operations leading to decisive battles, both of which in turn implied heavy casualties.

A similar kind of logic is evident in the now outdated definition of mass commonly associated with the Clausewitzian version of warfare. That definition was based on the numbers of soldiers in the opposing forces, with many being better than few.

Mass was a prime consideration in Napoleonic times, the American Civil War, World War I, the Russian Civil War, the Spanish Civil War, World War II, the Korean War, Vietnam, and the Iran–Iraq War. However, in today's era of rapid long-distance manoeuvre and precision weapons, the nature of mass has changed, in the following respects at least: a large, mediocre army is likely to be defeated by a small, high-quality army; there is no point in having vast numbers if those forces are not where they are needed when they are needed; and in the right circumstances technology can overwhelm mass, as in the case of precise long-range firepower from artillery, surface-to-surface missiles, and air-to-surface weapons applied against an exposed army. Long-range precision weapons and rapid manoeuvre have redefined the meaning of mass.

And this leads to the topic of attrition. The high level of attrition that is almost invariably but not exclusively associated with seizing and holding ground and mass warfare has become an unacceptable method of pursuing objectives. The US-led war in Indochina from 1962 to 1975 was a turning-point.

Vietnam stands as an object lesson in strategic confusion. The US cause was uncertain and the issues often unclear. The succession of South Vietnamese governments that US military power propped up were corrupt, fragile, and of dubious legitimacy, and many indigenous military units were incompetent and unwilling to fight. At the time the US commitment was starting to grow in the early 1960s, some senior US officials were largely ignorant of the country: of its customs, its culture, its values, its history, even its location.[8] As late as 1965 President Lyndon B. Johnson still had not articulated a coherent strategy for the conflict he was in the process of escalating. Not surprisingly, combat operations came to reflect that lack of policy direction. The result was another instance in which form was substituted for strategy.

Under the pedestrian leadership of General William C. Westmoreland, US and allied forces eventually adopted a strategy of search and destroy as their broad approach to defeating the communist army (which consisted of Vietcong and North Vietnamese soldiers) in South Vietnam. Search and destroy amounted to a series of limited duration, large-scale operations into communist-dominated territory, mounted from vast, secure – and, therefore, culturally isolated – US base camps. The intention was to demolish enemy strongholds, capture supplies, cut lines of communication, encourage surrender, and kill troops and their supporters.

If this particular version of attrition warfare had been related to the objective circumstances in Vietnam and to some over-riding strategic goal – to some clearly defined, desired, credible higher political effect – it might have been appropriate. In practice, search and destroy was operationally questionable, culturally insensitive, and strategically irrational. The alleged comment that 'we have to destroy this village to save it', a grotesque sentiment of uncertain origins, came to define the US approach to the war, together with Westmoreland's notorious response to a media question about high Vietnamese casualties: 'They're Asians, and they don't really think about death the way we do'. Search and destroy's most telling effect was to alienate many of the South Vietnamese civilians whose interests it was purportedly serving.

Additionally, reacting to the all-pervasive quantitative analysis of operational activities that was then in vogue in the Pentagon, and which was directed by Defence Secretary Robert McNamara and his immediate staff, nicknamed 'the whiz kids', US field commanders began to use statistics, first, as a measure of achievement, and second, as a de facto strategy. Numbers started to become ends in themselves as daily lists of 'achievements' were reported from Saigon back to Washington: so many bridges destroyed, so many food and weapons caches captured, so many villages pacified and, most perniciously, so many enemy troops killed in action.

Given the strategic lacuna at the highest level of government and McNamara's managerial passion for quantifying war, it was almost inevitable that ambitious field commanders would start to inflate the figures in their reports. Worse still, those figures, especially the daily reporting of the number of communists who had been killed in action, came to be seen as an indicator of progress. Just as technology had been substituted for strategy during the allies' bomber offensive in World War II, so counting body bags was substituted for strategy in Vietnam. The US experience in Indochina stands as a case study of strategic confusion.

Before concluding this discussion of the concept of seizing and holding ground and its hitherto defining characteristics of mass and attrition, two final observations should be made, the first concerning alternative models of land operations, the second the notion of unconditional victory.

Continental strategy has been a dynamic field of study for centuries, so it should not be surprising that military professionals have continued to seek innovative alternatives to the long-standing inclination simply to seize and hold ground through a series of sequential operations. The US army officer Robert Scales, for example, has proposed a combined arms methodology in which armies 'would not need to occupy key terrain or confront the mass of the enemy directly'.[9] Implicit in Scales' concept is the assessment that in many circumstances it will be preferable either to destroy an enemy's assets, or briefly but decisively to strike against one vital point, rather than routinely try to occupy and seize his territory. Under Scales' model, doctrinally and technologically advanced land forces would use fast-moving air and surface vehicles to make rapid and unexpected manoeuvre one of their primary characteristics. They would also work as an integrated whole with air strike-forces, with the lead element at any one time being decided by the enemy's disposition. Should the enemy concentrate, he would be identified and attacked with precision weapons launched from air platforms, operating at standoff distances. Should he disperse and go to ground, not only would he negate his own ability to concentrate force, but he also would leave himself vulnerable to attacks by numerically and qualitatively superior land forces exploiting their rapid manoeuvre capabilities. Prototypes of this kind of operation were evident on occasions during the US-led invasions of Afghanistan in 2001 to 2002 and Iraq in 2003.

Incidentally, in addition to challenging conventional wisdom, General Scales' concept represented one response to a rapidly growing characteristic of modern warfare, the dispersed or non-linear battlefield.

Up to and including World War I, armies and navies almost invariably lined up opposite each other before clashing front-on; indeed, one of the hallmarks of a great commander was his ability to bring his inherently slow-moving, massed forces together in the one place at the one time, in order to achieve maximum concentration. Battlefields were defined by the frontline, with the competing armies deployed on either side, and along which most fighting took place. World War I's Western Front is perhaps the best-known example. Flanking manoeuvres were, of course, a feature of this form of warfighting, but they were usually conducted not to disperse the fighting but rather to gain a battlefield advantage by outflanking the enemy's existing frontline. Even in World War II, by which time the ability to manoeuvre had been enhanced by an order of magnitude, theatres tended to be defined by lines, such as the Western Front in Europe and the Eastern Front in the USSR. The linear approach to engaging the enemy was largely followed in Korea in the early 1950s, and by the operationally inept forces of Iran and Iraq in the 1980s.

But during the US war in Indochina in the 1960s and 1970s, fighting in South Vietnam was characterised by distributed force concentrations and, therefore, by distributed battlefields. Vietcong and North Vietnamese soldiers could and did appear anywhere, from rice paddies to jungles to cities, throughout the length and breadth of the country; and their opponents could and did seek to engage them where they found them, rather than along any defined line. Whereas previously strikes behind enemy lines and outflanking manoeuvres had been the exception, now they were the norm. In subsequent campaigns in the Middle East, the Balkans and Central Asia, the non-linear model was the dominant form of land-force disposition and manoeuvre.

A radical alternative to the seize and hold ground mentality and the linear approach to (nominal) land operations was demonstrated during Operation Southern Watch, a largely unheralded but remarkable campaign conducted over Iraq from August 1992 to March 2003. Southern Watch was mounted against Saddam Hussein's government in response to its breaches of United Nations resolutions, and involved the successful enforcement of a no-fly zone for all Iraqi aircraft in the area south of latitude 33° North, a vast space which was blockaded by NATO air forces flying primarily from Turkey and off aircraft carriers in the Persian Gulf. There is little doubt that, if necessary, the air quarantine could have been extended to include major vehicular surface movement. In effect, air forces operating from their homebases occupied about one-third of Iraq's surface territory.

General Scales' concept of operations and Operation Southern Watch have their conceptual and practical limitations, arising in the one instance from the constrained size of a land force that could be rapidly airlifted into a contested area, and in the other from the tactical shortcomings of not having people on the ground. But they both make the point that we can expect continual challenges to conventional wisdom, of all varieties. At the same time, reality will demand that defence forces retain the capability to seize and hold ground. But that capability should only be exercised when it is relevant to the desired ends.

Few more professional military operations have been conducted since World War II than the occupation of Phuoc Tuy province in Vietnam by an Australian Task Force from 1966 to 1971. But within days of the ATF's withdrawal, the Vietcong had resumed full control of the province. Because the ends had been incorrectly defined by the US strategists running the war, the way – in this instance, the idea of territorial domination – was also incorrect. Like every other strategic consideration, the physical occupation of ground has no immutable strategic authority.

UNCONDITIONAL VICTORY?

Unconditional victory is sometimes assumed to be an automatic consequence of decisive battles, or of total as opposed to limited war. The term carries no qualifications: it means what it says; namely, that the victors can impose on the vanquished whatever terms they may choose. For defeated nations, in classical times that might have meant the massacre of all males and the destruction of the polity; in

World War II it meant the occupation and radical political and social reconstruction of Germany and Japan. But while perhaps superficially appealing, in practice the notion of an unconditional victory has become increasingly problematic.

In the past, unconditional victories have been comparatively rare; in the modern world they are almost inconceivable as a legitimate outcome. They are extraordinarily difficult to achieve, prohibitively expensive to pursue, and almost impossible to justify. World War II was a rare exception, and even then unconditional victory became the allies' declared political objective only halfway through the war, once the full depravity of the Nazi regime had become evident. Nothing less than the complete purging and rebuilding of German values was acceptable.

None of the protagonists in the subsequent major conflicts in Korea, Vietnam, and Iran–Iraq articulated a desired end-state remotely as absolute, settling instead for far more modest and realistic outcomes, such as a return to the pre-war geographic status quo or a face-saving withdrawal. The sheer difficulty and expense of modern warfare and the pressures arising from increasingly globalised economic and political systems militated against other more extreme objectives. Even during what was perhaps the most intense ideological contest in history, the Cold War between the United States and the Soviet Union, United States declaratory policy was never one of unconditional victory, but rather of containment. Nor is overwhelming military success any guarantee that the victor will be able to impose unqualified change, as the United States found when it was manifestly unable to enforce its political preferences on the Iraqi people following the comprehensive defeat of Saddam Hussein's army in early 2003.

In brief, the idea of pursuing an unconditional victory in the modern era is not only questionable but also could be unacceptably dangerous.

DETERRENCE AND RISK

Thus far this chapter has focused on compellence as one of the two major expressions of strategic action. It now turns to the second, coercion, which is more likely than compellence to involve only the threat, as opposed to the application, of physical violence or of some other disagreeable pressure. The main concepts associated with coercion are deterrence and risk, which between them incorporate the subsets of gradual escalation, incrementalism, and mutual assured destruction. While again acknowledging that a division of concepts can be somewhat artificial, and that overlap between categories is inevitable, the technique nevertheless remains useful in helping to bound the subject and therefore to understand it.

A strategy based on compellence will deny an opponent the opportunity to influence the nature or consequences of his planned demise. Change will be imposed compulsorily by the victor and accepted involuntarily by the vanquished, and should conform to the desired effects defined in the victor's pre-conflict planning. A strategy based on coercion, by contrast, will seek to impose change by convincing an opponent that the costs of further resistance are likely to exceed the benefits, and that by conceding he will retain some influence over his fate. Unlike compellence, coercive decision-making is a two-way process, with both protagonists having a voice in deciding how and when the discord will end.

Some measure of coercion is apparent every time protagonists compete in any kind of forum, from the battlefield to the bourse. Particular mention should perhaps be made of terrorists, for whom coercive violence is the weapon of choice. A classic tool of the weak against the strong, and which has unambiguous political overtones because it is directed against civilians, terrorism has been especially widespread since the end of World War II, a period that has coincided with communist insurgencies, the end of colonialism, and a variety of religious and nationalist independence movements.

The interactive nature of coercive violence was apparent in the bombing of the King David Hotel in Jerusalem in 1946, a terrorist act carried out by the Jewish underground movement Irgun Zvai Leumi, of which the future Israeli Prime Minister Menachim Begin was a member. At the time, Irgun was striving for the establishment of an Israeli state in Palestine, which was under British rule. The attack on the King David Hotel killed ninety-one people, and was one of a series of terrorist actions that eventually led the British government to conclude that the costs it was incurring exceeded any benefits, which in turn prompted its decision to withdraw from Palestine and support the establishment of an independent Israel in 1948. It is worth noting, however, that in general, other terror campaigns have been less successful.

If skilfully applied, coercion can facilitate conflict resolution without recourse to open conflict. That desirable state of strategic balance can be pursued through a variety of means and ways, including military, economic, diplomatic, social and cultural. None has been more important than deterrence.

Writing some 2500 years ago, Sun Tzu argued that supreme strategic excellence lies not in conquest on the battlefield, but in 'breaking the enemy's resistance without fighting'.[10] More commonly translated as winning without fighting, Sun Tzu's timeless aphorism is a classic expression of deterrence. A deterrent effect might be created offensively, through the possession of an intimidating attacking capability; or it might be created defensively, through the possession of protective capabilities that would make the perceived cost of an assault unacceptable. The concept can be subtle and elegant. It can allow all protagonists some opportunity to manoeuvre within the overall strategic setting and achieve some degree of satisfaction, depending on their definition of winning.

Not that deterrence is always subtle. At its crudest level it is likely to involve nothing less than an open threat of severe violence, as in the case of a military superpower forcing its will on a weaker state. And in turn, the dynamics of deterrence demand that weaker states believe that they will be subjected to violence if they are not deterred. In other words, for deterrence to work, force may have to be applied from time to time. The order from mighty Athens to feeble Melos in 416 BCE that the Melians should accede to certain Athenian political demands carried unmistakable implications. If war became necessary, then not only would it be one-sided, but the post-conflict retribution would be severe. As noted previously, in the event, when the Melians chose not to be deterred the consequences could not have been more terrible. Incidentally, the Melians decided to resist Athens because they believed their position was morally and legally justified. They were probably right, but perhaps they should have thought more carefully about their definition of winning in circumstances that were entirely beyond their control.

An equally merciless enforcement of one protagonist's will over another's, again partly with the objective of establishing deterrence broadly throughout the ancient world, was demonstrated some three hundred years later, following Rome's defeat of Carthage in the third and final Punic War. By about the mid-third century BCE, Rome was the dominant power in Italy, and Carthage in the Mediterranean, and their interests were starting to compete. Thus, the Punic Wars (a name derived from the Roman word for Carthaginians) were the consequence of a classic strategic tension, namely, the desire for powerful states to establish spheres of influence.

The first Punic War was fought from 264 to 241 BCE, with Rome eventually winning; the second from 218 to 202 BCE, when, among other things, the Carthaginian leader Hannibal used elephants to cross the Alps and invade Italy, a brilliant manoeuvre which nonetheless could not prevent Rome from once more emerging victorious, after several early reverses; and the third from 149 to 146 BCE, when a three-year siege of Carthage was ended by Scipio Africanus the younger's violent assault on the city. In order to end once and for all the Carthaginian challenge and to deter other potential competitors from questioning Rome, Scipio then spent some two weeks systematically destroying the entire city, including all buildings, walls, and the harbour. Every surviving Carthaginian citizen – perhaps 50 000 people – was sold into slavery, and Scipio might even have had the surrounding countryside sown with salt to prevent anything growing for years to come.

Enforcing deterrence via a demonstration massacre has by no means been confined to the ancient world. Shakespeare captured the horrific sentiment in his play *Julius Caesar*, written in the sixteenth century CE, when he had Mark Antony call out to his warriors at the end of a battle 'Cry "havoc!", and let slip the dogs of war'. Antony's merciless enjoinder reflected the common practice of allowing victorious troops to indulge in an orgy of slaughter, pillage, rape and destruction as a means of deterring possible future resistance from other polities. More recently, the twentieth and twenty-first centuries have provided any number of examples, from most regions of the world. Few have been more dreadful than the Rape of

Nanjing between December 1937 and March 1938, when a deliberate policy of slaughter and rape was inflicted on the Chinese citizens of Nanjing by invading Japanese troops. Some 400 000 civilians and prisoners of war were beheaded, bayoneted, burned, buried alive, or disembowelled; and some 80 000 women and girls were systematically raped and often mutilated or murdered, as the Japanese Army sent a message to the rest of China that any resistance would be met with the most savage consequences.

Deterrence can occur along a continuum of intensities. 'Power' is a relative concept and, depending on the circumstances, a solitary rifleman might constitute an effective deterrent capability if, for example, he were facing a small group of unarmed opponents. But to reiterate, like any deterrent capability of any magnitude, that rifleman (or warship, or air armada, or nuclear-armed missile) will only generate a deterrent effect if the object of the attention believes that, if necessary, the weapon will be used. Credibility is the essence of deterrence.

This observation leads to three critical points. First, the form of military power being used to deter must be relevant to the circumstances. Threatening to use, say, nuclear weapons against a state which was sponsoring minor international criminal activities would be neither appropriate nor believable.

Second, any organisation wishing to generate a deterrent effect may need to apply force from time to time, to demonstrate that its muscle is complemented by the will to use it; hence the examples cited above of the punishment meted out by the Athenians, the Romans, and the Japanese. More recently, it is sometimes argued that the Administration of US President Bill Clinton during the 1990s came to be regarded by terrorists as vulnerable to exploitation because of the weakness of its military responses to attacks against US interests. An extension of that reasoning has it that al-Qa'ida was emboldened to strike against New York City and Washington on September 11, 2001 by America's perceived moral weakness: that is, despite the United States' immense military power, the terrorists were not deterred.

Finally, the strategic balance that deterrence is intended to establish need not be the same as equivalence. For example, different cultures may be prepared to accept different – even wildly divergent – levels of casualties. Unless both protagonists have a clear understanding of each other's level of acceptance, then a perceived state of strategic equilibrium, as would be established by a mutually rational interpretation of the factors of deterrence which are in play, might be nothing of the kind. Any such misunderstanding clearly could be potentially dangerous.

Deterrence has existed explicitly and implicitly for as long as humans have sought advantage over each other, and overwhelmingly it has been achieved through the use of conventional force.[11] Examples from classical times have already been cited; similarly, in the modern era, for several centuries, the global power represented by the Royal Navy was the key to the British Empire, while during the period of international tension which immediately preceded World War II, the deterrent effect created by the Luftwaffe caused fearful British and French politicians to appease rather than confront the Nazi regime. Nevertheless, despite those and scores of similar cases, it is with nuclear weapons and their associated strategies that deterrence is most commonly associated.

The early nuclear strategy of massive retaliation represented deterrence in its most primitive form. No subtlety here: if we are attacked or believe we are about to be attacked with nuclear weapons, we retaliate with the full force at our disposal. Motivated in part by US President Dwight D. Eisenhower's 'new look' national security policy of the early 1950s, which planned to cut overall defence costs and exploit the United States' major military comparative advantage by emphasising air power, massive retaliation's all-or-nothing approach was so extreme as to be unfeasible. The sensible thing to do, therefore, was to avoid conflict – to be mutually deterred.

As noted in chapter two, nuclear strategy eventually evolved into mutual assured destruction (MAD), a concept which represents the apogee of deterrence. MAD explicitly recognised that defence against the nuclear threat was impotent, and that only deterrence in kind could act as a counter. MAD perfectly demonstrated the delicate balance that often is the key to deterrence, primarily through the need for both players to have a guaranteed second-strike capability. The reasoning here was that unless each side felt confident it could withstand a first strike and would always have the ability to retaliate, the 'mutual' component of MAD would be invalidated, and the temptation to launch a pre-emptive attack during a period of heightened tension might prove irresistible. A protected retaliatory capability stabilised a situation which otherwise could quickly become dangerously unbalanced. A corollary of this was that, should either of the protagonists develop his force structure in such a way as to jeopardise the other's second-strike capacity – for example, by acquiring an effective missile defence system – the whole basis of the deterrent effect on which MAD rested would be undermined.

The importance of the 'assured' factor within the MAD equation was evident in the effort and expense the USSR and the United States devoted to acquiring a variety of delivery systems, their objective being to establish a guaranteed level of second-strike redundancy. After initially relying on manned aircraft as the sole delivery platform, both countries developed intercontinental ballistic missiles, and then missile-launching submarines. The odds that any pre-emptive strike might simultaneously neutralise all platforms from that diverse triad were so long as to make the option irrational; that is, the second-strike capability was assured, and so MAD was validated.

Unlike other nuclear strategies, MAD was intellectually credible, and for fifty years it underwrote relative strategic stalemate by deterring direct military conflict between the United States and the USSR.

But there has been less cause for confidence in the nuclear balance between Pakistan and India, especially once Pakistan's need for an assured second-strike capability was compromised by the United States' decision in 1990 to halt the delivery of a number of F-16 strike/fighter aircraft, even though some had already been paid for. The problem for Pakistan was that while both protagonists had ballistic missiles as one nuclear-weapon delivery option, India's much larger strike/fighter fleet constituted a more potent alternative system. Additional F-16s were a critical component of Pakistan's nuclear warfighting calculus, and without them the temptation to act pre-emptively during any period of heightened tension might have proven uncontrollable. While some commentators claimed that the eventual lifting in 2005 of the US embargo on the F-16s would promote an arms race, others believed it would ease Pakistan's fears and enhance stability within the regional 'balance of terror'.

An important derivative of MAD has been the notion of deterrence within conflict. Often associated with the controversial US Defence Secretary from the 1960s, the sometime academic and businessman Robert McNamara, the idea was that nuclear-armed powers might still engage each other indirectly through proxies, but would observe self-imposed limits. Those limits might or might not be defined, and might include the proscription of certain weapons and targets, a cap on the level of force applied, and strict geographic boundaries. The concept was clearly in force throughout the Cold War, notably during the US involvement in Indochina, a conflict largely directed by McNamara.

CENTRE OF GRAVITY

'A centre of power and movement . . . on which everything depends' was the description with which Clausewitz formalised the idea of centre of gravity.[12] Regardless of whether we wish to compel, coerce or deter, there is no more important concept in strategic thinking. Directly related to Sun Tzu's timeless counsel to 'know the enemy and know yourself', and to the ends-ways-means construct, the suggestion that every protagonist will have one or more centres of gravity implies an essential focus for every strategic analysis and action, regardless of the level of conflict. A recent fad among some writers to describe the process of centre of gravity analysis as 'sensitivity analysis' provides another description without affecting the concept's logic, while parallels might also be drawn with the notion of *schwerpunkt*, an expression sometimes used in strategic debate to describe 'the focus of effort', or the 'key issue which all efforts must support'.[13]

Once revealed, the idea of centre of gravity is elegantly simple and powerful. If we can identify the entity or the issues which our adversary values or needs above all else, and on which his continued power, advantage and wellbeing fundamentally rest, all of our energies should be directed against those centres as the most effective way of achieving our desired end. Conversely, we must be prepared resolutely to defend our own centres-of-gravity, lest a successful blow by our opponent brings us undone. The concept is relevant to any competitive endeavour, ranging from sport to business to chess to warfare.

As is almost invariably the case, however, the translation of theory into practice can be challenging. One of the more straightforward examples of centre-of-gravity analysis would seem to be that of the totalitarian ruler. As all institutional authority resides within that individual, it would appear logical to aim our endeavours directly against him. Removing a dictator by, say, assassination, or by capture or death in battle, might seem obvious solutions. Both approaches have been popular historically, as illustrated by the fates of Darius, Julius Caesar, Napoleon Bonaparte, Nikolai Ceaucescu, and many more.

Yet the fact remains that dictators are notoriously hard to find and just as hard to kill. Adolf Hitler, Idi Amin, Saddam Hussein and Fidel Castro, for example, survived numerous assassination attempts to dominate their countries for years. And in more general terms, the effectiveness of sustained assassination campaigns, such as those conducted by Narodnik revolutionaries against Russia's ruling élite in the 1870s and by the Israeli Defence Force against various Arab groups in the late twentieth and early twenty-first centuries, seems highly questionable. Moreover, it is common for a despot to establish a pliant state apparatus which, on his death, ensures that one brutal autocrat is simply replaced by another. Lenin's eventual succession by Stalin in the USSR in the 1920s and Kim Il-sung's by Kim Jong-il in North Korea in 1994 brought no comfort to those hoping for more liberal regimes.

Nor is Clausewitz's now obsolete belief that the enemy's army invariably is his centre of gravity of much help. If Clausewitz had been correct, the challenge of deciding what to do would be simplified but it would not necessarily be clear-cut. Different armies might have different centres of gravity; furthermore, within any nominal centre of gravity there almost certainly will be critical subsets of key points. An army can be an exceedingly complex organisation, with a large array of strengths and weaknesses. Where precisely does its critical vulnerability lie? Is it the leadership, the supply system, a particular combat element, the morale of the soldiers' families back home? Numerous analysts believe that, because of the contemporary media's ability to flash sometimes shocking battle reports into millions of suburban homes, often in near real-time, sensitivity to casualties has become the superseding vulnerability of Western societies and their defence forces. Contrast this to the communists in Vietnam, who during the Tet Offensive of 1968 were prepared to accept appalling losses in order to achieve their political objective; or subsequently to terrorist groups such as al-Qa'ida, Hamas, Hezbollah and Jemaah Islamiah, many of whose members are not only prepared to die for their cause but actually seek a martyr's death.

Few better examples of the complexities of centre-of-gravity analysis exist than the attempt by operational research teams to identify a targeting strategy for the allies' combined bomber offensive against Germany and Italy during World War II. Seduced by the vision of a war-winning knock-out blow, planners in London and Washington poured resources into analyses of their enemies' war economies. Detailed studies were made of so-called industrial webs, vital points, choke points, strategic nodes and the like, always with the goal of identifying *the* single element which, if neutralised, would precipitate the enemy's collapse. Given the intricacy of the subject, it should not be surprising that different analysts identified different centres of gravity: for one, it was the transport system; for another, ball-bearing factories; for others still, oil, or the morale of factory workers, or submarine pens. Such was the regularity with which alleged knock-out blow solutions were presented that the officer in charge of the British heavy bomber fleet, Air Chief Marshal Sir Arthur Harris, became contemptuous of what he called the panacea approach to targeting.

Still, notwithstanding the vicissitudes of this particular case study, it is important to record two of its notable successes as a general observation on centre-of-gravity analysis. First, prior to the allies' amphibious landing at Normandy on D-Day, 6 June 1944, RAF and USAAF heavy bomber fleets were directed to concentrate their efforts against the transport system in France, to impair the Nazis' ability to rush reinforcements and supplies to crucial areas. Basil Liddell Hart later concluded that the air forces' paralysis of the transport system was the single most significant contribution to the success of the Normandy invasion.[14] Second, in the final year of the war, the bomber offensive's focus on the production and distribution of German oil supplies had a devastating effect on the Nazi war machine as tanks, trucks and aircraft largely ground to a halt as their life blood dried up. Centre-of-gravity analysis may be difficult but it is not impossible, and when it works the rewards can be immense.

There is a natural relationship between centre-of-gravity analysis and the ends-ways-means construct. Regardless of the level of conflict, and regardless of whether the person in charge is a general prosecuting a campaign or a corporal leading an infantry section, when confronted by any sort of hostile force, and if circumstances permit, that person should assess the likely consequences of any impending engagement in relation to the broader desired ends. Having made that assessment, he should then decide whether to try to compel, coerce, or deter, or to avoid contact, and so on. In similar vein, the enemy should be subjected to a centre-of-gravity analysis in order to best determine how he should be engaged: is there one vital person, or weapon, or external vulnerability?

It may of course transpire that circumstances deny one or both protagonists the opportunity for considered decision-making, as for example in the case of a sudden and unexpected encounter, or if there is an implacable determination on the part of one of them to pursue a certain course of action regardless of anything else. We also need to acknowledge that an instinctive decision can often work best, especially when a chance encounter demands an immediate response. Nevertheless, logic insists that, if at all possible, a rigorous centre-of-gravity analysis should be carried out.

Reflecting the truism that war ultimately is a contest of wills, in recent years centre-of-gravity analysis has tended to shift from physical vulnerabilities towards those of the mind and the emotions, at least at the higher levels of strategic competition. This axiological or values-based approach to targeting endeavours to identify the things the enemy leadership prizes most, and it is aimed directly at that élite rather than at the population, or armed forces, or national infrastructure. The reasoning is clear. Despots like the Nazis, the Imperial Japanese Empire, the Iraqi Ba'athists and their ilk have shown that they are prepared to let their citizens die and their countries be destroyed as long as they and their inner circle are safe. For coercion to work, therefore, the ruling élite must be personally targeted through attacks on such things as their wealth, property, businesses, hobbies, friends, families, and even their values.

Among other things, axiological targeting implies a profound understanding of an enemy's culture, which in turn exposes the concept's inherent complexity. How, for example, do we attack the values of a group like the Taliban, whose profound religious beliefs must be off-limits for both legal and moral reasons, but who otherwise as nihilists appear devoid of readily identified values? And what are the legal implications of strikes against individuals, families, and private property? Still, the idea of punishing those immediately responsible for the circumstances we wish to change instead of striking against their invariably more accessible rank and file is intuitively appealing, and there have been occasions when the approach may have been successful. It seems possible that value targeting applied by NATO forces against Slobodan Milosevic and his cronies in 1999 influenced the previously intransigent Yugoslav despot's decision to capitulate. And a variation was evident in the Middle East in 2004, when the Israeli Defence Force began to respond to attacks by Islamic Shi'ite Hezbollah forces from the Lebanon, not by attacking their bases, as they had usually done in the past, but instead by taking retribution against Syria, one of Hezbollah's primary sponsors.

The concept of centre of gravity comes with the variety of interpretations that is a characteristic of strategic studies. Some commentators will insist that there can only be one centre of gravity, as in physics; others believe that a more flexible interpretation is better suited to the workings of the human mind. As is the case with the definition of strategy itself, it is important to be aware of these variations, but more important not to let them assume intellectually inhibiting dimensions. A useful starting point is to study traditional warfighting concepts and practices – to understand what strategy has been – and to be capable of locating that understanding within the prevailing circumstances.

4

Manoeuvre and the application of force
Applying strategy

'GIT THAR FUSTEST WITH the mostest' replied the idiosyncratic Confederate cavalry commander, Nathan Bedford Forrest, when asked to explain his strategy for victory in the American Civil War. General Forrest may have been eccentric but he was an intuitive military genius for his times, and as usual he had got straight to the heart of the matter. In essence, he was talking about manoeuvre and the application of force. Once fighting either is about to start or has started, every decision a military commander takes should be informed by the superseding importance of manoeuvre and firepower. Like all good strategic thinking, the maxims of 'manoeuvre' and 'firepower' are elegantly simple, even though in practice the application of both can be extraordinarily complex.

A useful benchmark against which to test the authority of any alleged strategic maxim is to examine the extent to which it has or has not been affected by technological progress. In this case, regardless of whether the force to be applied will come from a lone infantryman, or from massed land, sea and air power working in unison, the principle of achieving an advantageous position and, if necessary, of then applying decisive firepower, remains as fundamental today as it did for Alexander, Genghis Khan, Napoleon, Nelson, and anyone else who has ever faced an opponent on the field of combat. The imperative for the jet-fighter pilot of the twenty-first century to be in the right position to detect and identify his opponent first (manoeuvre) and then to fire his missile first (firepower) to achieve a kill, as opposed to being killed, is precisely the same as it was for the Jewish shepherd boy David some 3000 years ago, when he managed to get close enough to the giant Philistine warrior Goliath to kill him with a slingshot-powered pebble.

Note that the emphasis with firepower is on 'if necessary' as opposed to 'without exception'; and on 'decisive' as opposed to 'heavier', or 'sustained', or 'concentrated'. It may be the case that superior manoeuvre will create a situation in which one of the protagonists concludes that the action should end there and then, such is his positional disadvantage, and he will avoid conflict: that is, coercion in the form of deterrence will have come into play. Additionally, it is feasible that a single shot could generate a greater strategic effect than, say, the massive but sometimes futile artillery bombardments of World War I. Note also that firepower and manoeuvre are complementary and interactive and that, depending on the circumstances, firepower can be used to facilitate movement.

The ability to manoeuvre forces to advantage is one of the premier skills of a strategist; it is fundamental to the art of war. As is the case with the definition of strategy, the most helpful definition of manoeuvre is one that does not elevate semantics above common-sense. Manoeuvre as a concept is best appreciated when it is regarded simply as an idea or a plan for getting someone or something, be it an army, or a section of soldiers, or a flight of aircraft, or a squadron of warships, or a suicide bomber, into the best position at the best time that circumstances permit. In the process, our exposure to the enemy's killing technology should be minimised and the effectiveness of our firepower maximised.

FIREPOWER AND MANOEUVRE IN THREE DIMENSIONS

Because the scale and variety of manoeuvre are almost infinitely variable, a selection of examples may be helpful to establish its nature and significance. The chosen episodes come from different eras and contexts, to emphasise the subject's enduring characteristics. First, however, the notion of 'speed' must be briefly discussed.

Speed is by definition relative, and as a component of manoeuvre its importance is difficult to overstate. The strategist who is the faster to make decisions and to move forces by deploying, advancing, retreating or outflanking almost invariably will generate an advantage of the highest order. Thus, at one end of the scale, the thirty or so kilometres a day that General 'Stonewall' Jackson's army would sometimes march during the Shenandoah Valley campaign in 1862 might not have been quick in absolute terms, but in relative terms it left his Union opponents floundering. A brilliant tactician who used speed and a skilful reading of the terrain to offset his army's numerical inferiority, Jackson in one five-week period marched his own division some 560 kilometres, even while halting on occasions to fight battles and skirmishes.

Modern fighter aircraft represent the other end of the speed scale. Saddam Hussein's invasion of Kuwait in August 1990, while alarming in itself, raised additional fears that his army might continue into Saudi Arabia to seize oil fields. Lacking forces in the area, the US President George H. Bush ordered a wing of twenty-four F-15C fighters to deploy from the continental United States to the Middle East. Flying at around 800 kilometres an hour, the aircraft made the fifteen-hour, 12 000-kilometre crossing non-stop, arriving fully armed. Whether or not this rapid manoeuvre was decisive in stopping Saddam's forces at the Kuwait–Saudi border is unknown; what is known is that the message of intent from the United States was unmistakable, and that the Iraqi Army did indeed stop. For both Jackson and the F-15 commanders, speed was the characteristic that defined their manoeuvring.

Turning to the broader examples, few better exponents can be found than Alexander the Great, who some 2300 years ago demonstrated a wonderful appreciation of manoeuvre at both the strategic and the tactical levels. Alexander's grand strategy during his conquest of the eastern Mediterranean, Asia Minor and South Asia between 334 and 323 BCE was defined, among other things, by the creative way in which he deployed his main army. The Macedonian king was not only a great battlefield commander and warrior but also a brilliant military thinker with a rare talent for identifying vital points that were not always evident to his opponents. His forces tended to appear unexpectedly in terms of time and place, as a consequence of which he was largely able to dictate the development of political and military events. In other words, he manoeuvred to advantage not only physically but also intellectually. Alexander's method of grand strategic manoeuvre, based as it was on his understanding of his various opponents' mindsets, the strengths and weaknesses of the respective forces, and his rare ability to read terrain, was characterised by Basil Liddell Hart as the indirect approach.[1]

A contrasting example from the nuclear age reinforces the enduring relevance of an indirect solution, within a dramatically different setting. In June 1948 the USSR exploited the arrangements under which the wartime allies had occupied Germany by closing off all surface access to the city of Berlin, which at the time was divided into four sectors controlled by the British, French, Americans, and the Soviets themselves. If left unchallenged, the communists' provocative action might not only have won them an important psychological victory, but also have given them permanent control of all of Berlin. Worried that an attempt to force the blockade on the ground might precipitate World War III, the allies instead 'built' a *Luftbrücke* – an air bridge – into Berlin. For the next fifteen months the 2.2 million inhabitants of the Western sectors of Berlin were sustained by air power alone as the *Luftbrücke* flew in 2.33 million tonnes of supplies in 277 569 flights. The USSR's eventual capitulation and lifting of the surface blockade changed the course of the Cold War and the face of Europe, without a shot having been fired.

A striking example of an indirect solution, the Berlin Airlift was itself underpinned by an equally striking application of an indirect flanking manoeuvre, which threatened the application of overwhelming force against the USSR. In July 1948 the United States deployed a number of apparently nuclear-capable B-29 bombers to the United Kingdom, a calculated demonstration of rapid global manoeuvre that did not go unnoticed in the USSR. The B-29s were not in fact armed with nuclear weapons but the Soviets did not know that and, as they had no operational nuclear warfighting capability of their own, they became more cautious in their handling of the confrontation they had precipitated in Berlin. Speed and coercion via manoeuvre deterred the USSR.

A return to Alexander's campaigns provides one of the earliest recorded instances of the indirect approach at the tactical level, this time involving a sequence of coordinated manoeuvres. Fighting numerically superior Persian forces at the Granicus River in 334 BCE, Alexander seems to have combined a feint attack by his cavalry with an oblique line of advance by his infantry to confuse the Persian commanders.[2] Confused they certainly were, because their hasty reaction to this unexpected approach was to reinforce parts of their line at the expense of others, which created weaknesses where none had previously existed. Alexander then manoeuvred his forces to exploit the Persians' self-inflicted defensive gaps and put his enemy to the sword.

Alexander's tactics relied on precise timing, with the key being the positional relationship between his cavalry and his phalanxes of foot-soldiers. The cavalry had to be sufficiently in advance of the phalanxes to draw the Persians into the trap, by inducing them to rush forces to their unexpectedly threatened flank, but not so far in advance that the phalanxes might not arrive in time to exploit the gaps left in the Persian ranks or to prevent their heavily outnumbered cavalry from being overwhelmed.

Tactical genius also characterised Napoleon Bonaparte's management of timing and speed, as he sought to overcome the innate slowness of the huge French armies he commanded at the turn of the eighteenth century. Napoleon was among the first strategists to appreciate that, given the technologies of the time, massed armies were a potentially war-winning force. The introduction in revolutionary France in 1793 of a broad-based system of national conscription (the *levée en masse*) provided him with the necessary authority to vastly increase the numbers of fighting men he could mobilise; the challenge then became one of manoeuvring that mass of men and matériel to advantage, in an era of primitive transportation systems.

Napoleon solved the problem through an ingenious combination of organisation, manoeuvre, timing and concentration. By dividing his armies into relatively autonomous corps he gave them the authority and the ability to move independently and, therefore, faster, but still in accordance with his overall campaign plan. It then became

Napoleon's task to bring the various corps together at the critical time, so that the entire force could be concentrated against the enemy at the one place. Admirably simple in concept, the tactic required masterful command and control in execution.

Suffice to say that timing and deception are central to manoeuvre at any level of combat. The allied invasion of Europe on 6 June 1944, for example, illustrates that truism at the opposite end of the scale to Alexander's comparatively simple application. For months leading up to the immense amphibious landing on the Normandy coast, the allies conducted a sophisticated deception campaign regarding their planned beachhead. Duly deceived, the Germans deployed tens of thousands of troops and their supporting arms too far from the actual landing beaches to be of any immediate use when D-Day finally arrived.

Air combat provides the next example of manoeuvre in practice, one that surprisingly may be less complex than Alexander's, even though it emerged more than 2200 years later. From the time systematic air combat first appeared in World War I, pilots who have been able to position themselves above their opponents and with the sun behind them have enjoyed a major tactical advantage. Even in recent years, when long-range missiles, and radars and other information systems have redefined the way in which air combat is conducted by providing better information sooner, thus facilitating quicker, beyond-visual range decision-making, pilots can still find themselves fighting at close range. And in that environment, the imperative to be the first to see and identify the enemy means that position relative to altitude and the sun can still make the difference between life and death. Note, by the way, the parallel here with the army axiom that holding the high ground almost invariably represents a major advantage. Indeed, this principle is so widely understood that 'taking the high ground' has become a metaphor within the English language for gaining an edge in any kind of endeavour.

General Helmuth von Moltke's unhappy experience with the von Schlieffen plan in World War I illustrates another important feature of manoeuvre. It is an adage of military staff work that no plan survives first contact with the enemy. While this overstates the case – the probability that a plan will have to be modified as circumstances unfold does not necessarily mean that its basic premises are false – it nevertheless highlights the importance of contingency planning and flexibility. As chapter two described, for von Moltke, manoeuvre effectively became an end in itself, and the consequences for him were severe.

Moltke's problems epitomised much of the campaigning during the early period of World War I. The whole point of manoeuvre is to gain an advantageous position which can then be used to apply decisive force if necessary. The source of that force is unimportant: it can come from infantry, artillery, naval gunfire, strike aircraft, or any other weapons system. What matters is that it is decisive. Throughout most of World War I generals struggled to find the right balance between manoeuvre and firepower. The available transport technologies of roads, railways and ships were neither sufficiently flexible nor sufficiently fast to facilitate the rapid manoeuvre of enough forces to seize a decisive positional advantage by outflanking, breaking through, or surrounding the enemy. By contrast, the killing technologies of the time, such as artillery and machine guns, were lethal against massed armies that too often amounted to little more than slow-moving targets. We should be dismayed but not surprised that World War I became a quagmire in which tens of thousands of entrenched troops slogged out savage battles for months over a few hundred metres of mud.

In those circumstances, generals began to use firepower as a substitute for manoeuvre, rather than as its partner. Again, we should not be surprised that sixty per cent of the casualties during World War I were caused by artillery, a figure which reveals the imbalance between manoeuvre and firepower. Only late in the war was some semblance of equilibrium restored, when innovative commanders began to exploit emerging technologies to break free from the predominant static mindset. At Hamel in July 1918, for example, the brilliant Australian General John Monash used a mobile, coordinated force of infantry, artillery, armour and aircraft to achieve an enhanced form of manoeuvre, which in turn led to a decisive victory.

And in the final hundred days of the war – a period which was marked by the extraordinarily sudden collapse of German resistance on both the Western and the Home Fronts – other allied leaders began to demonstrate a hitherto rarely seen degree of imagination in their use of existing technologies. Among other things, better target analysis, more guns, creeping artillery barrages, a shrewd admixture of high-explosive and smoke shells to both facilitate and disguise the advance of infantry, improved counter-battery fire against enemy artillery, the skilful use of mortar fire, better tanks, and much more use of aircraft to strafe and interdict hostile movements, all helped allied soldiers to manoeuvre far more effectively than had previously been the case.

An innovative application of manoeuvre and firepower was also the key to what is perhaps British history's most renowned naval engagement, Admiral Lord Horatio Nelson's victory over a combined French and Spanish fleet at Trafalgar in 1805. But where Monash, for instance, used both technology and ideas to break the prevailing mindset, Nelson relied solely on tactical ingenuity to manoeuvre his British fleet to winning advantage.

Prior to Trafalgar, naval commanders had shown little inclination to develop tactics which might have allowed them to annihilate an enemy. Fleets commonly sailed into battle in two opposing lines, with each ship's captain seeking to come up alongside a single opponent to deliver a broadside. Often, however, the engagement would be reduced to a tacking competition, as the two lines reacted in turn to each other's often-predictable (because it was governed by the prevailing wind) manoeuvring. At Trafalgar, Nelson dramatically broke this habitual pattern by dividing his fleet into two separate groups. The first attacked sections of the enemy's lines, thus breaking their defensive integrity, while the other, shunning the conventional broadside engagement, instead cut through the French and Spanish column at right angles, an unexpected manoeuvre which both divided the enemy's strength and closed his avenues for escape. Nelson's victory was to set the scene for a hundred years of maritime domination by the Royal Navy.

The tactic of crossing the enemy fleet at right angles reached its zenith at Tsushima exactly a century later, by which time sail and wood had been replaced by steam and steel. Described by Julian Corbett as the most 'complete naval victory in history', Japan's crushing defeat of the Russians in May 1905 rested in large part on superior manoeuvre, which itself was made possible by superior speed. But instead of sailing through the enemy's line, as Nelson had done, the objective now was to pass either in front of or behind him: as the tacticians of the era expressed it, to 'cross the T' by forming the horizontal crossbar of the letter T, with the enemy being the vertical bar. A line of warships that crossed the T was side-on to the enemy, and so was able to bring all of its heavy guns to bear simultaneously; by contrast, the opponent's barrage was restricted to those guns that could fire either forwards or backwards, depending on which end of the line was being crossed, and whose gunners could see past the other ships in their column.

By the time the Russian fleet reached Tsushima following its long transit from the Baltic Sea, it could make only about 15 kilometres per hour, the warships' hulls having been fouled by marine growth. The Japanese fleet, by contrast, was able to manoeuvre at 30 kilometres per hour, an enormous tactical advantage which its commander, Admiral Heihachiro Togo, exploited by crossing the T not once but twice. Togo further refined the tactic by unexpectedly bringing in a second line of ships from one side, which both prevented the Russians from escaping and subjected them to a withering crossfire. In two days Togo captured or destroyed twenty-one of twenty-five Russian capital ships and lost none of his own.

The evolution of longer-range guns, aircraft carriers and, eventually, very long-range missiles, transformed naval tactics, with beyond-visual range engagements gradually becoming the norm. A within-visual range tactic, the crossing of the T was performed for the last time at the Leyte Gulf in the Philippines in October 1944, when the largest naval battle in modern history was fought between American and Japanese fleets. It was a fittingly memorable encounter. Japanese commanders trying to enter the gulf through the narrow Surigao Strait in line left themselves open to the classic naval manoeuvre, and paid a heavy price when their force was subjected to a concentrated barrage of fire. Two battleships and three destroyers were sunk or knocked out of action, one heavy cruiser was badly damaged, and one destroyer damaged. Only one US ship was hit.

Manoeuvre, like beauty, can be in the eye of the beholder, as the final illustration reveals. General Ulysses S. Grant once asserted that, 'I never manoeuvre'.[3] Grant offered this laconic dismissal of the importance of position when he was commanding Union forces in the American Civil War, and was engaged in a grimly contested, fluctuating struggle with the armies of the Confederate States of America, led by General Robert E. Lee. Lee, by contrast, had engineered a series of unexpectedly successful actions against the Union largely through his skill in manoeuvring his forces to advantage.

For three years following the start of the war in April 1861, Lee had consistently second-guessed a succession of Union commanders by combining an incisive understanding of strategic objectives with a masterful appreciation of geography and logistics. As a result, his Confederate army, which almost invariably was outnumbered, sometimes by as much as two-and-a-half to one, and which was always inferior in terms of weapons, clothing, and nourishment, had regularly enjoyed positional superiority, which in turn contributed to a series of unlikely battlefield successes. Union President Abraham Lincoln became intensely frustrated with his generals, who proved incapable of translating their vastly superior numbers and material strength into a decisive warfighting edge.

Notwithstanding Grant's self-deprecatory comment, when he assumed command of the Union armies in the east early in 1864, he immediately began to outmanoeuvre Lee, in effect if not in the classical manner. Grant's great merit was that, unlike his predecessors, he had an unsentimental appreciation of the nature of warfare in the mid-nineteenth century, and of the strategic relationship between the Union and the Confederacy. His centre-of-gravity analysis consequently proved decisive.

The balance between manoeuvre and firepower in that era was such that the former was extremely difficult to manage, and the latter could be devastating. In those circumstances mass-on-mass fighting was the norm, which meant that casualties were likely to be heavy, a grim reality Grant accepted. Because of the North's immense financial, material and manpower superiority, Grant correctly concluded that the war could best be won by exhausting the South. As long as he kept closing with the enemy, leaving him little opportunity to regroup, recover, and reinforce, the odds were that the South's capacity to resist would eventually be ground down. Grant had done the maths, and, in the words of one historian, he was prepared to be the 'killer-arithmetician' Lincoln had been looking for.[4]

Those commentators who have criticised Grant's approach have missed the point. His application of manoeuvre may have been bloody, but in the circumstances it was rational. While Grant invariably sought the best geographic position from which to begin an engagement, it was not necessarily his first priority, and nor was it as critical for him as it was for the outnumbered and outgunned Lee. For Grant, the over-riding positional imperative was to attack the enemy constantly and relentlessly, regardless of who was where, which is precisely what he did. In his own words, the art of war in 1864 was simple enough: 'Find out where your enemy is. Get at him as soon as you can. Strike him as hard as you can, and keep moving.' He might not have manoeuvred his forces with textbook finesse, but he unquestionably manoeuvred them with a clear understanding of strategic imperatives and to war-winning effect.

REDEFINING MASS

Grant's ruthlessly pragmatic interpretation of manoeuvre was informed in large part by his clear understanding of the relationship between quantity and quality that prevailed during the Civil War. The case study is a telling one, because it serves to illustrate a general shift in the nature of quantity in warfighting, as represented by massed forces.

There was little difference in the standard of the fighting men of the Union and the Confederacy, but the Northerners' support services were vastly superior. Worse still for the South, their logistical inferiority was exacerbated by a numerical imbalance that only needed to be exploited by the right strategy to become almost insurmountable. Joseph Stalin once observed in a different time and setting that quantity has a quality all of its own, and, once Grant's unyielding determination to close at all costs started to negate Lee's previously inspired manoeuvring, mass was likely to prevail, which it did.

Since that era, however, the nature of mass has gradually been redefined. Technology has been central to the process, especially through the evolution of precision weapons. The self-propelled naval torpedo, which first appeared in the mid-nineteenth century, epitomises this process. Sufficiently small to be carried by patrol-boat-sized vessels and submarines, but sufficiently potent to sink capital ships, the torpedo at one stage threatened to end the age of the modern battleship almost before it had begun. Other challenges to the concept of mass continued to emerge throughout the first half of the twentieth century, but they only started to have a significant effect in the late 1960s. Three catalysts were especially important.

First, when the forces of the Warsaw Pact and the North Atlantic Treaty Organisation began to face each other down across the plains of Germany during the Cold War, the USSR's worrying advantage in numbers and conventional weapons (mass) led the United States and its allies to seek an offset through superior technology and tactics, such as substituting air-delivered tactical nuclear weapons for armies (precision, of a kind). Second, arguments in favour of pursuing that approach more broadly were bolstered by the United States' defeat in Indochina, where post-conflict analysis indicated a fundamental failure of strategy and force application. US military leaders consequently began to recast their warfighting doctrine, which started to emphasise precision, rapid movement, information dominance, advanced technology, and superior decision-making at the expense of sheer size. And finally, the stunning victories won by heavily outnumbered but high-quality Israeli forces in the Middle East in 1967 and 1973 provided a demonstration of the new model in practice.

That trend has continued, the end result being that, today, numerically small but intellectually powerful, technologically advanced, fast-moving defence forces routinely out-think and outmanoeuvre larger but mentally and physically less agile opponents. At the start of the twenty-first century, Stalin's dictum regarding the innate power of sheer size has lost its authority.

OFFENCE AND DEFENCE

Just as firepower and manoeuvre share an interdependent relationship, so too do the two basic expressions of their application, 'offence' and 'defence'.

Clausewitz believed that, in general, defence was the stronger form of warfare, a judgment which was accurate enough for the Napoleonic times in which he lived, and also for the mass-on-mass warfighting of the latter half of the nineteenth century, of World Wars I and II, and of the Iran–Iraq War (1980 to 1988). The histories of those conflicts are depressingly replete with unsuccessful mass attacks, often into the teeth of terrifyingly deadly entrenched defensive firestorms. Too often planned by generals with a near-theological belief in the presumed innate, even moral, superiority of the offence, and who either could not or would not exploit manoeuvre sufficiently, such campaigns reflected a dogma that frequently resulted in the most dreadful slaughter within the attacking ranks.

Clausewitz's thinking was influenced by the fact that terrain often provides a powerful defensive advantage, reflected in the long-standing army rule of thumb that an attacking force needs a numerical advantage of three to one over its opponents. And it is the case that natural features such as high ground, rivers, jungles and mountain ranges can be used by defenders to swing the balance; to leave their opponents with few offensive options, perhaps only a frontal assault against well-entrenched positions, a situation in which the assessed costs of mounting an attack might seem to outweigh the benefits.

This interactive relationship between the offence and the defence has in the past engendered a distinctive form of warfare, namely, the siege. Also a long-standing expression of the balance between manoeuvre and firepower, the siege provides an instructive model of how strategy has been applied, and warrants detailed discussion.

Sieges typically have been mounted by forces that were sufficiently strong to compel their opponents to retreat into defensive redoubts like walled cities, castles, jungles, mountains and caves, but insufficiently strong to successfully assault that redoubt without risking unacceptable losses, or even defeat. The upshot for the attackers has been a kind of defensive-offensive operation, in which they continue to exercise the initiative, but do so within carefully defined limits to contain their potential losses. Only when they assess that the besieged defenders have been sufficiently weakened by privation, continual bombardment, disease and the like should the attackers resume their all-out offensive.

According to the Greek poet Homer's epic the *Iliad*, the siege of Troy in about 1200 BCE lasted ten years, and eventually succeeded only by deception. Having ostensibly finally given up and sailed away, the Greeks left behind a large wooden horse which the Trojans wheeled triumphantly into their city; later that night, soldiers hiding inside the horse opened the city gates, allowing the Greek Army which had stealthily returned to enter and sack Troy. Sources for the Trojan wars can be vague, but it seems that the Greek siege might not have been as meticulous as the concept implies, and that Troy might have been covertly resupplied by allies, thus allowing its citizens to avoid the disease and starvation which frequently are a key indirect weapon of the attacking force. Three thousand years later, during the six-week siege of Vicksburg in mid-1863, the Confederate soldiers and citizens trapped inside the city enjoyed no such relief, and ultimately had little option other than to surrender to the surrounding Union army commanded by General Ulysses S. Grant.

Grant, of course, profited from being able to bombard the inhabitants of Vicksburg with cannon fire, a technology and form of coercion unavailable to the Greeks at Troy. Prior to the invention of gunpowder and the emergence of cannons or 'bombards', retreating behind robust barriers was often the best option for an army confronted by a stronger foe. While by doing so the retreating army forfeited its ability to manoeuvre, the strength of its defensive position might outweigh the disadvantages. But cannons that could breach defences, a warfighting revolution associated most notably with the fall of the mighty walled city of Constantinople to Muslim forces in 1453 CE, changed all that. An immobile target which can be bombarded is at the wrong end of the continuum of firepower and manoeuvre.

Geography, weather, and access to lines of communications can profoundly affect both sides in a siege, in an extreme case to the extent of turning the hunter into the hunted. The 900-day blockade of Leningrad by German forces from 1941 to 1944 saw both sides suffer dreadfully from starvation, cold and disease. But the inhabitants of Leningrad received occasional relief from resupply convoys which were able to evade the Germans, who by contrast were eventually cut off from their own supply lines and potential reinforcements by

Soviet armies and air forces manoeuvring to their rear. The besiegers now became the besieged, and the Nazis finally had to surrender.

Yet another noteworthy variation of the siege – in broader terms, of the interaction between the offence and the defence – was the Royal Navy's blockade of Germany during World War I, an action that was so effective that some historians believe it was the single most important factor in the allies' eventual victory. Among other things, the social revolution which broke out in Germany near the end of the war was due in part to the increasingly severe privation citizens had suffered for four years. A feature of the blockade was its extension to other hostile or even neutral nations, with third-party ships that supported the Germans being refused passage or impounded.

Since the mid-twentieth century, manoeuvre and the application of force from the air have made the siege an increasingly uncertain strategy. The Berlin Airlift of 1948 and 1949 has already been mentioned as an episode in which an innovative use of manoeuvre and the threat of force were used to outflank and coerce an attempted surface blockade. Three subsequent sieges reflected the dynamic nature of the balance between the offence and the defence.

The first began in November 1953 near the border of North Vietnam and Laos, at the remote French fort of Dien Bien Phu. Attempting to lure their Viet Minh opponents away from guerilla operations into a large set-piece battle which they believed would be to their advantage, French commanders deployed a 'bait' of some 13 000 soldiers and their supporting arms to Dien Bien Phu. A central assumption of the French plan was that air transport would be able to fly supplies and reinforcements into the airstrip inside the compound.

By early 1954 the trap appeared to have been sprung, as Dien Bien Phu had been surrounded by about 50 000 soldiers from the People's Army of Vietnam, commonly known as the Viet Minh. But when the Vietnamese assault led by General Vo Nguyen Giap started in earnest on 13 March, the French were shocked to come under sustained artillery fire, which against all odds Giap's troops had manhandled across rivers, through jungles, and over mountains onto the hilltops overlooking Dien Bien Phu. The artillery barrage dramatically changed the offence-versus-defence equation by both exposing the French fortifications and effectively closing the airstrip. Dien Bien Phu's capitulation on 7 May signalled the end of French rule in Indochina.

Fourteen years later during the US war in Indochina, a similar situation seemed to be unfolding when the heavily fortified US base at Khe Sanh, also near the Vietnam–Laos border but south of Dien Bien Phu, was besieged by communist forces, once more under the command of General Giap. This time, however, vastly superior air-lift and airdrop capabilities meant that the Americans were never cut-off from their supply lines, as the French had been. Perhaps even more importantly, Khe Sanh's defenders were able to call in massive air strikes, which, when combined with aggressive combat patrols mounted from within the fort, made the communists' position untenable. By the time General Giap decided to withdraw in mid-March 1968 he had suffered some 12 000 casualties compared to the US force's 200.

The final example comes from 1992, when Serbian militants seeking to secede from the newly independent state of Bosnia decided that their best military option was to lay siege to the disputed city of Sarajevo. Serbian paramilitary forces seized the heights around Sarajevo, closed off all surface access and, like General Giap's army at Dien Bien Phu, began to bombard their target relentlessly, in this instance with artillery, rockets and mortars. Initially the siege was militarily successful as Sarajevo's citizens suffered heavy casualties and the city's infrastructure was severely damaged. But by mid-1993 a tunnel which allowed supplies in and people out had been dug, and a UN-sponsored airlift was providing a steady supply of humanitarian aid. At this stage, in strict military terms, the campaign might have been regarded as a failure for both sides, neither of whom seemed capable of breaking the impasse unaided. In a sense, the balance between firepower (the Serbian bombardment) and manoeuvre (Sarajevo's tunnel and airlift) had reached an equilibrium. The stalemate continued until a political solution was reached in 1996, by which time the siege of Sarajevo had become the longest in modern history.

Sieges provide an instructive model of the inherent tension between the offence and the defence because they demonstrate that between the two extremities there are many shades of grey. For example, while sieges may be largely static, they can on occasions feature innovative and extensive manoeuvre, as the three illustrations cited above showed. Sieges are also a useful model of another basic form of land operations, positional warfare, which by definition is the opposite of manoeuvre warfare.

Plainly, any soldiers who place all of their strategic options on holding a particular piece of ground have committed themselves to a war of position; to a mode of conflict whose outcome will ultimately be decided by the custody of that position. Any geographic feature or structure might serve as a position to be defended, ranging from a shallow ditch, to a hilltop, to a port blockaded by a fleet, to an island base. In turn, the attackers' response might range from a frontal assault, to a complex series of flanking manoeuvres, to an extended siege, or, as demonstrated by Douglas MacArthur in his 'island hopping' campaign in the Pacific in World War II, to simply bypassing defended locations.

Land campaigns during World War I and the 1980 to 1988 Iran–Iraq War are examples of positional warfare which, in a sense, were only one step removed from a siege, because the frontlines along which the protagonists fought remained relatively static. Similarly, after initially involving rapid, long-distance manoeuvring, the Korean War degenerated into a positional stalemate for its final 2½ years, with the battle front stabilised along the pre-war boundary. In certain circumstances there can, of course, be strong reasons for adopting positional tactics, the most common of which include the powerful imperative for a weaker force to try to use terrain to defend itself, and the need to halt the advance of a superior force. The heroic defence of the narrow pass at Thermopylae by 300 Spartans supported by a thousand or so Thebans and Thespians in the fifth century BCE against a quarter of a million Persians is a timeless example of the latter, with the Spartans' eventual defeat buying valuable time for their Greek allies.

Returning to Clausewitz and the balance between the offence and the defence, the Prussian was, like all of us, a creature of his time, which in his case meant that he was writing only about war between armies, for whom historically defence has been the easier to organise and conduct. Nor were armies which were on the defensive in Clausewitz's era able to call for fire support from aircraft or ships, a capability which in more recent times has routinely changed both the balance between the offence and the defence and, often, the course of land battles. Indeed, the nature of warfare at sea and in the air further confuses generalisations which in the past have favoured the defence. The reduced effect of geographic features in the maritime environment makes the weighting given to a defensive posture problematic at best for navies; while the complete absence of geographic features from the skies makes any such weighting dangerously misleading for air forces, as the history of the fight to control the air has demonstrated.

Traditionally there have been two schools of thought on how best to win air superiority. The classic model formalised by Giulio Douhet contends that it is preferable to destroy an enemy's air force on the ground, an offensive outlook which promises a rapid, decisive outcome.[5] The alternative model advocates aerial combat between opposing fighters, a defensive outlook which often involves a battle of attrition, and of which the American William 'Billy' Mitchell was an early adherent. In fact, neither proposition can claim enduring dominance.

Until 1990, winning control of the air generally did not follow Douhet's offensive prescription but was achieved defensively. The destruction on the ground of the Red Air Force by the Luftwaffe in mid-1941 and the Arab air forces by the Israelis in June 1967, for instance, were historical aberrations. Most air forces have preferred to structure themselves for the defensive counter-air role because it is easier to organise and plan, is politically less contentious, and can be concentrated around vital national assets such as the leadership, the infrastructure, and the army. The predominance of the defensive counter-air model has been evident on the Western Front in World War I, in the Battle of Britain (1940), during the destruction of the Luftwaffe over Germany in 1944–45, and in Korea (1950–53), Vietnam (1965–72), the Falklands (1982), and the Beka'a Valley (1982).*

---

* The destruction of the Luftwaffe over Germany in 1944–45 has been characterised as 'defensive counter-air operations' because it was achieved by allied fighters which were protecting their bomber stream. The bomber stream may have been moving in space, but in effect it was a single 'vital point' around which its escorting fighters flew DCA. The Luftwaffe was drawn up to attack the bombers and was gradually destroyed in a war of attrition

But starting with the 1991 Gulf War against Iraq, technology appears to have swung the pendulum the other way, with potent weapons systems such as long-range radar, electronic jamming, stealthy platforms, long-range weapons, and high-speed anti-radar missiles having given attackers a decisive edge. The US-led campaigns in the Balkans (1995 and 1999), Afghanistan (2001–2) and Iraq (1991 and 2003) were overwhelming testimonies to the supremacy of the offence over the defence – at least in the air, and for the time being.

To be fair to Clausewitz, we should acknowledge that he firmly qualified the case for the defence by stating that victory was unlikely in the absence of an offensive campaign.[6] That crucial caveat once again raises the issue of knowing what we mean by winning, and it also challenges commanders to demonstrate their mastery of the art of war by preparing an offensive campaign which can overcome the inherent strengths of the defence.

Technology in the form of manoeuvre vehicles and killing power has been central to answering that challenge in all eras, situations and geographic settings, noting that technology unaccompanied by sound doctrine and competent leadership is unlikely to provide an answer by itself. For example, the reintroduction of the horse as a manoeuvre vehicle into North America by the Spaniards in the sixteenth century revolutionised the way in which Native Americans could fight, with their new-found mobility dramatically enhancing their capacity to take the initiative – to go on the offensive and as mentioned previously, precisely the same outcome was achieved by General Monash 400 years later at Hamel, when he too exploited new manoeuvre vehicles and innovative tactics as a means by which hitherto ponderous armies might overcome the devastating killing power of artillery batteries and entrenched machine guns.

THE SEARCH FOR DISCONTINUITIES

Strategy at every level has always involved a search for discontinuities – it has always been a contest to create mismatches in which our strengths can be directed against the opponent's weaknesses. Initiatives such as the indirect approach and the exploitation of speed, terrain, and technology are intended to confer an edge in the constant struggle for positional superiority. At the risk of lapsing into semantics, those kinds of gambits might be regarded as a tactical application of manoeuvre and firepower. Two other initiatives which assumed prominence in the strategic debate at the start of the twenty-first century might be regarded more as strategies in their own right. They are so-called asymmetric warfare, and the doctrine of pre-emption. Neither is original, but the profile of each rose sharply in the wake of the attack on the United States by al-Qa'ida operatives in September 2001. Asymmetric warfare has become the method of choice for the application of force by the weak against the strong: it is the preferred recourse of a protagonist who lacks both the resources and the political strength to challenge an opponent within a conventional military setting. Conversely, and partly in response to the growing use of asymmetric means and ways against them, militarily powerful nations such as the United States and Israel increasingly have used pre-emption as a way of dealing with this new threat, obviously with the intention of acting before asymmetric attacks can be made. As the post-September 11 slogan has it, they have been seeking prevention through pre-emption.

The starting point for the concept of asymmetric warfare is our natural predilection to maximise any comparative advantages we may hold over current and potential rivals. The United Kingdom's development of the Royal Navy as a primary instrument of power and empire between the sixteenth and twentieth centuries is an exemplar. Alfred Thayer Mahan's treatise on maritime strategy related a nation's wealth directly to its ability to control and use the seas, and was drawn largely from his analysis of the Royal Navy's status as the world's dominant offensive, defensive, and deterrent force for several centuries.

Few nations enjoy the security of being surrounded by sea, a positional and asymmetric advantage that predisposed successive British rulers towards making the most of their maritime environment for exploration, trade, colonisation, empire-building and, not least, defence. We might regard this accident of geography as nothing more than good luck, which it was, up to a point, but there was no luck associated with the series of political, social, religious and economic reforms which in combination made possible the United Kingdom's early embrace of mercantilism and industrialisation, which in turn both underwrote and was sustained by British naval dominance. The ditty 'Britannia rules the waves' was far more than vulgar propaganda: it was a populist expression of comparative advantage at its best.

Britain's European rivals Spain, France, Russia and Germany all built substantial fleets, but none was ever able to compete consistently with the Royal Navy. A key factor here was not so much the existence of a maritime comparative advantage, but its absence. As continental powers sharing land borders with other powers, those states knew that their greatest military threat came from invading armies. Unsurprisingly, therefore, during the period under review, they placed their priority on building strong armies to defend their homelands. Such was the nature of European politics that those armies were routinely called upon to earn their keep. Eventually, the mass slaughter of World War I was to demonstrate how evenly matched those forces were. In other words, none of the protagonists had been able to identify and exploit a decisive national military comparative advantage. Perhaps in the circumstances that was not possible, but the general observation remains instructive.

Technology, social factors and demographics have probably been used to an even greater extent than geography in various attempts to develop national comparative advantages. For example, at the turn of the twentieth century, France was one of the early leaders in the development of submarines, as officials sought a technological asymmetric response to the naval supremacy of their then rival, the United Kingdom; in the event, for a variety of reasons, the initiative was unsuccessful. Similarly, during the standoff between China and the United States over Korea in the 1950s, economically poor but population-rich China based its war plans on mass assaults, close-up fighting, and attrition; while the United States sought to leverage its powerful economy, well-educated population and immense technological superiority, a combination which facilitated the ability to fight with smaller numbers, knowledge and precision, at a distance. A rapidly growing economy in the later years of the twentieth century has enabled China increasingly to focus on improving its military technology, but the capacity to field overwhelming numbers on the ground continues to be the defining characteristic of its military power.

Few countries can hope to match China's mass or the United States' technology, which leads back to the asymmetric practices of guerilla warfare and terrorism as distinctive forms of manoeuvre and the application of force.

Guerilla operations have been a traditional response by organisations that have otherwise lacked the means to challenge their opponents' military comparative advantage. Representative small-scale examples include the Indonesian independence movement led by Sukarno and Mohammed Hatta that won freedom from the Dutch in 1949, and Fidel Castro's campaign which overthrew the regime of President Fulgencio Batista in Cuba in the late 1950s, thereby replacing one dictator with another. Among the large-scale examples, Mao Tse-tung's extended campaign to seize state power in China which finally succeeded in 1949 is the most noteworthy.

Guerilla or partisan tactics are sometimes ascribed only to conflicts involving non-state actors, but they have been used at one time or another by many states and most military organisations. There have been few larger standing armies than that of the USSR's in World War II, but as the Soviet Union faltered before the Nazi invasion in mid-1941 its commanders initially had little option other than to adopt guerilla methods – retreating, harassing, delaying, ambushing, destroying food supplies and infrastructure – as they fought desperately to stabilise the situation. The Red Army's greatest battlefield commander, Marshal G. K. Zhukov, made skilful use of two of his most potent comparative advantages, severe weather and the USSR's strategic depth, by employing tactics which slowed the Nazis' advance and overextended their lines of communications, an approach that eventually trapped the Germans in a brutal Russian winter. Zhukov had adopted the classic guerilla ploy of trading space for time. Overshadowed in history by massed battles the scale of which dwarfed anything subsequently witnessed on the Western Front, and which to all intents and purposes ultimately destroyed the Wehrmacht, Zhukov's foray into guerilla warfare was a crucial component of his overall strategy.

More generally, élite units like commandos and special forces which are present in most professional armies reflect many of the characteristics of guerillas. Indeed, such units sometimes tread precariously along the often narrow line that separates guerilla warfare from terrorism. The objective of the United States' notorious Operation Phoenix in South Vietnam in the 1960s and 1970s, for example, was to 'neutralise the Vietcong' by 'eradicating its political apparatus', a euphemism for officially sanctioned political assassinations. Yet at the same time, the US Administration was denouncing as terrorism a comparable campaign mounted by the Vietcong against uncooperative South Vietnamese officials.

Operation Phoenix was not unique. State-sanctioned terrorism has always been a feature of political–military competition. It stretches chronologically from the severe sanctions such as execution, torture, slavery and ostracism routinely applied to recalcitrant citizens and slaves by the ancient Greeks and Romans, to the systematic brutality of colonial powers like the British, Spanish, Dutch, French and Portuguese, to the almost incomprehensible scale of the terror inflicted on Soviet society by Stalin and his Politburo collaborators, and on China by Mao Tse-tung. And since World War II there has been the institutionalised repression of regimes such as those of Castro, apartheid South Africa, Idi Amin, Saddam Hussein, Robert Mugabe, and scores more.

Even though those and similar regimes have employed terrorism as a tool of government policy, the method is more commonly associated with radical groups operating outside the state apparatus. The list of perpetrators runs to thousands and covers the duration of recorded history: Zealots, Assassins, Narodniks, Irgun Zvai Leumi, Red Brigades, the Baader-Meinhof group, Hezbollah, Hamas, Jemaah Islamiah, and so on. Such movements almost invariably have been associated with the pursuit of a particular cause and end-state, which often has been more overtly ideological than those sought by more broadly based political movements.

No terrorist/asymmetric action has been more successful than al-Qa'ida's stunning attack on America on September 11, 2001. For sheer effect and ingenuity, the raid rewrote the terrorism handbook. Not only was the political impact immense, but so too were the

economic and social consequences. Airlines and their many subsidiary industries lost business for months, the United States was
forced onto a near-war footing, with all of its associated costs, many
people became afraid to travel, and extremist movements generally
received a major morale boost. Astonishingly, as part of the United
States' immediate response to try to prevent repeat attacks, US fighter
pilots ordered onto standing air defence patrols over major cities were
authorised to shoot down hijacked US airliners, filled with US citizens. It is hard to conceive of a more extraordinary strategic effect.
Nor has the full impact of the attack yet become apparent, as it is likely
to be years before the consequences of the subsequent US military
response – the invasions of Afghanistan in 2001 and Iraq in 2003 –
can be fully assessed.

Like every act of terrorism, September 11 was reprehensible. It was
also, however, a textbook illustration of how to exploit comparative
advantage and fight asymmetric warfare. In a sense, it marked a logical if depraved response to military events of the preceding thirty-four
years. Israel's crushing victory over Egypt, Syria and Jordan in only
six days in June 1967 marked the beginning of a period in which
the warfighting capabilities of the United States and its allies seemed
to have become almost incontestable within a conventional setting;
that is, when using conventional weapons in a theatre-level campaign and, in the main, complying with the Law of Armed Conflict.
Following its humiliation in Indochina, the US defence organisation had reinvented itself intellectually, to the extent that between
1991 and 2003, in coalition with various allies, it had utterly routed
ostensibly formidable opponents twice in Iraq and the Balkans and
once in Afghanistan. Any sensible enemy could only conclude that
an armed challenge to the United States would have to be made by
unconventional means.

The Israelis' and the United States' battlefield successes were
underwritten by their overwhelming air power, which allowed them
to use the skies for intelligence gathering, troop movement, and
resupply, and for powerful strikes in support of surface forces or
immediate strategic objectives. Air power of that dimension has
invariably been the sole preserve of the handful of states that have
had the wealth, technology and education base which are essential

for a conventionally organised air force to prosper. A corollary of that has been the assumption that less advanced countries and non-state organisations cannot raise and sustain an effective air force. Yet on September 11, by way of lateral thinking, for some two hours al-Qa'ida possessed and operated one of the most lethal air forces in history. Its pilots gained control of the air by deception, in the process defeating the most advanced integrated air defence system in the world, and they then struck in broad daylight against New York City and Washington, unchallenged by the combined air defence might of the US Air Force, Navy, Army and Marines.

Al-Qa'ida exploited two comparative advantages in particular. First, the United States' relatively open society allowed the terrorists to enter America, merge into the community, train at local flying schools, and book seats on the commercial flights they subsequently hijacked and converted into an instant if wholly expendable air force. No responsible person inside the US air defence system recognised what was happening until it was too late. And second, al-Qa'ida's operatives were willing, indeed, passionate, to die for their cause. The entire US defence apparatus and approach to strategy had been built up over centuries on the assumption that, ultimately, most combatants want to survive the experience of battle. Al-Qa'ida had matched its ruthless, closed-society mindset against the United States' openness, and had emerged the winner. By any measure the attack was a brilliantly conceived and executed asymmetric operation.

Pre-emption was the US Administration's initial strategic response. Like asymmetric warfare, pre-emption has always been a feature of human conflict. Japan's devastating strike against Pearl Harbor in December 1941 has been perhaps the most successful example to date: other notable episodes include the German invasion of the USSR in June 1941; and Israel's victory in the 1967 Six Day War and its precision strike against the Iraqi nuclear reactor near Baghdad in June 1981. But again, like asymmetric warfare, the notion of pre-emption achieved an unusually high profile at the start of the twenty-first century, again primarily because of September 11.

During a speech in June 2002, US President George W. Bush stated that instead of relying on deterrence as its principal declaratory defence policy, the United States would now act first and explain later – it would 'take the battle to the enemy [and] confront the worst threats before they emerge'. Pre-emption had become policy. Bush contended that September 11 had shown that a national security strategy predicated on an essentially defensive outlook left the US militarily vulnerable and made the country seem morally weak. A defensive posture not only conceded the initiative to an aggressor, but also allowed him to prepare and grow strong in his own time. Because waiting for something to happen in a world seemingly vulnerable to large-scale terrorist attacks was no longer an option, 'prevention via pre-emption' was the logical reaction (at least to the Bush Administration).

Two concerns loomed large during the determination of the policy. The first was the perceived need to buttress the credibility of deterrence by actually applying extreme force from time to time – by demonstrating that US military power was not a paper tiger but was backed up by the will to use it vigorously if necessary. Implicit in this was the belief that previous Administrations had been weak in their military responses to terrorism and had thereby emboldened the United States' enemies generally. And second, there was the danger that future terrorist attacks might involve the use of weapons of mass destruction (nuclear, chemical, biological), the consequences of which would be so fearful as to demand the most forceful preventive action. The subsequent invasions of Afghanistan and Iraq translated that policy into practice.

THE LAW OF ARMED CONFLICT

The basic principles for conducting manoeuvre and applying force have varied little over the centuries. But deciding how much and what kind of force to apply – that is, successfully interpreting those principles – has often been an extraordinarily complex and difficult task. The Law of Armed Conflict provides a starting point for resolving that complexity.

Self-interest was an early source of motivation for regulating war, and has remained so. The Greeks in about the fifth century BCE and later the Romans both developed formal and informal practices for limiting the application of force, which typically related to post-victory behaviour and was intended to restrict the damage rampaging soldiers might cause to property the victors now wished to utilise themselves. Some two thousand years later, in 1648, the treaty of Westphalia formalised the rise of nation-states and simultaneously prompted interest in a system of international law, albeit one which was again characterised by self-interest. Today, International Humanitarian Law and the Law of Armed Conflict which started to emerge in the mid-nineteenth century are the basis of efforts to regulate war.

Among other things, that body of law addresses war crimes, crimes against humanity, and genocide, all of which relate to 'how much' and 'what kind' of force might be applied. Genocide, for example, is likely to be pursued only as a matter of grand strategy – as the consequence of a decision taken within the highest councils. The Holocaust in World War II, the war between the Hutus and the Tutsis in Rwanda, Burundi and the Congo from the 1970s to the 1990s, and the ethnic cleansing conducted by all protagonists but most comprehensively by Serbs against Muslims in Bosnia in the 1990s, demonstrated that genocide remains an acceptable strategy for some leaders in the modern world. Hatred based on racial, religious and tribal differences is the common stimulus for this darkest of human emotions.

There are three concepts fundamental to the contemporary Law of Armed Conflict: military necessity; humanity; and proportionality. Each of those concepts clearly differentiates between combatants and civilians, and each is concerned in part with the questions of how much and what kind of force, if any, can be justified in the prevailing circumstances. In essence, limits are placed on the application of force. Only targets which represent a legitimate military objective can be attacked; civilians are excluded (a caveat which automatically categorises terrorism as a war crime); and the force used must be proportional to the military need for the particular objective. The remainder of this section is concerned with the notions of military necessity and proportionality as they relate to the application of force, noting that the issue of humanity is examined in detail under the broad heading of 'just' wars in chapter eight.

The subjectivity inherent in those concepts simply reflects reality. Two parties disputing offshore resources might settle in the first instance for a mere show of force by, say, deploying ships to the area; conversely, states and organisations that believe they are involved in a fight for their very survival might decide that the maximum application of force, including even genocide and the use of weapons of mass destruction, represents a proportional response.

A deft demonstration of matching the application of force to the prevailing circumstances was given by China during its brief incursion into Vietnam early in 1979. Irritated by a series of perceived insults and alleged illegal behaviour, on 17 February China's leaders sent 120 000 troops across the shared border to conduct 'punitive military operations'. Population centres were occupied and assets seized as Chinese soldiers penetrated some forty kilometres into Vietnam. Then, after only three weeks, they withdrew. Although the fighting had often been intense, the scale of the incursion had been carefully controlled, and the Chinese were satisfied that they had, in their words, 'taught Vietnam a lesson'.

The fact remains, though, that such carefully measured actions are unlikely to be contemplated in more dire circumstances. At Kursk on 5 July 1943, for example, Soviet dictator Joseph Stalin believed that defeat would presage the end of the USSR, which under Nazi rule would have become a slave state. When the Soviets' 1.3 million troops, 3600 tanks and 2400 aircraft clashed with the Germans' 900 000 troops, 2700 tanks and 2000 aircraft in the decisive battle of World War II, the Red Army had no doubt that it was to use every means at its disposal to win, and that if necessary every soldier was expected to fight to the death. Kursk represented one extreme of the continuum of force application, with the Soviets prepared to fight a battle of annihilation.

An analogy of sorts might be drawn with the 1970 Treaty on the Non-Proliferation of Nuclear Weapons, which has since been ratified by some 190 countries. The argument is often made by advocates of the so-called realist school of international relations that most states have signed that treaty simply because they are not themselves threatened by nuclear weapons and their national survival is not at risk. Should that situation change, the argument continues, affected states capable of building the bomb would quickly do so. The examples of non-complying nations such as India, Pakistan, Israel and North Korea would appear to validate that reasoning. The point here is that in extreme circumstances any application of force is more likely to be defined by the dictates of necessity than by those of proportionality.

That is not to say that the Law of Armed Conflict is impractical and should only be paid lip service. On the contrary, the code is fundamental to our efforts to preserve some level of civilised behaviour within the uncivilised activity of war. It is to say, though, that force is relative, and that proportionality and military necessity are subjective. The allies' bomber offensive against Germany in World War II illustrates the point.

There is no doubt that, had Germany won the war, the commander of the RAF's bomber offensive, Air Chief Marshal Sir Arthur Harris, would have been tried and executed as a war criminal. For most of the campaign Harris made no pretence of trying to target the Nazis' war economy directly, concentrating instead on 'de-housing' the civilian men and women who worked in the factories. Most nights for four years Harris's squadrons carpet-bombed German cities, killing some 500 000 civilians and displacing millions more. Like Stalin at Kursk, Harris – supported by Churchill, Roosevelt, and the other allied leaders – believed he was fighting a war of national survival, a desperate situation which justified desperate measures. It is noteworthy, by the way, that the general consensus among legal specialists is that under the Law of Armed Conflict as it existed at the time, Harris did not act improperly. That would not be the case today.

A distinctive application of the notion of proportionality emerged in the United States during the tenure of General Colin Powell as chairman of the Joint Chiefs of Staff from 1989 to 1993, a period which included the 1991 Gulf War. Powell was a combat veteran from the United States' war in Indochina, in which US strategy was typified by its inappropriateness to the political, cultural and military setting. From Powell's perspective as a soldier, one of the consequences was that, too often, the fighting men ended up paying the price for political ineptitude. Subsequently, as chairman of the joint chiefs, Powell articulated a doctrine for the commitment of his men and women to battle which among other things declared that the 'force used [by the United States] should be overwhelming and disproportionate to the force used by the enemy'. At first glance the doctrine might seem contrary to the Law of Armed Conflict. Yet Powell might reasonably have contended that his intention was to achieve a rapid, decisive victory, which could mean comparatively few casualties and, therefore, a more humane outcome.

A similar argument was made by those air-power theorists whose concepts were used to justify the carpet- and fire-bombing of German and Japanese cities in World War II, in which instance the gap between theory and practice proved to be horrifically wide. By the same token, had a land invasion of Japan become necessary, some analysts estimated that US forces would have sustained around 500 000 casualties, a number which decision-makers in Washington could not ignore when they contemplated the military necessity and proportionality of using atomic bombs which, in the event, convinced Japan to surrender without a single allied soldier having to set foot on the Japanese home islands.

The crew of the American B-29 Superfortress the *Enola Gay* (named after the mother of the mission commander) who dropped the atomic bomb on Hiroshima on 6 August 1945 observed principles of manoeuvre and the application of force that would have been familiar to generations of strategists and warriors, from Alexander to Nathan Bedford Forrest to al-Qa'ida. Whether Alexander and Forrest could have rationalised the questions of 'how much' and 'what kind' of force in relation to Hiroshima, and then Nagasaki three days later is, of course, another matter altogether.

MORALITY AS STRATEGY

Any application of force can generate ethical concerns, which might range in level and intensity from an individual's conscience (is it moral to kill, even in an officially sanctioned war?) to the national will (is a particular course of action 'just'?, and so on). A unique interpretation of 'application of force' which drew on that ethical dimension was developed by the Indian revolutionary Mohandas

Karamchand Gandhi, who led his nation's struggle for independence from Britain in the first half of the twentieth century.

Gandhi's strategy is often described as civil disobedience, as a non-violent campaign of passive resistance expressed through such actions as non-cooperation (refusal to pay taxes, rates, and other official imposts; refusal to perform civic duties; etc.), strikes, fasts, protest marches, sit-ins, and the like, a technique which was later successfully adapted into other settings by other revolutionary leaders, including Martin Luther King in the United States in the 1950s and 1960s, and Lech Walesa in Poland in the 1970s and 1980s. In Gandhi's case, however, the description 'civil disobedience' is only partly correct because his strategic concept was far more profound than mere disobedience or non-compliance.

The name Gandhi gave to the technique he developed to undermine British authority in India was 'satyagraha', a compound of Sanskrit nouns which translated as 'a search for truth'.[7] Satyagraha incorporated the kinds of protest activities mentioned above, but, perhaps more significantly, also expressed a philosophical and moral position by rejecting violence. By refusing to react to the systematic political, social and physical aggression of the British oppressors, the satyagraha would achieve a state of moral authority which, Gandhi believed, would expose the illegitimacy and immorality of British rule, thereby leading to its defeat.

Historically, the application of force in the pursuit of a strategic objective almost invariably has been precisely that; namely, the use of organised violence to impose physical costs such as pain, the destruction of assets, and death. Gandhi turned that method on its head by making passive resistance a powerful psychological weapon which, in effect, turned violence back against its perpetrators by invalidating the military concept of valour, and the legal notions of humanity, proportionality, and just war. If soldiers who beat or killed passive protesters became stricken with self-loathing, as sometimes happened, then, paradoxically, the non-violence of the protesters had become a coercive weapon. Satyagraha was a morally derived, passive asymmetric strategy.

Reference was made in chapter two to Machiavelli's conclusion that 'all armed prophets have conquered and [all] unarmed ones

[have] failed', a sentiment later endorsed by Mao Tse-tung, who asserted that all political power comes from the barrel of a gun, and Stalin, who, during a discussion on the influence or otherwise of the Catholic church, asked rhetorically: 'How many divisions does the Pope have?' Satyagraha represented a notable exception to such coldly calculated expressions of power politics. But it is important to appreciate that, like every other strategic concept, satyagraha was a creature of its time and context. Had Gandhi and his followers been confronting less civilised colonists than the British, the probability is that they would have been subjected to a degree of brutality that no philosophical search for the truth could have conquered.

* * *

The means of conducting manoeuvre and applying force have changed beyond recognition over the centuries. Marching has been either replaced or complemented by, among other things, horses, ships, mechanised land vehicles, aircraft, and space vehicles; as have slingshots been replaced by bows and arrows, bombards, machine guns, precision missiles and, soon, space-based weapons. But the principles for exploiting manoeuvre and firepower have largely remained the same. Relative position and having the right weapon remains just as important to today's fighter pilot moving at 1000 kilometres an hour as it did to the Old Testament's David, moving at five kilometres an hour. And, to take a cross-section from history, Alexander, Genghis Khan, Lee and Giap would all have been familiar with and, perhaps, professionally impressed by, the deception, surprise, and use of position, and the matching of force to the objective, demonstrated by al-Qa'ida's attack on New York City and Washington. 'Manoeuvre and the application of force' is far more than a tactical catch-phrase: it is the essence of applying strategy.

5 | Shaping the strategic environment
Making strategy work

ANY RESORT TO ARMED conflict is likely to indicate a policy failure of some kind, since ideally our grand strategic activities should enable us to achieve our goals without resort to force. As is always the case there will be exceptions, for instance, when one protagonist is determined to use organised violence as his method of first choice, regardless of anything else. Examples include Hitler's policies to exterminate the Jewish race and subjugate Slavic nations as slaves, and the ethnic cleansing pursued through open warfare in the Balkans in the 1990s. But generally, interest groups prefer to achieve their policy goals by shaping the strategic environment: by influencing attitudes and events in favour of their objectives.

SHAPE-DETER-RESPOND

The idea of trying to make strategy work for us reflects the classic strategic hierarchy of 'shape-deter-respond', under which the order of priorities is: first, influence the environment in which we function – political, diplomatic, economic, social, cultural, military, geographic – towards our interests; second, if shaping is not entirely successful, deter behaviour that might be inimical to those interests; and last, if deterrence fails, respond as necessary anywhere along the spectrum of influence from, say, soft sanctions at one extreme to war at the other. Shaping strategies will be directed towards our own strengths and preferences, and typically will involve diplomacy, alliances, trade and economic agreements, military exercises, and cultural exchanges.

Diplomacy and alliances are the most commonly used strategic shaping mechanisms. Consistent with the aphorism that in foreign relations there are no enduring friendships, only enduring interests, the history of alliances has seen many strange bedfellows. Few have been more ill-matched than Soviet foreign minister V. M. Molotov and his German counterpart, Joachim von Ribbentrop, who in August 1939, only days before the start of World War II, signed a non-aggression pact. Implacable ideological opponents, the communist Soviets and the fascist Nazis knew that sooner or later war between them was almost inevitable. But in mid-1939, Soviet dictator Joseph Stalin needed time to strengthen his military forces before any such clash, and German dictator Adolf Hitler needed temporarily to remove the possibility of having to fight on his eastern (Russian) front as he prepared for his imminent invasion of Poland, the Low Countries and France.

Nominally intended to last ten years, the non-aggression pact was broken in less than two when German forces invaded the USSR in June 1941. But in the meantime, typifying the opportunistic domain of power politics, the pact had helped shape the environment favourably for both signatories. Stalin in fact had hoped desperately that the arrangement would have given the Soviets at least another year's breathing space and, notwithstanding irrefutable evidence from his intelligence sources in the preceding months that a Nazi invasion was certain, was shocked when it happened. Still, had the Germans attacked two years earlier, it is likely that the USSR would not have survived.

The Molotov–Ribbentrop Pact illustrates two-way strategic shaping at a national level; that is, it is representative of the inherently interactive nature of competing strategies. While dramatic, it is only one of many possible shaping models. Perhaps the most complex example from recent times was the global shaping attempted by the United States and the USSR during the fifty years of the Cold War. The United States' use of two distinct approaches that in effect were opposed to each other, and which both enjoyed some success, is particularly noteworthy.

Both approaches were incorporated within the overall strategy of containment, a proposal for dealing with emerging Soviet power articulated in a now famous article published in 1947 by the celebrated US foreign relations officer, George Kennan.[1] Illustrating yet again the elusive nature of the word strategy, containment as described by Kennan was both a strategy and an objective. The important definitional issue here is not so much the meaning that might or might not be attached to any use of the ubiquitous noun 'strategy' but, rather, that we clearly understand what our desired objective is, how we intend reaching it, and whether it is within our capabilities.

Kennan advocated a firm but sensitive policy towards the USSR, in which the United States' actions would be determined primarily by what the Soviets would probably do and not by what they might do. In essence, that meant the US policies should be informed by best-case rather than worst-case analyses of the USSR's probable military, political and economic behaviour. Soviet expansionism as perceived by the United States would still be opposed, but that opposition would be expressed in the first instance through diplomacy and negotiation rather than by military confrontation. Kennan argued that containment should focus on the key geographic areas of Western Europe and Japan, in the one instance by protecting friendly European states from Soviet coercion, and in the other by building up post-war Japan as the mainstay of liberal democracy and, therefore, as a bastion against communism, in North Asia.

Kennan's emphasis on diplomacy and negotiation as the basic tools of containment is sometimes not fully appreciated, perhaps because of the overwhelming profile of the nuclear standoff that became the defining characteristic of the Cold War. Ironically, Kennan's version of containment was conceived in part to try to avoid the potentially apocalyptic military competition that he feared an arms race between the world's first two nuclear powers might fuel. The use of military power as a shaping mechanism for the strategic environment was not part of his vision, and history would suggest that he was more right than wrong. Of the two major armed conflicts from the Cold War in which the United States and the USSR were either direct or de facto participants, Korea from 1950 to 1953 was militarily inconclusive and politically frustrating for the United States, and Vietnam from

1962 to 1975 caused perhaps the greatest disunity in the United States since the civil war a century before.

At the same time as Kennan's version of containment was being debated, his ideological opponents within official US circles were promoting an alternative shaping strategy, which was defined by National Security Council document number 68. Prepared in 1950 by Kennan's contemporary Paul Nitze, NSC-68 stated that the global promotion of democratic values and institutions was an interest of the highest order for the United States. But unlike Kennan, Nitze believed the United States should pursue that end primarily through the use of military power, preferably via coercion, but with compellence as an acceptable alternative. NSC-68 presented the case for military containment as both the means and the strategy for preventing the spread of communism, and among other things it subsequently provided the intellectual justification for the war in Vietnam.

Containing communism undoubtedly was the United States' objective in Southeast Asia generally and Vietnam specifically, but the question that must be asked is whether different means and ways might have been used. A number of prominent commentators, notably Singapore's pre-eminent political figure Lee Kuan Yew, and former US Secretary of State Dean Rusk, have argued that the West's intervention in Vietnam was a success, and that although Saigon fell to the communists in 1975, the intervening years gave other Southeast Asian states time to strengthen themselves sufficiently to avoid the same fate. Perhaps that was so, but it is an argument which assumes that Cambodia, Laos, Thailand, Malaysia and Singapore would have fallen without those extra ten years, which is by no means certain; and it ignores the consequences for Cambodia, where a case can be made that the West's war in Vietnam made possible the accession of Pol Pot's genocidal regime in 1975. Moreover, the US intervention was an unmitigated disaster for Vietnam in terms of casualties, social dislocation and economic disruption.

Culture matters, which was why the US government's dismal ignorance of Vietnamese history was noted in chapter three. North Vietnam's leader Ho Chi Minh and his senior colleagues may have been communists, but they were first and foremost nationalists who might well have been receptive to the kind of diplomatic and economic shaping favoured by Kennan. The United States' choice of a military strategy also illustrated the dangers inherent in the common temptation to let the means determine the course of action, particularly when those means seem to offer an easy answer. In this case, the United States perhaps turned too quickly to its armed forces, first, because they appeared overwhelmingly superior and therefore promised a quick solution; and second, because the option to go to war simplified what would have otherwise been an exceedingly difficult and complex policy decision. That this is not the way to manage decision-making seems self-evident, but it is indicative of an approach that is frequently applied.

Containment via compellence in Southeast Asia was the opposite of containment via soft power in post-World War II Europe, where the visionary Marshall Plan translated Kennan's policy into practice. Launched in 1947 by US Secretary of State George C. Marshall, the plan provided some US$20 billion in aid to reconstruct devastated European economies and social systems, a process which Marshall believed would block competing Soviet overtures. A feature of the plan was its requirement for participating states to act as a unified economic unit, an arrangement which forced them to develop common interests. So successful was the initiative that it can be regarded as the necessary precursor to the formation of the European Economic Community in 1958 and the European Union in 1993, and to the growing unification of Europe generally.

The inclusion of West Germany was another of the Marshall Plan's inspired initiatives, ensuring as it did the re-integration into Western Europe of at least half of one of the continent's most influential nations. In the event, it was West Germany's stunning economic progress in the post-war decades that as much as anything else highlighted the superiority of the Western economic and political system to that of the USSR's and East Germany's, and which contributed to the collapse of the USSR in 1991.

Kennan's policy was also applied in North Asia where, driven by the imperatives of global politics, the Western powers implemented a remarkable episode of strategic shaping. Japan was the centrepiece.

At the formal surrender ceremony held on the USS *Missouri* in Tokyo Bay on 2 September 1945, documents and statements issued by the allies were severe and uncompromising, as might be expected following unconditional victory over a most cruel and brutal enemy. Japanese warriors were told they were neither honourable nor gallant foes, but rather would be remembered only for their treachery and atrocities, sentiments which would have been shared by the great majority of allied servicemen who fought against them. Sentiment, however, counted for little in the pragmatic world of realpolitik. Well before the ceremony on the *Missouri*, American and British politicians had decided that a strong, rehabilitated Japan would be an essential bulwark against the Soviet Union and, most probably, China, where it seemed likely that Mao Tse-tung's communists would gain power in their civil war against Chiang Kai-shek's nationalists.

Prime Minister Churchill, President Truman and Marshal Stalin had agreed at the Potsdam Conference in July 1945 that, while Japan's military forces were to be completely disarmed and stern justice meted out to all war criminals, the Japanese were not to be destroyed as a race or a nation. The Potsdam Declaration placed direct responsibility on the Japanese government for removing all obstacles to the revival and strengthening of democratic tendencies among the Japanese people, an objective which was to be pursued under the supervision of an allied occupation force. General Douglas MacArthur was appointed Supreme Commander for the Allied Powers in Japan, in effect becoming the country's proconsul during its early rehabilitation, a task he was to perform with characteristic imperious intellect and skill.

Replicating events on the other side of the world, Japan's subsequent economic and social 'miracle' was no less remarkable than West Germany's. Located at the geographic eastern and western extremities of communist power, the emergence of two newly democratic, modernising, economically dynamic states had a profound effect on international relations.

Soviet shaping strategies during the Cold War were in a sense more sophisticated, but in application proved to be inchoate. Even in its dual guises, containment at least reflected a certain consistency, namely, the United States' determination actively to oppose Soviet and communist influence at every turn. Propped up by the United States' enormous economy, the policy could be applied extravagantly both diplomatically and militarily, which it was.

The Soviets' response was, in contrast, inhibited by self-imposed pressures. According to the doctrine of Marxism–Leninism which allegedly guided the USSR's development, capitalism contains within itself the seeds of its own destruction. Theoretically, therefore, all the Soviet leadership had to do was bide its time until its ideological opponents in the West self-destructed. Rarely, of course, has there been a greater dichotomy between theory and practice than the Soviet experiment between 1917 and 1991. In particular, the attempt by Lenin, Stalin and their successors to build socialism in one country in the USSR was diametrically at odds with Marx's 'scientific' analysis of the universal nature of socio-economic development and class warfare.

Because of that dichotomy, which the USSR's leaders either denied or rationalised away, Stalin was constantly preoccupied with the challenge of trying to build a socialist economy in the face of continual reminders that he could do so only by the systematic application of brute force against his own citizens, a caveat which doomed national productivity and, therefore, Stalin's spending power, to fall further and further behind that of his ideological opponent's. External factors exacerbated the problem after World War II, with the USSR now required to maintain forcible control over not only its own citizens, but also those of its newly acquired satellite states in Eastern Europe. And additional complications started to emanate from China, where the accession of Mao Tse-tung introduced a competing source of communist primacy.

Incidentally, the Soviets' attempt to build socialism in one country remains a stunning example of strategic delusion. By no means is this observation offered as brilliant hindsight, or as a gratuitous dismissal of the Soviet experiment. The last thing that could be said of Stalin and his colleagues is that they were fools; on the contrary, many, not least Stalin himself, were towering intellects. Perhaps the best and the worst that can be said of them is that they were idealists who came to allow extreme missionary zeal and then hubris to fatally cloud their strategic judgment and their morality.

Nevertheless, it seems that the majority of the Kremlin's inner sanctum continued to believe in the historic mission and inevitable triumph of communism: that is, they held firm to their vision of the future as defined by Marx and Lenin. Their great and unforgivable mistake was to endorse state terrorism as the way to achieve that idealised end.

Outside the boundaries of the USSR, Stalin and his successors' shaping policies tended to be as much opportunistic as they were consciously strategic. Stalin's encouragement of Mao Tse-tung and North Korean dictator Kim Il-sung to invade South Korea in June 1950, thus precipitating the Korean War, seems to have been motivated by little more than the fact that the opportunity to do so had arisen, although it might also be seen as the action of an aging supremo trying to unsettle potential challengers inside the Kremlin. Self-interested cynicism on such a monumental scale may not be strategy, but nor is it an uncommon characteristic of strategic decision-makers.

Soviet efforts to develop a coherent shaping program for communism internationally were equally cynical, with the Communist International (Comintern) being quietly put to rest in 1943, and its nebulous successor, the Communist Information Bureau, in 1956.* The circumstances behind the demise of the Comintern epitomised realpolitik. Stalin had never had much interest in the organisation, which by 1943 had in any case outlived whatever purpose it may have served, but he was able to portray its liquidation to his Western wartime allies of convenience as a gesture of goodwill. After the war, Stalin's major shaping interest was in maintaining his grip on the sphere of influence he had established around the USSR, in the form of the newly occupied, newly communist satellite states, although, as noted previously, if an opportunity to make life difficult for the United States presented itself, he was happy to take it.

The concept of a 'sphere of influence' as a strategic shaping mechanism warrants further comment.

---

* The Communist International (Comintern) was an amorphous organisation formed in 1919 to promote the soviet system of governance on a global scale. In practice, it often was used to serve the interests and dominance of the USSR's leaders over those of other communists, and its activities were rarely coordinated

SPHERES OF INFLUENCE

Generally established by powerful states to promote their own well-being, spheres of influence are as old as strategy itself. Whenever one nation achieves some form of influence over others, it has extended its capacity to shape or control events. That outcome is most commonly associated with military control, as in the Roman Empire (Rome's ruthless competition with Carthage over spheres of influence, for example, was discussed in a different context in chapter three), the Spanish Empire, the British Empire, the Soviet Union's domination of its East European satellites, the Pax Americana, and so on. In those and similar instances, the deployment of military forces to the location or sphere the central power wishes to influence represents the way in which its desired ends are to be achieved. The degree of influence sought and attained can vary, with, say, the sheer size of the Soviet Union's military presence in its satellite states during the Cold War indicating the USSR's determination to enforce its will absolutely; and the smaller presence of US armed forces in Western Europe being indicative more of a message of intent.

A sphere of influence can be established without the deployment of military power to the area of interest. Depending on the circumstances, a declaration of intent backed up by a remotely based but readily available, credible deterrent or compellence capability can be sufficient to achieve the objective. The Monroe Doctrine is one of the better-known examples of this approach. In 1823, US President James Monroe announced that, henceforth, the New World, broadly defined as North and South America, and the Old World of Europe were to be regarded as separate spheres of strategic influence, and that in particular, the colonisation of Latin America was to cease immediately. Any future European interference in the Americas, Monroe continued, would be regarded as hostile to the United States. As a corollary, Monroe declared that the United States would not interfere in European affairs. The Monroe Doctrine was underwritten by the naval might of the United States and the United Kingdom, the latter's government having supported the policy.

Deciding whether or not a particular sphere of influence is a 'good' thing or a 'bad' thing is, of course, entirely subjective. Thus, it should not be surprising that, some eighty years and twenty-one presidents later, the aggressive and adventurous President Theodore Roosevelt chose to interpret the Monroe Doctrine as a licence for the United States to pursue its own form of 'new' imperialism by formally extending its influence to the Philippines and Latin America. A quick search through the records will unearth any number of sphere of influence doctrines – Truman, Brezhnev, Nixon, Carter – which generally have been time-limited, and which served their purpose for the era in which they were enunciated.

While military force has been a primary means of establishing spheres of influence, other instruments of power have often been more effective, even if slower to create change. Persuasion via economic incentives and disincentives, for example, is a favoured tool of diplomacy. The approach's attraction is self-evident, and the techniques involved should be familiar, given that the principles apply to almost any kind of social interaction, from the workplace to sporting clubs to family events. Two case studies have been chosen to illustrate the point. The first, involving Iran, Europe and the United States, is noteworthy for the complexity of its interactive politics and for its unexpected consequences; the second, involving China and Japan, provides a contrast through its mixture of emotion, culture, history, and pragmatism.

Early in 2004 the United States repeated its long-standing allegation that Iran was a major supporter of international terrorism; simultaneously, the UN again expressed concerns that Iran harboured ambitions to acquire nuclear weapons, which would place it in breach of the world body's protocols. Iran's government was accused of being one of the most dangerous in the world. In an attempt to coax the country's rulers away from sponsoring terrorism and developing nuclear weapons, a group of European states offered to underwrite a program of foreign investment intended to boost Iran's economy and modernise its workforce skills. At the time, however, Iran's export earnings from oil production were so large that its leaders were able to pick and choose from such offers; indeed, they were probably more capable of exerting international financial pressure than many first-world states. In the circumstances, Europe's attempt to shape Iran's behaviour through the incentives of development aid and financial transfers held no attraction, and it should not have been surprising that the initiative was rejected.

A danger with this kind of two-way dynamic is that the protagonist seeking to modify a competitor's behaviour might turn too quickly to the strongest element of his national power, without first establishing which of those elements best suits the circumstances. An example often cited is that of the United States, which, the argument goes, can be too hasty to turn to the use or the threat of military force, simply because it can, not necessarily because it should. And indeed, as if on cue, in this instance, US political leaders began to issue thinly veiled military threats against the Iranian government. Which leads to the unintended consequence: namely, that gratuitous pressure from the United States – a nation characterised in Tehran as the 'great Satan' – may have hastened Iranian efforts to acquire weapons of mass destruction.

China's exploitation of its admittedly traumatic history with Japan has, on occasions, been no less belligerent. Using tactics that were described in some news reports as 'violent, crude and anachronistic', in April 2004 China's leadership authorised anti-Japanese demonstrations in a number of cities, allegedly to express anger at Japan's continuing refusal to acknowledge wartime atrocities such as the Rape of Nanjing. The accusation was legitimate, but the sometimes violent nature of the protests was not. In any case, there was much more to the incident than Beijing admitted.

China's leaders were using history as a convenient medium to attack several important Japanese policies indirectly. The Chinese objectives were to: undermine Japan's efforts to gain a permanent seat on the Security Council of the UN; intimidate them over disputed offshore oil fields; and remind them not to interfere in China's dispute with Taiwan. Reminiscent of the forceful but calibrated way in which it had 'taught Vietnam a lesson' in 1979, China was now putting its main rival in North Asia in its place; that is, it was attempting to shape the strategic environment.

Economic and diplomatic shaping fall into the category of 'soft power', as opposed to military 'hard power'. Culture also plays a role here, one which in the longer term may be the most potent of all shaping mechanisms. So-called American cultural imperialism is perhaps the best-known, in the form of films, popular music, fashion, speech, dance, food, and the like. Joseph Nye's study of soft power ('the means to success in world politics'), for example, notes that the United States is by far the world's biggest exporter of film and television shows, has the largest population of foreign university students who are then exposed to American values, and publishes more books, has more music sales, and hosts more Internet websites than any other country.[2] Similarly, the Soviet Union 'spent billions' publicising its 'high culture' such as ballet, music and literature, promoting sporting successes, and sponsoring peace movements and youth groups; France and Spain invest in the international dissemination of Francophone and Iberian cultural values; and so on.

To suggest that any regime has consciously tried to shape the strategic environment exclusively by the promotion of its culture would not only be facile but also patronising to those hundreds of millions of people who happily embrace foreign customs; however, to deny the long-term impact of culture as a strategic instrument would be to ignore the obvious.

BALANCE OF POWER

Somewhat analogous to 'sphere of influence' is the notion of 'balance of power'. One of the basic concepts from the theory and practice of international relations, balance of power means precisely what it says. Competing states and alliances seek to maintain a balance with which all are comfortable across a range of means and ways, in furtherance of strategic ends. Military power is the most readily identifiable of these means, but others such as economic strength and political influence arising from, say, the control of a vital resource, can be significant. Should any of the competitors perceive an unacceptable imbalance developing, he is likely to seek recourse by strengthening his alliances or by rearming. Balance-of-power contests include those between the Triple Alliance and the Triple Entente prior to World War I, the axis and the allies before and during World War II, and the USSR and the United States during the Cold War. In the twenty-first century, China, India, Brazil, and perhaps Japan and the European Union are all likely to join the equation as major players at the global level.

Fear over a perceived imbalance in military power was one of the motivating factors behind Soviet Premier Nikita Khrushchev's decision to deploy nuclear-capable missiles to Cuba in 1962, an action which took the world to the brink of nuclear war. Khrushchev knew that the United States held a substantial numerical advantage in inter-continental ballistic missiles armed with nuclear warheads; furthermore, the United States had stationed shorter-range missiles in Europe where their proximity to the USSR greatly reduced the flight time of any attack, which in turn imperilled the Soviets' second-strike capability. The ensuing Cuban missile crisis of October 1962 is a study in strategic decision-making in itself; for the point of this exercise it is sufficient to record that Khrushchev eventually withdrew his missiles, and to note the balance-of-power considerations that prompted his original decision.

Continuing with the Cold War setting, the shaping instruments of spheres of influence and balances of power intersected during the high noon of that confrontation, in the 1950s and 1960s, when both major protagonists sought to construct geographically defined alliances against each other to enhance their power by extending their influence. For the United States, those barriers eventually comprised the three security alliances of NATO, CENTO, and SEATO that bounded the USSR geographically from Western Europe, through Central Asia, to the Far East; while the Soviets achieved a similar if less comprehensive effect with their Eastern European satellites and the Warsaw Pact.

As the preceding discussion illustrates, shaping at the grand strategic level during the Cold War was primarily an interactive competition between the world's two superpowers. However, at the height of that competition, a number of nations that believed they had been disenfranchised as strategic players attempted to impose themselves into the calculus. The backdrop was the city of Bandung in Indonesia and the occasion was a meeting in 1955 between twenty-nine African and Asian states to promote economic and cultural ties and to combat colonialism. An incidental outcome from the meeting provided another instructive insight into strategic shaping.

Among the more influential figures at the Bandung conference was the charismatic Indian Prime Minister, Jawaharlal Nehru. Supported in particular by Indonesia's mercurial President Sukarno, Yugoslavia's strongly independent (from Soviet hegemony) President Josip Tito and, for a time, senior Chinese officials, Nehru played a key role in translating the relatively low-key Bandung experience into the high-profile Non-Aligned Movement. Eventually reaching a membership of more than a hundred states, the Non-Aligned Movement met formally for the first time in Belgrade in 1961.

The defining principle of the Non-Aligned Movement was the rejection of the East–West confrontation and of colonialism. In other words, the participants' informal and entirely reasonable objective was to establish their own collective spheres of influence. But just how successful the movement has been in observing its principles is open to question. What can be stated with certainty is that, almost inevitably, realpolitik intervened. Even at Bandung, many member-states were already linked to one of the superpowers, thus compromising their non-aligned status; while others such as China and India soon began to pursue superpower status themselves, an ambition seemingly at odds with the movement's ethos.

These two purportedly non-aligned nations went to war with each other only a year after the Belgrade meeting, in late 1962. China's first nuclear test was conducted in 1964, India's in 1974. By then, both nations were openly seeking regional influence, if not hegemony; and by the turn of the twenty-first century both were exploiting rapidly growing economies to fund the modernisation of their already impressive military forces. China had established a sphere of influence in North Asia, India likewise in South Asia. Each continues to monitor the other's military developments closely to ensure that an unacceptable imbalance of power does not develop, and occasional clashes along their shared borders have served as reminders of the continual jostling over their contiguous spheres of influence.

Before concluding this section, a final comment on the interactive and dynamic nature of shaping activities is necessary. George Kennan's policy of containment provides an informative illustration.

Since the collapse of the USSR in 1991, containment increasingly has come to be regarded as a great success, and, of course, hindsight indicates that it was. The policy managed to strike a fine balance within an enormously complex range of sometimes contradictory demands, including, where appropriate, sensitive engagement, mutual deterrence, and measured aggression. For some fifty years, containment provided a plausible framework within which thousands of US politicians, diplomats, generals, economists, business people and the like could work towards an identifiable common end. It is essential, however, to appreciate that while the goal of containment remained admirably clear intellectually, the ground on which the protagonists manoeuvred was continually shifting.

The USSR's leaders did not simply sit back and allow themselves to be contained. On the contrary, they were dynamic, adaptive opponents who constantly reacted, changed their minds, made decisions, and took the initiative. Frequently neither they nor their American adversaries knew how something they had done would be interpreted, especially when poor communications between Washington and Moscow exacerbated periods of extreme tension such as the Berlin blockade in 1948, the start of the Korean War in 1950, the launch of the world's first artificial space satellite by the Soviets in 1957, the shooting-down of an American U-2 spy plane over the USSR in 1960, and the Cuban missile crisis in 1962. There were many occasions when US policy-makers had to act with little if any consideration for the strategy of containment, having instead to respond to the imperatives of the moment.

None of this is especially remarkable within the opportunistic world of power politics, even more so within the world of superpower politics. The point here is that at any one of a number of flashpoints over almost half a century, containment might have been perceived to have failed, or it might have been radically modified, or even abandoned. And when in 1991 the USSR did collapse – when it had been contained out of existence – it did so with a rapidity that was entirely unforeseen by Western policy-makers. That is, our appreciation today of Kennan and containment rests very much on our post-facto understanding of what the protagonists did and did not know during the Cold War, and what they did and did not do, and on our knowledge that the Soviet Union was indeed ultimately contained. This is not to disparage Kennan and his far-sighted policy; on the contrary, events have properly assured his place in history. It is, however, to place the greatest possible emphasis on the inherently interactive nature of strategy.

KNOW THE ENEMY

The belief that we can shape our strategic circumstances implies a sophisticated understanding of the environment in which we operate. Central to any such understanding is knowledge, about ourselves, our enemies – and our friends. As the army maxim has it, time spent on reconnaissance, on gathering information, is never wasted.

It is for that very good reason that espionage is often called the second oldest profession (a distinction sometimes also claimed for politics), a description which may be supported by the Hebrew Bible. Prior to the battle of Jericho some 3200 years ago, the Israelite leader Joshua dispatched two spies with instructions to find out what they could 'about the land, especially Jericho'. In a nice confluence of historical aphorisms, Joshua's agents spent the first night of their mission at an inn owned by a prostitute named Rahab, prostitution of course being regarded as the oldest profession. In fairness to the reputations of the two spies, an inn would have been a good place to listen and ask questions in those times, when information was gathered primarily from first-hand meetings.

Joshua's concern was with the short-term: with getting enough good intelligence to give him an advantage in the imminent battle. Troop numbers, force disposition, defensive works, reserves, supplies, morale and similar details which reveal the opponent's immediate warfighting capabilities are of most interest in such situations. If time permits, that kind of capability derived intelligence can be combined with a considered assessment of the enemy's likely intentions, to inform our decisions for longer-term manoeuvring and, possibly, the overall campaign as opposed to single-battle objectives. For example, depending on what we learn about our opponent, we might still have time to change our plan of attack, or to recast our force disposition, or perhaps even to avoid conflict for the time being. And at the strategic level, intelligence of exceptional quality can be exploited to shape the direction of an entire campaign. The allies' success in decoding the German Enigma cipher machine during World War

II is an outstanding example, with the knowledge gained being so valuable as to constitute a strategic weapon.

The confrontation between the USSR and the United States during the Cold War offered one of the more dramatic illustrations of the connection between intelligence and strategic shaping. The great danger in that most interactive of strategic competitions was that ignorance on the part of one protagonist of the other's capabilities might precipitate a pre-emptive nuclear strike, because of the possibly unfounded fear of the consequences of inaction.

A glimpse into that sensitive perception-reaction dynamic was provided in the late 1950s and early 1960s, when both the US Air Force and a committee reporting to President Dwight D. Eisenhower separately concluded that the Soviet Union enjoyed a substantial numerical advantage in nuclear-armed inter-continental ballistic missiles (ICBMs). This so-called 'missile gap' caused grave concern in the United States and heightened tensions between the superpowers. In truth there was no gap; on the contrary, the United States had many more ICBMs than its rival. With the benefit of hindsight, we should be seriously concerned that US leaders were making decisions related to possible nuclear warfighting on the basis of such dangerously wrong information.

High-quality intelligence is the key to preventing decision-makers from taking peremptory action, in any circumstances. While opponents might not always understand each other's intentions, they can at least understand each other's capabilities. In this instance, those capabilities consisted of nuclear-capable missiles and bombers, which could be counted and qualitatively assessed. If both sides were confident that they understood the other's strengths and weaknesses, and if both knew that an acceptable balance of power existed, then a satisfactory degree of reassurance presumably would be established.

In the event, the term 'reassurance' came to encapsulate the calming effect knowledge can generate, and the concept developed into one of the foundations of the nuclear balance of terror between the USSR and the United States. Technology in the form of air- and space-based sensors played a major part in lifting the fog of uncertainty and in building reassurance. Beginning in the late 1940s, the United States in particular employed an increasingly effective variety of aircraft to spy on the USSR's nuclear warfighting capabilities. But because cameras were the primary sensors, aircraft had to overfly targets and, notwithstanding the extreme altitudes at which many of them operated, the risk of being shot down was a constant worry. Some forty American spy aircraft were lost on flights over communist countries between the end of World War II and 1980, with some 180 aircrew being killed.[3]

Photo reconnaissance satellites which offered absolute security and, because of their extreme operating altitudes, much greater area coverage per pass, were the answer. Both sides developed extensive spy satellite programs which achieved remarkable results. The US Corona project, for example, which ran from 1960 to 1972, took about 800 000 photographic images of targets inside the USSR, a number which, according to unofficial reports, included every nuclear-capable ICBM silo, submarine site, and bomber base. As a result of the knowledge gained, the fears of US officials were greatly eased; presumably satellite-derived intelligence engendered a similar level of reassurance in the USSR.

Once the Cuban missile crisis had been safely negotiated in late 1962, the Cold War slowly started to thaw. Knowledge rather than fear began to shape the strategic environment. Ostensibly objectionable strategic spying missions were in fact vital in making the nuclear standoff more transparent, and in building reassurance into what was an otherwise extraordinarily dangerous competition.

A footnote on espionage and shaping must be added. In addition to learning about our opponents, we also need to understand our friends and allies. What we do in a crisis and how we do it can depend just as much on our allies' intentions and capabilities as on those of our enemies. Will our allies support us in all contingencies? Do they really have the influence and firepower they claim? If circumstances prevent them from contributing combat forces, will they at least provide logistics and intelligence support? These are not hypothetical questions. During the 1982 Falklands War, for example, the two combatants, Argentina and the United Kingdom, both had formal security ties to the United States, and both needed US aid to mount effective campaigns. In the event, the United States chose to provide the British with vital assistance and the Argentineans with none.

While many Argentineans fought bravely, the general incompetence of their campaign suggests that their leaders had not considered the status of their alliances, among other things, before they precipitated the war.

Not all regimes are as inept as that of Argentina's generals. We should not be surprised, therefore, that the history of spying on friends parallels that of spying on foes. The Israelis perhaps are the exemplar, having gained illegal access to the most sensitive technical and political information held by some of their most steadfast supporters, including the Americans, the British and the French. Whatever we may think of the moralities of this, noting that all states spy on each other and that Israel has simply been better at it than most, we should acknowledge that we cannot shape our strategic environment to best effect if we do not fully understand all of its critical variables, including the intentions and capabilities of our friends.

IDEAS AND REALITY: THE FORCE STRUCTURE

Karl Marx once observed that 'the philosophers have only interpreted the world, in various ways; the point, however, is to change it'. With due alteration for context, Marx's comment could be applied to the theory and practice of strategy. Specifically, at some stage in the process, abstract strategic thinking has to be translated into a tangible force structure – into the means needed to turn ideas into actions.

A force structure comprises the people, hardware, command-and-control systems, doctrine and, in more recent times, software that in combination constitute the essence of a military or paramilitary organisation. A force structure will indicate a number of crucial attitudes: how a nation intends to defend itself; the priority it places on military capabilities as an instrument of national power; its strategic outlook and preferences, especially in relation to the shape-deter-respond construct; and the quality of its defence force.

A specific force structure can shape, even determine, the strategic environment in which it exists. World politics were to a considerable extent held hostage to the Roman Army from about 500 BCE to

500 CE, to the Royal Navy from the eighteenth to the twentieth century, and to atomic weapons in the second half of the twentieth century. Responding to the experience that a certain military posture can shape events, at the start of the twenty-first century a number of nations and organisations were ignoring the UN-sanctioned treaty on the non-proliferation of nuclear weapons as they sought to acquire the 'bomb' as a means of either achieving a measure of international influence they believed they otherwise lacked, or of strengthening their deterrence and defence capabilities.

At the operational level of war, force structures largely decide how a nation can and will fight. A defence force without a navy plainly is unlikely to fight at sea, while one with a powerful army plainly will prefer to fight on land. Prior to World War II, Germany and the USSR sensibly placed their force development emphasis on powerful armies: as continental powers, both had previously been invaded by land, and both had won great victories on land. By contrast, it was no coincidence that in the years leading up to World War II, the United Kingdom and the United States paid far more attention to strategic aerial bombardment as a warfighting concept, protected as they were in the one instance by oceans and in the other by oceans and distance.

The examples of Rome's army, Britain's navy, and the superpowers' nuclear weapons are representative of force structures that were suited to their times and circumstances. Equally, there is no shortage of examples of force structures that were unsuited to the dual demands of shaping their strategic environment and of fighting the wars with which they coincided. Australia and Indonesia provide representative case studies.

Following the attack on Pearl Harbor in December 1941 and the fall of Singapore in February 1942, Australians faced the possibility of a Japanese invasion, which could come only by sea. The threat was not new, having been identified by Australian defence planners in the early 1920s. We might question, therefore, why, in the period between World Wars I and II, Australia spent some 60 per cent of its defence budgets on a small, very expensive and ineffectual navy, when for the same money it could have assembled a predominantly maritime-strike air force of sufficient size and power to have defeated any invasion fleet. The same general criticism can be made of Indonesian security planning during the 1950s and 1960s. At a time when the main threat to Indonesia's national security came from various internal insurgent movements, its substantial investment in long-range bombers, fighter aircraft and submarines made little sense, even more so because its defence personnel were manifestly incapable of operating those weapons systems effectively. In both instances the force structures lacked strategic logic; consequently, they exerted no shaping influence on their respective strategic environments.

A rational approach to force structuring will follow one of two broad methods. Under the first, planning is threat-specific; under the second, it is threat-ambiguous. While the former is relatively straightforward, the latter is complex. In both cases, though, the starting point is the same, namely, a rigorous analysis of the prevailing strategic circumstances, including national interests, strengths, vulnerabilities, geography, population, infrastructure, the economy, internal political factors, alliances, and credible threat assessments.

Few better examples of threat-specific force-structure planning can be found than that of the Israeli Defence Force prior to the 1967 Six Day War. The threat was crystal-clear, amounting to nothing less than the destruction of the Israeli nation by armed force; and the source of the threat was also crystal-clear, namely, the surrounding Arab states, especially Egypt and Syria.

Geography and demography largely determined the way in which the Israeli Defence Force structured itself to fight for national survival. Israel is a very small country, measuring only 370 kilometres from north to south and as little as fourteen kilometres across. In 1967 its population was 2.5 million compared to the 52 million of its enemies. Land borders were shared with Egypt, Syria, Jordan and Lebanon, the first three of which were overtly hostile to Israel's existence. A jet bomber could fly from Cairo to Tel Aviv in thirty-five minutes, from Suez to Tel Aviv in twenty minutes, and from Damascus to Haifa in nine minutes. Invading armies similarly could reach key population and government centres within hours. Egypt and Syria maintained ostensibly powerful land and air forces and, in the event of war, could expect substantial reinforcements from Jordan and Iraq. In broad figures, the Arab forces amounted to about 750 combat aircraft, 1650 tanks and 300 000 troops, against which the Israelis could field 320 combat aircraft, 800 tanks and 264 000 troops.

Lacking strategic depth and dangerously outnumbered, the Israelis made two critical planning decisions. First, it was clear that they needed to fight on enemy territory, not their own. And second, they had to take the initiative and seek a rapid victory to deny other Arab states the time to mobilise against them. Dominating the air thus became a *sine qua non* of their campaign plan. Air power alone offered the speed of action, strategic reach, and striking power which could seize the initiative from the outset, eliminate the danger of Arab attacks on Israeli population centres, and expose enemy surface forces to strikes from the sky.

The Israeli Air Force was structured precisely to achieve that objective, consisting predominantly of jet fighter/ground attack aircraft which could be used either for pre-emptive raids to destroy the Arabs' air forces on their ramps or, failing that, for a 'dogfight' campaign in the skies to gain control of the air. Flexibility was an important consideration since most aircraft had to be able to change quickly from one role to another – for example, from air defence to ground attack – depending on the state of the battle. In contrast to its large numbers of strike/fighter aircraft, the Israeli Air Force possessed relatively few airlifters, because the short distances to borders and the open, flat terrain meant that land forces could move to trouble spots almost as quickly by truck and armoured personnel carrier as they could by air. For similar geostrategic reasons, the Israeli Air Force had invested little in other air support capabilities such as maritime patrol and rotary-wing transport.

That rational assessment of operational priorities was complemented by an emphasis on quality. The Israeli Air Force was an élite organisation, well trained, aggressive and confident. Its strike/fighter aircraft, mostly French, represented leading-edge technology. The contrast with their well-equipped but operationally and doctrinally inept enemies was conspicuous.

It is a matter of record that, when the theory behind the Israeli Defence Force's force structure had to be transformed into practice, Israel's airmen all but destroyed their primary threat, the Egyptian air force, on the ground in some three hours, and then meted out the same treatment to the Syrian and Jordanian air forces in less than half an hour. Having achieved its first objective, the Israeli Air Force was then free to pursue the remaining two: interdiction of the enemy's lines of communications; and close air attack. The prosecution of those two roles was just as successful as the first. While many factors contributed to what was one of the most brilliant campaigns ever conducted, it is clear that the Israeli Defence Force was ideally structured to confront the existing threat to the Israeli nation.

Forty years later the Israeli Defence Force continues to apply the same threat-specific methodology to its force-structuring determinations. The translation of informed analysis into precise planning which underpinned Israel's success not only in 1967, but also in the equally crushing victories of the 1973 Yom Kippur War and the 1982 conflict in the Beka'a Valley, remains evident. The basic structure of the Israeli Defence Force has remained much the same, albeit extensively modernised. There have, however, been two notable additions.

First, it is now widely believed that by 1967 Israel had built two nuclear warheads, and that by the early twenty-first century that number had increased to between 100 and 200. Those weapons serve a dual purpose. First, they contribute to the threat-specific force structure with which Israel confronts its long-standing regional enemies; and second, they generate a broad deterrent effect against any kind of threat from any kind of potential enemy. In other words, they are used to shape the strategic environment.

And second, in the late 1990s, Israeli strategists assessed that Iran's development of medium-range surface-to-surface missiles and nuclear technology was starting to represent a major threat; consequently, new weapons systems intended to counter that danger began to appear in the Israeli Defence Force's order of battle. These included very long-range strike-fighters, perhaps capable of attacking Iranian nuclear production facilities as per the raid on Iraq's Osirak nuclear reactor in 1981; an anti-ballistic missile defence system; a very long-range, precise, high-speed air-to-surface missile; two long-endurance, high-altitude unmanned aerial vehicles with the ability to loiter over a threat area for about sixty hours, one fitted with standoff missiles and the other with information-gathering sensors; airborne early-warning and control aircraft; and a space program centred on Israeli-owned and -operated spy satellites.

In summary, for half a century, Israeli planners have provided a textbook model of threat-specific force structuring, in which the clearly understood end of national survival has been unambiguously complemented by the endorsed way of the military defeat of any armed threat and the available means.

Before turning to the intellectually most challenging force structuring task – namely, where there is no obvious threat – Singapore's experience represents a worthwhile case study because it falls halfway between the threat-specific and threat-ambiguous models. On the one hand, Singapore is not subject to the kind of overt hostility that exists between, say, Israel and its neighbours, Greece and Turkey, North and South Korea, and India and Pakistan. On the other hand, Singaporeans are sensitive to their position as an economically successful nation which, lacking natural resources and a large domestic market, has built its wealth largely on intellectual capital; and which, as a small, predominantly Chinese society, is bordered by the much larger, less developed Islamic nations of Indonesia and Malaysia, both with an historical distrust of expatriate Chinese communities. Furthermore, like Israel, Singapore has almost no strategic depth: a jet fighter can cross the island from north to south in only three minutes, and from east to west in just a few seconds more.

Consequently, Singapore's leaders have worked assiduously to ameliorate their perceived vulnerability by developing a deterrent force which sends a powerful message to any potential aggressor. Specifically, the Republic of Singapore Air Force has been designed in the first instance for pre-emptive strikes, to be conducted as far away from the city-state as possible. If pre-emption is precluded, offensive operations, again at the maximum distance from Singapore, are clearly Singapore's preferred option. There is no doubt that the general threat posed by Singapore's defence force is well understood throughout the region, not least by the Malaysians, with whom Singapore has had an ambivalent relationship; and nor does any neighbouring government doubt that the Singaporean military is capable of performing the task for which it has been structured. Singapore's pragmatic leadership does not have to be reminded that, in order to be effective, a deterrent force must be recognised for what it is by those it is intended to deter. In summary, Singapore's armed forces shape perceptions within Southeast Asia, generate a broad deterrent effect, and are capable of responding to a range of regional defence contingencies.

The difficulty of assembling a force structure that matches the endorsed ways should never be underestimated. Even in threat-specific circumstances, such as those that have motivated Israel's approach, numerous complications remain. Among other things, planners need to establish priorities, identify the most suitable capabilities to match those priorities, decide how much of the existing force structure might be relevant, harmonise the various environmental combat components with each other, establish an effective command-and-control system, and acquire funding for new acquisitions. But at least in the threat-specific setting, the starting point – the threat – is obvious.

By definition, the same cannot be said for the second main approach, the threat-free or threat-ambiguous setting. Referring back to Marx's observation on philosophy and action, how can we figuratively change the world if we cannot interpret it? NATO's intellectual confusion at the end of the twentieth century provides a broad illustration of the problem in terms of roles, missions and force structuring; while Australia's experience during the final three decades of the same century offers a more detailed case study.

For fifty years, NATO's planning staff had one of the less taxing jobs in international security. The organisation had been explicitly founded to confront the post-World War II military threat posed by the emergent Soviet Union, a task it was to undertake either through an apocalyptic exchange of the American–French–British nuclear arsenal on the one side and the USSR's on the other, or through a massive confrontation of conventional forces on the plains of Germany. An enormous amount of detailed analysis was needed to prepare the contingency plans that gave effect to those conclusions, but the broad strategic thrust and its associated force-structuring requirements were largely self-evident.

Then in 1991 the long-standing threat disappeared almost overnight with the collapse of the USSR, a political earthquake that among other things precipitated a dramatic decline in Russian military capabilities. In the circumstances, it was unsurprising that NATO's leadership promptly fell into something of a strategic vacuum. Without the intimidating spectre of the 'natural' enemy, what was its *raison d'être*? What were the member-states to do with nuclear weapons and a massive conventional military force that had been shaped to fight World War III? NATO's intellectual anxiety deepened when, during the 1990s, the main security problems it faced turned out to be stabilisation operations and terrorism, neither of which fitted comfortably with its Cold War mentality and force structure. In the years since then, NATO has struggled to redefine itself intellectually and practically.

On the other side of the world, Australia had been facing a no less perplexing strategic challenge. In the early 1970s it started to become apparent that the various communist insurgencies which had shaped regional security attitudes since the end of World War II did not represent a genuine threat either to the liberal democracies or to most of the emerging states of Southeast Asia. Having spent decades structuring their military services to fight as an expeditionary force alongside Western allies in distant lands, Australian strategists suddenly had to confront the uncomfortable truth that there was no immediate threat against which they could conveniently shape their force structure.

After a good deal of uncertainty, two key planning judgments were reached. The most important was that the central business of Australia's military forces was the direct defence of national territory. That judgment was not as self-evident as it might seem. For many regions of the world, especially the Pacific which, with the exception of World War II, has been as peaceful as its name indicates, the idea of one state conducting armed attacks against another with the intention of subverting sovereignty is so remote as to be almost incredible. Nevertheless, the global strategic environment remains one of uncertainty and change. It may be the case that in two or so decades most nations will feel sufficiently confident not to worry about their territorial integrity, noting, however, that a very high level of confidence is likely to be needed before any kind of unilateral disarmament were contemplated. In the meantime, for most national leaders territorial security continues to assume over-riding importance.

Incidentally, decision-makers who conclude that protecting national sovereignty is not their defence force's main business should reconsider their need for a military organisation, and think instead about coast guards, enhanced police services, paramilitaries and the like, with which they can still conduct constabulary tasks but at a fraction of the cost of a regular military organisation.

Having defined the defence force's central business, the second step is to test that business against the nation's enduring strategic characteristics of geography, economy, population and infrastructure. In Australia's case, it is obvious that the country is an island continent surrounded by an air/sea gap, and that it has a strong economy, a small population, and a sparse infrastructure outside the main residential areas. Yet the strategic implications of those characteristics apparently had not been fully appreciated by preceding generations of Australian strategists, who for decades believed that their country could only be defended with British or American help. By contrast, Japanese planners who examined the problem less emotionally during World War II reached a different conclusion. When staff officers at the Imperial General Headquarters in Tokyo did their sums, they found that they would need twelve divisions and 'more shipping than Japan could provide' to cross the air/sea gap and make an opposed lodgment in Australia. In other words, the effort required to invade Australia was disproportionate to the likelihood of success, primarily because the air/sea gap was a formidable barrier which could be defended relatively easily by a modestly sized but capable and appropriately structured force.

A couple of points should be made at this stage. First, cases of the apparently obvious are not always so. Consequently, defence planning needs to proceed on a basis of rigour and process rather than intuition, bias, visceral fear and the like. Second, the methodology being outlined here is general, not specific. The key is to structure defence forces to maximise enduring comparative advantages. Switzerland's experience corroborates this truism. Throughout the second half of the twentieth century the Swiss, who also defined their central defence business as the protection of national territory, exploited their land-locked, mountainous terrain by maintaining a huge citizen-based army which would literally take to the hills to make an attempted invasion so difficult and potentially so costly as to be irrational.

Eventually applying the same logic but arriving at vastly different force-structure conclusions because of vastly different objective circumstances, in the 1970s Australian planners began to place their priority on the kinds of capabilities needed to conduct operations in the air/sea gap, namely, surveillance, reconnaissance, air superiority, and maritime strike-forces. Although observing a similar methodology, Switzerland and Australia arrived at two very different strategies, the one favouring defensive land forces, the other offensive maritime forces.

It may, of course, be the case that for, say, economic reasons, a country's leaders will decide that their nation cannot be defended unaided against a major external threat; or they may decide that internal pressures constitute the greatest danger to their regime. If they are rational they will shape their forces accordingly, perhaps in the first instance by trying to bolster their security through alliances, perhaps in the second by giving priority to counter-insurgency and anti-terrorist capabilities. Regardless of individual circumstances, defence strategies should be based on assessments of central business and enduring strategic conditions.

Once those judgments have been made, the question becomes one of defining systems, numbers and preparedness states. To again use the example of Australia: What is the best way to defend a large air/sea gap? How many platforms, weapons systems and people will be needed to provide confidence at home, deter potential aggressors abroad, and conduct successful operations? How long will indicative rates of effort have to be sustained? How much money will be needed to maintain those forces at a suitable level of preparedness? With due alteration of detail, those questions are germane to force-structure planning anywhere.

MOTIVE, INTENT, AND CAPABILITIES

Among the concepts strategists can use as a means of exploring such issues, warning time and the nature of credible contingencies are critical. Both are complex, and warning time in particular can be a contentious planning tool. Specifically, can we establish with an acceptable degree of confidence when an incipient threat is likely to assume substantial form; or, perhaps more cautionary still, can we identify previously unrecognised threats in time to take action?

A threat is generally regarded as having three components: motive, intent, and the military capabilities needed to translate ambitions into actions. Motive and intent can be difficult to measure, since both are subjective. The motivation for one country to attack another may or may not be apparent, while the intention to attack can be even more difficult to predict, as demonstrated by Pearl Harbor, the start of the Six Day War, Iraq's invasion of Kuwait, and al-Qa'ida's attack on New York City and Washington. And even when hostility is overt, emotional preferences may make us want to deny the truth, as, for example, when Stalin refused to acknowledge irrefutable evidence that Hitler was about to invade the Soviet Union in June 1941. On the other hand, many threats are crystal-clear long before they result in open aggression. In each of the examples cited above, the danger represented by Japan, Israel, Iraq and al-Qa'ida had been recognised by their opponents years beforehand, yet none of them was adequately prepared when the attacks came.

There are other, not uncommon, complications that can also confound efforts to use motive and intent as primary planning indicators. For example, unexpected regime collapses can suddenly alter alliances, military capabilities, balances of power, and spheres of influence. Western leaders were stunned by the rapidity with which the modernising Shah of Iran's pro-US government disintegrated in 1979, to be replaced by a conservative, theocratic, anti-US Administration. Among other things, the end of US influence in Iran meant that the Shah's heavily subsidised, high-technology military forces quickly began to lose their effectiveness, which in turn almost immediately changed the regional military balance. A somewhat similar pattern unfolded when the USSR unexpectedly began to unravel with startling speed following the fall of the Berlin Wall in 1989.

None of the foregoing is to suggest that we should not try to assess motive and intent, or that we should exclude them from our deliberations. On the contrary, both are properly recognised as critical strategic-planning determinants, which is one reason why states practise diplomacy – to understand each other – and conduct espionage – to gain an advantage over each other. It is to suggest, however, that we need to be aware of the complexities associated with subjective analysis.

The third component of any military threat, force capabilities, seems easier to assess. Unlike possibly arcane motives and intentions, the technical dimensions of military capabilities can be confidently measured. We know the performance characteristics of various tanks, ships, aeroplanes and weapons; we can count numbers of platforms, soldiers, technicians, and scientific research personnel; and we can assess the effectiveness of logistics support services and national economies. Consequently, in an attempt to reduce the complexities of the force-structuring process, planners sometimes use a capabilities-based approach, which involves evaluating the tangible capabilities of nominal competitors and then configuring one's own forces to be technically superior.

The fact that a country whose military capabilities are measured and used as a benchmark may have no obvious hostile motives or intentions is, under this methodology, irrelevant. This is not as illogical as it might sound. Within a given region of strategic interest, the most likely defence contingencies are those based on existing military capabilities; that is, a 'threat' which is not supported by the right kinds of capabilities is not credible. By focusing only on existing capabilities, planners should be able to determine the kind of force structure they will need both to counter those nominal capabilities and prosecute their own defence strategy. The problematic nature of motive and intent is thus circumvented.

However, despite its pragmatic rationale, the capabilities-based methodology is not entirely convincing. To start with, motive and intent might be difficult to judge, but their removal from the planning equation is cause for unease. So too is the possibility that a threat might be invented, or at the least exaggerated, simply because of another nation's geographic proximity and existing military capabilities. To take an extreme instance, should the United States regard Canada as a threat, simply because Canada has a competent, modern defence force, and the two countries share a border? Any such suggestion would be nonsensical. In other words, motive and intent cannot be wholly excluded from the threat-assessment equation.

Furthermore, it is a fundamental assumption of this methodology that any significant shift in a nominal country's capabilities will be detected in time for a corresponding force-structure adjustment to be made; that is, the notoriously unreliable concept of warning time assumes major proportions. And the fact is that there have been many instances of undetected, dramatic increases in capabilities. For example, in 1988, Saudi Arabia secretly obtained about fifty CSS-2 intermediate-range ballistic missiles from China. By any standards, ballistic missiles with a 3000-kilometre range represent a major offensive capability, with the potential to disturb prevailing regional balances and stability. Because the acquisition of the CSS-2s did not require any of the in-country development and testing which reconnaissance systems look for and generally detect, the missiles were discovered only after they had arrived in Saudi Arabia, too late for any preventive action to be taken. Similarly, following the reunification of Germany, NATO security planners were startled to discover that some East German army units held stockpiles of weapons three times greater than had been reported by Western intelligence.

More recently, the growing incidence of terrorist attacks such as the release of sarin gas in the Tokyo subway system, airliners flying into the World Trade Center and the Pentagon, and the Bali, Madrid, London, and Amman bombings, as opposed to the use of conventional military forces, has exacerbated the problems associated with undue reliance on warning time as a force-structuring tool. Whereas it is hard to disguise substantial alterations to armies, navies and air forces, it is relatively easy to conceal potentially major capability shifts within the small-group activities typical of terrorists. The increasing availability of weapons of mass destruction will only intensify the problems inherent in trying to detect clandestine capability changes.

The relative ease with which terrorists can strike compared to conventional military forces also carries significant implications for the relationship between strategy and force structures. There is a trend within advanced defence forces to decentralise authority, thereby permitting small, highly lethal components such as special forces, snipers, and long-range stealthy weapons systems like submarines and air vehicles to act with minimum response time should the opportunity to pursue a strategic effect suddenly present itself.

But with the best will in the world, national defence forces remain fundamentally bureaucratic and their organisational arrangements remain fundamentally hierarchical, with all of the decision-making inhibitions that implies. Delays will almost invariably arise, particularly when the prosecution of a target has sensitive legal implications, for example, if it involves a breach of sovereignty, decapitation, or objects of cultural significance. By contrast, organisations such as al-Qa'ida, Hezbollah and Jemaah Islamiah are characterised by the independence of their global networks of operatives, who might share a loosely defined objective such as the forced removal of Americans from Saudi Arabia, or the establishment of a caliphate from the Middle East to Southeast Asia, and who pursue that end through the common way of terrorism, but who do so largely when and how each independent cell chooses.

Additionally, the phenomenon of globalised terrorism tends to invalidate the capabilities-based methodology of force structuring for at least two reasons. First, because the objective of that methodology is to build a superior force structure to those of nominal regional competitors, its process clearly will be challenged by a competitor – terrorism – whose base is global and which recognises no state boundaries. And second, the measurement of capabilities on which the methodology relies becomes far less certain when applied against terrorists, who have no readily visible presence, who constantly seek to use new and unexpected means, and who reject the rule of law.

* * *

Strategy works at numerous levels and is inherently interactive. Decisions made and actions taken by one protagonist should induce responses from other protagonists, perhaps to do nothing, perhaps to make a radical change of plans. We can try to control this often unpredictable dynamic by using strategy to shape the environment within which events occur. Strategic shaping is likely to take place through the shape-deter-respond construct, an approach that reflects a logical progression of ideas and influence, of desired effects, and, as a last resort, of actions. Ideally, shaping should manipulate the strategic environment in favour of our own strengths and preferences and against our competitors' weaknesses.

Spheres of influence and balances of power are crucial expressions of the shape-deter-respond methodology. Alliances and military force traditionally have been key components of both expressions, noting that alliances can often be cynical in origin and Machiavellian in practice, and that military force structures must remain relevant to the prevailing circumstances. Determining those circumstances can be a challenging process, especially during times of shifting loyalties and unpredictable threats. Regularly defining what we mean by winning, and then testing our circumstances against the ends-ways-means construct, will help to minimise the inherent risks.

6 | Strategic paralysis
Strategy as an ideal

IN AN IDEAL WORLD, every strategic action would achieve its desired outcome as quickly and efficiently as possible. Precisely how we might measure those descriptors is likely to vary from case to case, but the criteria would usually include minimum costs in terms of casualties and treasure, minimum damage to the environment and to any infrastructure, and an end-state acceptable to most parties, including the vanquished. It has been the allure of that kind of rapid, decisive outcome that has motivated such long-standing concepts as the decisive or great battle and the knockout blow, and which more recently has seen attention turn to strategic raids.

A central feature of each of those concepts is the priority placed on speed. All things being equal, a rapid conclusion offers the best chance of achieving the best outcome, for the obvious reason that the shorter the fight, the less time there is for both sides to kill people and break things. Speed can also make a major contribution to surprise, a tactical advantage which in itself can shorten conflicts.

Speed is a relative term and it has a number of dimensions. The Mongol armies that rampaged through Asia and Europe in the thirteenth and fourteenth centuries CE travelled light and drove their horses relentlessly, sometimes covering 200 kilometres in two days, a previously unheard of rate of advance for armies. Indeed, according to the Venetian explorer Marco Polo, the Mongols 'could travel up to ten days, subsisting only on horse's blood, which they drank from a pierced vein'. The ability to appear unexpectedly gave the

Mongols a tactical edge, and created an aura of unpredictability and terror. Similarly, during the era of sailing ships, it was the unexpectedness of a fleet's arrival on the horizon, perhaps on the far side of the world, that as much as anything made British, Spanish, Portuguese and Dutch warships the pre-eminent strategic weapons of their age. In other words, for both the Mongols and those naval powers, speed amounted to a de facto form of surprise. While technology has long since made horse-mounted cavalry and sailing ships obsolete, the general point remains valid.

The dimension of speed represented in those examples is that of movement, of being able to get from one place to another within a timeframe that, regardless of whether it is two hours, two days or two years, generates shock. But movement represents only one half of the physical aspect of the speed equation. The other half is intensity of force application. An army that creates surprise by arriving quickly but which then is incapable of applying enough pressure for any one of a number of reasons – insufficient firepower, insurmountable defences, adverse geography, inadequate logistics – may well have wasted the time and effort it expended getting from A to B.

Encapsulated partly in the principle of war of concentration, the rapid application of force can, like rapid movement, create shock and overwhelm. At one end of the scale, rapidity of application can be generated by the sheer number of weapons employed, while at the other end it tends to be associated with the continually increasing efficiency derived from new weapons technology. For example, with its rate of fire of 500 rounds per minute, a single Maxim machine gun from the late-nineteenth century was the equivalent of 100 riflemen; thus, in one engagement during the Matabele War (1893 to 1894), fifty British soldiers equipped with four Maxim guns were able to fight off some 5000 Matabele warriors. As the British man of letters and politician Hilaire Belloc whimsically noted, in a more general context:

> Whatever happens, we have got
> The Maxim gun, and they have not.

An alternative form of rapid application emerged twenty years later in the form of strike aircraft, with their singular ability to revisit and so reattack the same target in a comparatively short timeframe. In the example of the Maxim gun and aircraft, the de facto speed of application represented by mass was replaced by the true speed of the weapons system, with its inherent economy of effort.

Rapid manoeuvre and force application are not ends in themselves; rather, they are operational methods, whose purpose is to give us the initiative and throw the enemy off-balance – to prevent him from implementing his preferred plan of action while enabling us to implement ours. That is, they are tools to be used in the broader contest of decision-making on the battlefield.

There is nothing new in any of this: the competition of intellect and will has always been the essence of strategy, and successful strategists have always looked for better tools to serve their cause. What is new is the pace at which that competition can now proceed. And this has introduced a third dimension to the concept of speed. Advanced communications, computing and intelligence systems have dramatically increased the speed with which information can be collected and transmitted, and with which decisions can be made and, ultimately, actions taken, to the extent that *tempo* has become a strategic quality as fundamental as firepower and manoeuvre. It is a significant development.

TEMPO AND STRATEGIC PARALYSIS

At the start of the twentieth century, sheer firepower was the overriding determinant in force structuring and campaign planning. Armies based on massed infantry supported by heavy artillery and machine-gun fire were seen as the key to victory. Because of the limitations of the railways, road transport and shipping which shifted and resupplied those armies, and given the advantage firepower and position conferred on the defence, the approach was understandable if uninspired, as World War I demonstrated (and as the American Civil War had revealed fifty years previously, but whose lessons many European generals chose to ignore).

Towards the end of World War I, manoeuvre began to supplant, or at least to equal, sheer force as the primary desirable characteristic of combat formations. The increasing mechanisation of armies was central to this change, as was the emergence of air power and a quantum improvement in communications systems, which revolutionised a commander's ability to know who was doing what, where, and to whom, not least his own troops. Primitive communications, or more often their complete absence, had been a major factor in the ability of the Mongols and sail-era warships to arrive unexpectedly, to generate speed via ignorance and, therefore, to achieve surprise. The impact on the application of strategy that the communications revolution started to have about the end of World War I was enormous. It was that revolution that enabled the concept of strategic paralysis.

The blitzkrieg technique which the Wehrmacht trialled during the Spanish Civil War and then employed to full effect in the early phases of World War II symbolised the full return of comprehensive manoeuvre to the battlefield. In general, fighting in World War II achieved a balance between force application and manoeuvre, with both being necessary and neither likely to succeed without the other. There were of course exceptions. On the Eastern Front, the Red Army eventually overcame its early tactical ineptitude through sheer brute force based on mass and position; by contrast, operations in North Africa and the Pacific were characterised by frequent movement, often over great distances and sometimes very fast. The maritime nature of the Pacific campaign in particular placed a priority on manoeuvre, noting that, once the allies had all but severed Japan's shipping lines of communications by mid-1944, the firepower of the emperor's armies which were stranded on bypassed islands became irrelevant to the final outcome. The re-emergence of manoeuvre was an event of the highest order.

Major wars fought between 1950 and 1990 confirmed this shift. Fighting in Korea initially featured rapid movement as the competing armies surged up and down the peninsula, before they settled into a positional stalemate along a frontline just north of Seoul in mid-1951. Americans during their war in the jungles of Indochina from 1962 to 1975, Soviets during their invasion of Afghanistan from 1979 to 1989, and Iranians and Iraqis during their clash in the marshlands and deserts of the Middle East from 1980 to 1988, all failed to appreciate the changing balance between fire-power and manoeuvre, and paid a price. In Vietnam, US commanders confused technology and firepower with strategy and were constantly outmanoeuvred by their enemy, both on the battlefield and politically, an experience subsequently shared by the Soviets in Afghanistan; while in the Middle East, the technical and intellectual incompetence of both combatants condemned them to a reprise of the static slaughter of World War I.

Campaign planners from all four countries would have profited from a careful analysis of the Israeli Defence Force's tactics during the 1967 Six Day War and the 1973 Yom Kippur War. Acutely conscious of their numerical inferiority and geographic vulnerability, Israeli strategists exploited their superior decision-making and technology to generate an operational tempo which overwhelmed their Arab enemies. During the Six Day War especially, the speed with which the Israelis collected information, made decisions, manoeuvred, and applied firepower was so powerful as to become irresistible. The Israelis made tempo a factor in warfighting that was the equal of force application and manoeuvre.

Drawing on both the good and bad lessons from Vietnam and the Middle East, and incorporating important technological developments in computing, communications, information sensors and precision weapons into their thinking, in the early 1980s a handful of Western strategists began to develop an updated version of the knock-out blow. Variously described as 'hyperwar' and 'control warfare', the concept eventually became known as strategic paralysis. The idea was to subject an opponent to an overwhelmingly swift combination of decision-making, manoeuvre, and firepower, all directed against his centres of gravity. Unable to cope with the tempo and metaphorically outflanked in the clash of wills, the enemy would be strategically paralysed. That was the theory, anyway.

The concept of strategic paralysis demanded fast, furious, simultaneous precision strikes against an opponent's vital points and focused on breaking his will from the very start of hostilities. Lesser targets which might lie in-between attacking forces and the enemy's true centres of gravity would simply be ignored. Speed of decision-making, manoeuvre and force application were of over-riding importance. Also called parallel or concurrent warfare – descriptions chosen to distinguish it from gradual, incremental or sequential warfare – the technique sought the rapid degradation of the whole of the enemy's system, a process that in theory would precipitate strategic collapse. Some analysts believe that prototypes of the model were evident on occasions during the US-led military campaigns in Iraq (1991 and 2003), Bosnia (1995), Kosovo (1999), and Afghanistan (2001 and 2002).

The conceptual framework for strategic paralysis was provided by two US Air Force fighter pilots, Colonels John Warden and John Boyd. Each developed his ideas as a discrete contribution to strategic thought, although Warden was familiar with Boyd's work, which predated his own. Warden was the architect of the air campaign conducted by coalition forces against Iraq in the 1991 Gulf War, and Boyd was a flier of legendary skill who developed into an influential strategic thinker. Warden's beliefs were developed exclusively in relation to air power and focused on the physical element of strategic paralysis and thus were concerned primarily with compellence; Boyd's thinking applied to the art of war generally and focused on the psychological element, and thus was concerned primarily with coercion. Regardless of the respective authors' intentions, both sets of concepts have broad relevance; that is, they can be used to inform strategic thinking in any environmental setting, especially when the best features of each are combined.

FORM AS STRATEGIC PARALYSIS

Three aspects of Warden's work are especially noteworthy.[1] First, he applied a rigour to target classification and selection which too often had been absent in the past. Central to that rigour was his depiction of an enemy's centres of gravity or vital points as a series of five concentric rings, which he symbolically portrayed as a bull's-eye. While each of the rings denoted a worthwhile target set, the innermost represented the highest-value, the outermost the least. Starting with the centre representing the highest-value targets, Warden's model identified the five critical components of an enemy's system as follows: leadership; organic essentials ('those facilities or processes without which the state or organisation cannot maintain itself'); infrastructure;

population, with the emphasis on attacking the national will, not people themselves; and finally, the fielded military forces.

According to Warden, all five rings will be present in most socio-economic systems and, if possible, the entire system should be attacked concurrently. If our own force-structure limitations prevent the prosecution of this idealised parallel campaign, then the centre – the leadership – should invariably be the priority. In practice, however, it might not always be possible physically to reach more than one or two of the outer rings. For example, by about the middle of World War II, the allies' superiority in the air and at sea meant that German and Japanese strike-forces were capable only of reaching the outer rings of the allies' systems, a shortfall that inhibited their ability to exert strategic pressure.

The logic is clear enough. Victory depends on convincing the competing leadership to capitulate, and because that effect is more likely to be generated by the application of pressure to an inner ring than to an outer ring, the inside targets must be prosecuted first. This method differed in practice, if not in theory, from most previous military strategies, which generally presumed that any campaign would have to start at the outer ring – that is, with the enemy's fielded forces, which almost invariably would be placed between any attacking force and the more critical rings – and work sequentially inwards, towards the ultimate target of the leadership. Warden's reversal of that traditional approach was captured in the slogan 'inside-out warfare'.

The second notable feature of Warden's concept was its tacit incorporation of the revolutionary effect of emergent technologies, especially precision-guided munitions. In World War II the destruction of a notional target required 9000 bombs; in Vietnam, improved weapons accuracy had reduced that figure to thirty bombs; in Iraq in 1991, a single PGM could do the job. This was a technological advance of the first order, one which redefined the meaning of mass. Without that revolution in weapons technology, Warden's need for irresistible speed of force application and concurrent operations could not have been met; with it, his model became feasible. The immense efficiency gains inherent in PGMs enabled a comparatively small offensive force to prosecute a large number of targets simultaneously, thus generating a disproportionate effect. Technology provided Warden with the tempo his concept demanded.

The final noteworthy feature of Warden's thinking was the emphasis he placed on understanding the opposition's culture, of 'getting inside the enemy's head'. The United States' bombing campaign against North Vietnam, for example, had often reflected cultural confusion, with US planners imposing first-world values onto a third-world socio-economic system. Yet there was little point and even less leverage in subjecting an agrarian society to an offensive campaign predicated on demoralising an industrial society. Consistent with the truism that war is always a clash of wills, Warden understood that correct targeting relies on knowing what the enemy leadership values. Furthermore, placing the leadership at the centre of his five-ring targeting model unambiguously reminded campaign planners where their strategic priorities must always lie.

Warden's work was the subject of considerable criticism following the 1991 Gulf War. The most common reproach was that his methodology was one-dimensional; that its single-minded focus on attacking a pre-planned list of targets was mechanistic and linear. As a consequence, the argument continued, the targeting list became an end unto itself, to the extent that it effectively was the strategy. This indeed seemed to be the case eight years later, during NATO's air campaign against the Milosevic regime in the former republic of Yugoslavia in 1999, an operation clearly based in part on an interpretation of Warden's model. But the problem there was more one of application than of theory. When the campaign began to falter, the response of the US army officer in command, General Wesley Clark, was to demand more and more targets to attack, regardless of their relevance to any ends-ways-means construct, let alone to Warden's hierarchy of strategic importance. One observer later described Clark's bombing campaign as little more than a disconnected series of 'random acts of violence'. It was only after NATO finally began to observe Warden's fundamental principles by concentrating on leadership targets, including the personal assets of Milosevic and his inner circle of supporters, that the campaign began to generate the desired effect.

Nevertheless, Warden's preoccupation with the form of strategic paralysis (how things are done) at the expense of purpose (why things are done) does reflect a theoretical weakness. While his model indicates that war invariably is a combination of physical and psychological competition, in practice, Warden's personal belief that the psychological factor is excessively difficult to measure, or even to identify, led him to direct his attention primarily against the enemy's physical nature. But this is an approach that presumes that as the enemy's physical system collapses so too will his capacity to resist, and this is by no means certain. In brief, his model makes insufficient allowance for unintended and unforeseen circumstances, and for people's resilience in the face of adversity.

At the same time, Warden brought an admirable clarity to target analysis. Specifically, his unambiguous focus on leadership – on the minds of the enemy élite – was an overdue reminder that war is indeed a clash of wills. In an era when information technology, advanced communications and smart weapons are continually enhancing the ability of all forms of combat power to achieve high rates of operational tempo, and are increasing the opportunity for commanders generally to pursue a strategic effect from the onset of hostilities, the significance of this is considerable. If we substitute 'centre-of-gravity analysis' for 'target analysis' – that is, if we translate Warden's thinking from its comparatively narrow air-campaign origins to strategy in the broad – the true merit of his contribution becomes apparent.

PURPOSE AS STRATEGIC PARALYSIS

The emphasis on purpose lacking in Warden's model can be found in Boyd's self-styled 'universal logic of conflict'.[2] Whereas Warden sought to compel by imposing change on the enemy – by denying him a role in deciding how and when conflict would be resolved, by physically collapsing his strategic environment – Boyd sought to coerce, to convince the enemy that his best option would be to modify his unacceptable behaviour. Reflecting his familiarity with Sun Tzu's philosophy, Boyd noted that the key to winning or losing is always the opponent's perceptions. In terms of ways and ends, Boyd was suggesting that the only purpose in attacking, say, a particular command bunker, or bridge, or power station, or dictator's mansion, is the effect that that action will have on the true target, namely, the enemy leader's mind.

Boyd is best-known for his 'OODA' loop, an acronym for Observation-Orientation-Decision-Action. A fighter pilot in the Korean War, Boyd was intrigued by the F-86 Sabre's remarkable kill rate of 10:1 over the MiG-15 in air-to-air combat, given that the performance of the two aircraft was similar. He deduced that the Sabre pilots' success was due primarily to their aircraft's hydraulically operated flight controls and adjustable horizontal stabiliser, which allowed the US fighter to transit from one manoeuvre to another faster than its Soviet counterpart. After further thought, he began to see the implications of this particular example for competitive decision-making generally.

Regardless of whether we are flying an F-86, or fighting a one-on-one gunfight, or leading a section of riflemen, or commanding a theatre-level campaign, or practising grand strategy, or anything in between, the OODA cycle represents a universal logic of conflict. Simply put, the protagonist who is the faster to act intellectually and physically is likely to win. The OODA loop explains this competitive process. As the loop indicates, we first need to observe our opponent, to assess what he is doing, and how. We must then orient ourselves to the prevailing circumstances; that is, we must assess what we know about our opponent and ourselves, including such things as experience, culture, support, geography, alliances, firepower, and the desired or acceptable objectives. Having observed and oriented, we decide what to do; and, having made a decision, we act. Immediately we have acted, the OODA process recommences, as we observe our opponent to assess his response to our decision and action, and we reorient ourselves, and so on, until the particular decision/action contest is resolved, ideally in our favour.

Boyd regarded orientation as the most important phase of the process. Whereas poor orientation is likely to lead to bad decisions, informed orientation is likely to produce good decisions and, therefore, superior actions. From that, it follows that our first responsibility is to understand the strategic environment. Only then, Boyd argued, is originality of thought and action likely to flourish, a necessary condition if we are to exploit non-linear thinking and asymmetries in our effort to 'find and revel in mismatches'.

If orientation is the intellectual core of Boyd's theory, then time is the key to its application. Demonstrating elegantly simple logic, Boyd noted that time simply exists, that it does not have to be transported, sustained or protected, and that everyone has equal access to it. In other words, time is a free good which a skilful decision-maker should exploit and a less skilful decision-maker is likely to squander. In particular, time will be the ally of the protagonist who is best able to compress the OODA cycle, who can repeat the loop faster and more intelligently, and who can eventually get inside his opponent's decision-making cycle and thus control the clash of wills.

The criticism is sometimes made that Boyd's model is vulnerable to groups such as terrorists and guerillas who, the argument goes, can control tempo and invalidate the OODA cycle simply by refusing to respond to their opponent's actions. But this reasoning cuts both ways. On the one hand, the criticism misses the essential nature of the OODA process. Because the cycle is continuous, any decision a protagonist might take, including not responding to his opponent's preceding action, should be observed and oriented. It is then up to the active protagonist to decide on a presumably modified course of action, to implement that action, and immediately to begin the process again by observing the response, and so on. On the other hand, if an opponent's responses continue to frustrate the application of sufficient pressure to induce an outcome, then the objective of imposing strategic paralysis would seem problematic.

The theoretical basis of strategic paralysis is best represented by a combination of Warden's form and Boyd's purpose, with the strengths and weaknesses of the two models tending respectively to complement and mitigate each other. Unsurprisingly, tempo emerges as a critical factor. In theory at least, overwhelmed by the speed with which he is being attacked both psychologically (Boyd) and physically (Warden), the subject will collapse into a state of strategic paralysis. The US-led campaigns in Iraq in 1991 and 2003 best represent the translation of theory into practice thus far, in conspicuously different ways. Those campaigns also indicated that the concept of strategic paralysis, while intrinsically worthy of study, remains a work in progress.

THE EVOLUTION OF STRATEGIC PARALYSIS

In 1991 the Iraq invasion proper began with the most focused air campaign in history, as hundreds of aircraft and surface-to-air missiles attacked scores of carefully selected targets with unprecedented discrimination. Because the centre of gravity as represented physically by the dictator Saddam Hussein and his inner circle was hard to find and hit, the leadership target set was undermined indirectly, via strikes against its command-and-control apparatus. Within days Iraq's communications and information systems were barely functional, and Saddam and his lieutenants were experiencing extreme difficulty in speaking directly to their field commanders, let alone knowing what was going on. Concurrent strikes against key components of the other four target rings compounded their shock and confusion. Saddam had been attacked 'inside-out', and his OODA loop had been expanded almost beyond management. Well before the coalition armies rolled into Iraq some six weeks later, Saddam's ability to compete in the decision-making contest had effectively been paralysed. It was no coincidence that the land war lasted a mere hundred hours.

Before turning to the 2003 invasion of Iraq, the opportunity to make an observation in passing must be taken. This book has continually stressed the point that military victory is not an end in itself. Notwithstanding the remarkably one-sided nature of the 1991 war, President George H. Bush's inability to define a satisfactory political outcome beforehand and to arrive at one afterwards illustrated that truism. Bush's political failure enabled Saddam Hussein to remain in power, and the Iraqi dictator was soon again perceived as a threat to regional stability and to US security. Once al-Qa'ida had attacked the United States on September 11, 2001, and links, however tenuous, had been asserted between that terrorist organisation and Saddam, the presence in the White House of the first President Bush's son, George W. Bush, made a second war with Iraq more likely than not.

As a study of strategic paralysis, George W. Bush's 2003 campaign in Iraq provides a contrast to the 1991 experience. The crucial distinction arises from the form of combat power – the means – with which the model was pursued. Following the 1991 war, the key characteristics of strategic paralysis of sustained high tempo, extreme precision and discrimination in force application, and a focus from the beginning on leadership targets, had been evident in three other campaigns, twice in the Balkans (1995 and 1999) and once in Afghanistan (2001 to 2002). On each of those occasions the force application from NATO in 1995 and 1999 and from the US-led coalition in 2001 and 2002 came predominantly from air weapons, as it had in Iraq in 1991. In 2003 in Iraq, however, the centrepiece of the military campaign was a high-speed dash from Basra to Baghdad by a joint air/land force, with the lead role in the fighting falling primarily to the armies. While some components of the strategic paralysis model were still the province of discrete air operations, notably the attempts to decapitate key Iraqi leaders, this time it was the land forces that sought to overwhelm the enemy through sheer tempo and by dominating decision-making on the battlefield. That they were just as successful as their air force predecessors had been in 1991 indicated a broader relevance for the notion of strategic paralysis than some critics might previously have acknowledged.

But again an important point must be made in passing, also again related to the political dimension of strategy. It may be the case that on occasions a military campaign or strategy can be too successful for its own good, particularly, perhaps, in the case of strategic paralysis. The Nazis' invasion of the Soviet Union in June 1941 provided an early illustration of this apparent contradiction, which was later also evident in Iraq in 2003.

As had been the case during the blitzkrieg through Poland, the Low Countries and France at the beginning of the war, the Germans initially swept all before them in the USSR. Among other things, the Nazis destroyed the infrastructure of the Red Air Force as they overran air bases and factories west of Moscow. The distinctive nature of this destruction was, however, to create an unexpected problem for the Luftwaffe. Because the Red Air Force was crushed so quickly on the ground, many of its most valuable assets – trained pilots

– survived. In terms of centre-of-gravity analysis, skilled pilots are a much more important, expensive, long lead-time and perishable resource than bases, factories and aircraft. Thus, several years later, once the Nazi advance had stalled, and when modern aircraft were pouring out of Soviet factories which had been rebuilt beyond the Germans' reach, those same pilots were able to return to the conflict and eventually assert their dominance. Had the German invasion been protracted and had the Soviet pilots been killed in a war of attrition in the skies, that could not have happened.

The experience was repeated sixty-two years later in Iraq, but in a different form. So rapid and comprehensive was the US-led coalition's victory that when the military campaign ended after only five weeks, the Iraqi Army had suffered relatively little physical damage. Consequently, large numbers of Saddam's soldiers were able to slip away and later join an insurgency which, within months, had turned the initially triumphant coalition forces into a deeply unpopular army of occupation, and which had brought Iraq to the brink of civil war. Once again, it seemed, strategic paralysis had been too successful.

It would of course be facile, indeed immoral, to contend that a less efficient military strategy, such as the campaigns of attrition fought in World Wars I and II, and which had shattered the enemy's forces by the time victory was achieved, should have been applied in 2003. A swift, low-cost victory is by definition a good victory. The issue for the Nazis in 1941 was that their blitzkrieg against the Soviet Union came agonisingly close to winning, and if it had succeeded the immediate survival or otherwise of the Red Air Force's pilots would have been irrelevant. Once the decision to invade the USSR had been taken, and given the extent to which German forces were already committed in other theatres, the gamble on a quick victory in the east was not only justifiable but probably essential.

Nor should any criticism be made of the stunning military campaign fought by the US-led coalition in Iraq in 2003. The problem there was the failure of the Administration of President George W. Bush to reconcile the United States' desired political ends (the democratisation of Iraq and then the broader Middle East) with the chosen way (invasion) and means (armed forces). In turn, that problem arose because of the Bush Administration's ignorance of Iraqi history in particular and Islamic culture in general, and not because of any military strategic shortcomings. Thus, the conclusion we should draw about strategic paralysis at this stage is that the sheer speed with which the concept can produce results increases the already powerful imperative for decision-makers to understand precisely what it is they are seeking to achieve, and what that end-state implies, not least in relation to the chosen means and ways.

EFFECTS-BASED PLANNING

The pursuit of strategic paralysis is dependent on two complementary concepts, effects-based planning (EBP) and network-centric warfare (NCW). Like so many ideas associated with strategy, neither is necessarily new, but each has been revitalised by emerging technologies.

Since the mid-1990s, EBP has been adopted as the name for a methodology in which the desired effect of any action, regardless of its scale, should be identified before that action is initiated, and then harmonised with its associated ways and means. Plainly, leaders usually have had a particular outcome in mind when they have developed strategies and initiated courses of action. But if the history of warfare and international relations is any guide, we might question the extent to which many of those decision-makers have, in the first instance, located their desired end-states within the overall prevailing strategic circumstances. Furthermore, it seems that, too often and too quickly, there has been a tendency to turn to the maximum application of force as the preferred means. EBP is intended to address those logic flaws.

The background to EBP is worth examining, not least for the illustration it provides of a common intellectual sequence in strategic studies, namely, one in which existing or emerging military capabilities shape concepts, rather than the other way around. In this instance the philosophical catalyst has been the tactical capability represented by PGMs.

PGMs were used in World War II and the US war in Indochina, but reached maturity only in the 1990s, when they comprised about 9 per cent of all munitions expended by coalition air forces during

Operation Desert Storm in 1991 and 70 per cent during Operation Iraqi Freedom in 2003. The trend revealed by those numbers is clear and the implications far-reaching. What they mean is that, for the first time on a large and sustained scale, if a target can be identified, it can be hit. As noted above, in the past, the relative inaccuracy of weapons encouraged the physical destruction of targets, and because it took 9000 bombs to eliminate a notional target in World War II, there was no point in finesse. Consequently, overkill in terms of the technique employed (area attacks) and the kinds of weapons used (large high-explosive bombs) was a rational if intellectually crude response. The fact that one PGM could now achieve the same effect as World War II's 9000 dumb (unguided) bombs represented a new capability of the first order.

But hitting something precisely turned out to be only the starting point of a process in which a tactical/technical capability has been translated into a methodology for planning and warfighting for all three traditional services, and which may have the potential to embrace not just military activities, but a whole-of-nation approach to security. The conceptual breakthrough came with the simple but powerful realisation that, given that a target would be hit precisely, did it need to be destroyed? Could a more tailored, suitable, subtle, even psychological *effect* be generated by calibrating the weapon both to the target and to the ultimate campaign objectives? In other words, could a better fit be achieved with Clausewitz's enduring strictures on ends and means, and on war as policy?

The targeting of electrical facilities in Baghdad in 1991 provides a classic case study of EBP at the tactical level. Instead of destroying power grids with high-explosive bombs, the US-led coalition used weapons that dispensed thousands of carbon fibres to short-out transformers for periods varying from hours to days, depending on the prevailing operational demands, and how long it took the Iraqis to remove the fibres. The same principle has since motivated research and development into increasingly flexible weapons in order to facilitate the pursuit of a wide range and scale of effects: examples include warheads that can be calibrated immediately prior to release to deliver a specific explosive intensity; non-lethal weapons; inert warheads; miniaturised weapons which permit more effects per platform per mission; and so on. The objective is to realise an effect tailored to the prevailing circumstances, rather than to accept the somewhat mindless destruction of every target.

If it makes sense to try to achieve a precisely defined effect from every nominally tactical action, which it does, then it makes even more sense to adopt the same approach to national security objectives and to planning and conducting military campaigns. In that context, EBP has come to define a *philosophy* for national security, thus differentiating the concept from other developments such as the so-called Military Technical Revolution and the Revolution in Military Affairs which, as technology without doctrine, were one-dimensional.*

Given that warfare ultimately is a clash of wills, it was almost inevitable that this rediscovered interest in precisely linking actions to desired outcomes would be extended, first, to all levels of operations and decision-making from the tactical to the strategic; and second, to the pursuit of cognitive as well as physical effects. It was no coincidence that the rise of EBP was paralleled by an invigorating debate on the mind of war, perhaps best represented by the US Marines' use in the 1980s of John Boyd's work on competitive decision-making on the battlefield. Indeed, the fact that Boyd's OODA loop and phrases such as 'getting inside the enemy's decision-making cycle' have almost become clichés is an indication of the contemporary influence of this set of ideas.

Two actions from the second US-led war in Iraq, in 2003, illustrate different kinds and levels of EBP in practice. The first concerns the United States' approach to securing control of the air, an outcome which traditionally has been achieved by physically destroying the enemy air force in the air and on the ground. This time, however, consistent with the concept of achieving a carefully defined *effect* – namely, negating the Iraqi air defence system to facilitate unimpeded use of the air by friendly forces – comparatively little effort was directed towards destroying Iraqi aircraft and their supporting

---

* The notion of a Military Technical Revolution is generally associated with US Cold War plans to offset the USSR's overwhelming numbers with advanced technologies that facilitated deep and punishing strikes. The term 'Revolution in Military Affairs' encompasses any combination of new technologies and innovative operational concepts, such as the emergence of mechanised warfare in the 1930s, and of nuclear weapons and ballistic missiles in the 1950s.

infrastructure. Instead, the Iraqi air defence system was nullified by a series of tailored and connected EBP actions, including deterrence (Iraqi memories of their rout in the air in 1991, which in 2003 predisposed their pilots to stay on the ground), selective hard strikes against key command-and-control nodes (if pilots have no instructions, no radar to guide, and no communications they are unlikely to be effective), and selective soft strikes (feeding false data into Iraqi information systems, spreading computer viruses). It is noteworthy that the Iraqis launched more than 1600 surface-to-air missiles and made some 1200 anti-aircraft artillery attacks against coalition air forces but shot down only seven aircraft, numbers that indicate their air defence system had been largely negated without having been destroyed.

Second, the reported successful bribing of senior Iraqi officers to surrender rather than fight is representative of perhaps the most cost-effective approach to EBP, one which is wholly cognitive/informational.

It should be evident from the preceding discussion that EBP is applicable at any level of conflict, and that it facilitates the application of minimum, as opposed to maximum, or excessive, force. Furthermore, it is a defining characteristic of EBP that, invariably, it will be an implicit aim of the active protagonist to try to turn a tactical or operational gain into a strategic gain.

A fundamental step in implementing an EBP-derived approach to security is to have a clear understanding of what we do and do not mean when we talk about an effect we wish to establish as an objective, and which we wish to generate from a set of actions. Regardless of the kind and the extent of any effect we may wish to achieve, if we are successful, then, in our terms, we will have won. And to remind: because winning is a relative concept, an open-minded interpretation of the term is likely to be most useful because it will generate options and encourage flexible thinking.

By its nature, the successful application of EBP will, like the OODA process, demand a profound understanding of an opponent's culture, society, economy, and system of governance, which in turn will place an even greater premium than already exists on the skilled collection, analysis and dissemination of information. This process must include measuring the post-facto effects that have actually been caused as opposed to those that were sought, incorporating an appreciation of the effects the *opponent* saw, as possibly distinct from what *we* saw. What this means is that the application of EBP at a campaign or similar level will require a degree of strategic professionalism presently possessed by very few nations or organisations. Essential components will include highly trained people, good ideas, and advanced equipment, all supported by a robust economy and a strong indigenous research and development base.

Notwithstanding the utmost endeavour, efforts to determine desired effects with precision will to a greater or lesser degree remain an inexact science. Furthermore, as is the case with every form of coercion, the application of EBP will be interactive. In other words, any effect we pursue may trigger unforeseen or unintended second- and third-order effects, perhaps within our own system as well as that of the enemy's, the end results of which could feasibly be worse for us than accepting the pre-conflict status quo. This is true of most coercive actions, but the warning still needs to be sounded.

Desired effects might be defined by descriptions which locate them within one or more of the physical, cognitive and informational domains. For example, we might require our defence forces to be capable of generating shaping as a method of influencing our strategic environment; annihilation as an extreme physical effect; deterrence as a combination of physical and cognitive effects; manipulation as a combination of cognitive and informational effects; and so on. Any rational application of such guidance would lead to distinctive force-structuring conclusions for each required effect and its associated method.

It is important to appreciate that any immediate or short-term desired effects will have to be generated by our existing force structure, or by one that can be rapidly assembled; that is, we may have to manage possibly unexpected emerging threats with existing, perhaps unsuitable, legacy defence capabilities. There are inherent problems in relying on capabilities derived from hardware like strike aircraft, warships and tanks which not only can take twenty years from conception to operational service, but which also then typically remain in service for thirty or more years. That kind of timeframe will certainly see dramatic and unexpected shifts in threat perceptions, noting unexpected events like the sudden end of the Cold War, the sudden emergence of al-Qa'ida, and mass illegal immigrant flows following natural disasters.

Those possibilities point in turn to the potential of strategies that value cognitive, non-kinetic effects above physical effects, the reason being that the former are less likely to rely on legacy hardware and are more likely to exploit dynamic practices. Such non-traditional means and ways might also increase the chance of quick conflict resolution with minimum casualties and physical destruction. For example, information operations which undermine the confidence of the opposition élite, encourage defection and surrender, infiltrate enemy command-and-control systems, spread misinformation and computer viruses, and so on, have all been used to increasing advantage in recent years. And unlike physical effects which almost invariably require the deployment of forces and the risking of friendly lives, cognitive effects can be pursued from a secure base, perhaps even in the homeland, and for extended periods, with little if any danger to the executors.

A corollary of the preceding argument is that a radically different attitude might be needed towards the capabilities currently generated by legacy (existing) weapons systems, given that the very long operational timeframes often associated with major systems such as ships, tanks and aircraft are inimical to the EBP philosophy. Among the initiatives being examined, rapid prototyping and tranche acquisition are currently the most fashionable. Selecting a particular platform for rapid prototyping involves a degree of technological risk, and can also lead to accusations of favouritism from companies whose products are not chosen for what amounts to a form of preferential treatment. However, if a platform's potential were strong, the benefits of reducing the time to bring it on-line by perhaps as much as ten years would justify confronting those kinds of issues. And introducing platforms in discrete tranches rather than through the traditional method of continual delivery of the total order could also decrease the time needed to make a portion of the capability productive, by reducing the effort associated with having to set up new logistics, prepare and conduct new training courses, and develop operational concepts.

Other initiatives which facilitate EBP are already in place. Many defence forces now utilise outsourcing, leasing, and commercial off-the-shelf acquisition as early, indirect and partial solutions to the problem of legacy systems. Robotics and unmanned aerial vehicles, among other things reduce the need for costly, long lead-time machines and, for operators such as pilots and principal warfare officers, are representative of another set of emerging options.

The challenge of translating the theory of effects-based planning into a practical model should not be underestimated. It will be very demanding. Two points made previously are relevant here. The first is that, because of the nature of EBP, any broad application of the technique will demand a profound understanding of an opponent's culture, society, governance, and economy, skills which have not been especially evident in most of the military campaigns of the past half-century, regardless of who has been involved; and the second is that any immediate effect we generate may trigger unforeseen or unintended second- and third-order effects, perhaps within our own system as well as that of the enemy's, the consequences of which could feasibly be worse for us than accepting the pre-conflict status quo. Some case studies may help to illustrate EBP's inherent complexities.

Thus far, EBP has been exercised almost exclusively in the form of offensive air operations, in which pre-selected targets have been prosecuted with explosive hard-kill (kinetic) weapons. While the selection of the right targets and the choice of suitable weapons is a highly specialised task and can be complex, strike operations nevertheless remain one of the more manageable options within the full range of EBP possibilities, which can extend to the considerably more opaque dimensions of social and cognitive effects. Additionally, the direct results of a kinetic attack are among the easiest to measure, physical damage being more immediately obvious than, say, social disintegration. Yet even within this relatively straightforward model there are potential pitfalls. For example, a strike against an enemy's electrical power generation system might shut down his war industries, but it might also cut off power to humanitarian services such as hospitals, aged-care complexes, and water supplies which could breach the

Law of Armed Conflict and cause damaging international publicity. Competent campaign planners will try to anticipate those kinds of secondary effects, but experience suggests that war is unlikely ever to be entirely free from Clausewitz's fog and friction.

COMPLEX, ADAPTIVE COMPETITORS

The planning matrix becomes even more complicated when we try to directly target the human dimension of warfare – when we try to predict how our opponent's decision-makers will respond to actions we initiate in pursuit of a desired effect. Human beings are innately complex and adaptive, an emotional and intellectual combination that ensures we can never forecast with absolute confidence the outcome of any action-reaction cycle. The confrontation between Australia and Indonesia in 1999 over the planned military intervention into East Timor, authorised by the United Nations and led by the Australian Defence Force, illustrated this uncertainty.

Indonesia is Australia's largest and most important neighbour and, because of its vast population, contrasting culture, and sometimes erratic political system, has often been perceived by Australians as a security concern. Consequently, successive Australian governments have poured resources into intelligence programs intended to provide a sophisticated understanding of how Indonesians think and behave, with the objective of making informed judgments regarding Indonesia's probable reaction to various contingencies. Yet according to off-the-record reports, when UN forces landed in East Timor, senior Australian officials had little idea of the effect the intervention might trigger. Would humiliated Indonesian Army officers honour their government's undertaking to cooperate with the UN, or would they yield to emotion and attack? In the event, they observed the UN compact, but if they had not, the effect could scarcely have been more serious for Australia.

If one protagonist which tries so hard to understand another cannot confidently predict first-order effects, let alone possibly catastrophic second- and third-order effects, how useful is similar planning likely to be when competitors who know comparatively little about each other are involved? The obvious case study here is the US-led invasion of Iraq in 2003, in which the Bush Administration's ignorance of the cultural and historical dynamics in Iraq unleashed massive unforeseen follow-on effects. Clearly, the last thing US officials expected after their apparently decisive military victory over Saddam Hussein's army was Iraq's subsequent disintegration into insurgency and near-civil war, and the probability that the eventual outcome they will have caused will be a conservative, theocratic government, hostile to US interests. As former Australian Foreign Minister Bill Hayden dryly noted, 'Talk about unintended consequences'.

To summarise, at the moment, complex effects-based modelling is extremely challenging. But that is not to suggest that EBP is unworkable. On the contrary, the notion of planning our actions around clearly defined, desired effects, both physical and cognitive, as opposed to the routine practice of simply destroying targets, is self-evidently good. However, we need to be aware of EBP's complexities and to proceed accordingly. At this early stage, two approaches to exploiting the technique seem plausible, the one theoretical, the other practical.

As far as theory is concerned, planning for effect should simply be regarded as a state of mind. All EBP planning should be conducted within the ends-ways-means construct, and should start with a determination of the effects we require and those our actions are likely to generate, including subsidiary and unwanted effects. Using this method, we could reasonably expect that we would start operations with a clearer idea than would otherwise have been the case of where we want to go, how we want to get there, and what kinds of means we should use. As it happens, evidence from strategic studies journals and military staff college curricula indicates that, within advanced military forces at least, the merit of thinking in terms of effects rather than of destruction, or of seizing and holding ground, or of attrition, and so on, is already accepted as a given.

And as far as practice is concerned, EBP should be allowed to evolve through its relatively straightforward and thus far fairly successful application to pre-planned strike operations. The immediate, primarily kinetic effects of a precision strike can be reasonably anticipated during the planning phase, and the results of physical damage can generally be measured after the event. In other words, we can let technology take the lead.

There is something of the 'build it and they will come' approach to this method, which seeks to manage the otherwise ambiguous dynamic that has always characterised the relationship between theory and technology.* Does theory lead technology, or vice versa? Regardless of the answer we might favour, the relationship is symbiotic. In this instance, because of the inherent complexity of the theory component, the suggestion is that we should consciously let the technology component take the lead. For example, one existing technology that could readily be adapted to enhance effects-based operations is the data link.[3] Presently, carrying out a strike and then measuring its effect usually involves two separate tasks, which are often separated by significant time delays. If data links were built into weapons, operational staff would be able to observe and measure the results of every strike immediately it took place, thereby considerably improving their ability to control both desired and actual effects.

There is also the example of the separate defence services acquiring common technologies such as communications and electronic warfare equipment to facilitate joint operations. Almost invariably, equipment commonality will improve inter-service cooperation, which in turn can exert a positive organisational influence. And when that equipment is related to information activities, there may well be an associated EBP follow-on.

In short, the 'build it (the technology) and they will come (the theory)' approach to EBP minimises the complicating cognitive factors while exploiting the more manageable technical factors.

Just as EBP as a mindset has become a given within many advanced defence forces, so too has the application of the OODA cycle. There is a powerful linkage between EBP and the OODA process in general and its orientation phase in particular. Given the inherent complexity of trying to predict and measure effects, the constant application of the OODA cycle to EBP imposes logic and discipline on both the

---

* The saying 'Build it and they will come' is from the 1989 motion picture *Field of Dreams*, itself an allegory for belief. An American farmer hears voices which he eventually realises are telling him to build a baseball diamond in his cornfields. He does so, and the ghosts of the 1919 Chicago White Sox baseball team (notorious for 'throwing' the World Series) appear on his 'field of dreams'.

planning and the conduct of operations. The end result is a technique which seeks to exploit the conceptual strength of EBP while at the same time managing its practical limitations.

EBP represents the intellectual antithesis of the mass and force-on-force mindset that has largely typified warfare and which is still favoured by many armies. Even as recently as the US war in Indochina and the Iran–Iraq War, services that ostensibly were well prepared doctrinally and technologically joined battle with the primary objective of applying force-on-force, of relying on mass and firepower, and of winning through attrition. Such an approach is prohibitively expensive, morally dubious, and inherently self-limiting. By contrast, EBP establishes a logic flow between ends, ways and means at all levels of strategic thinking and conflict; breaks the irrational but widely shared force development mentality in which platforms, rather than desired effects, are used to define capabilities; facilitates the exploitation of dynamic ideas and technologies; and provides a security-planning philosophy designed to meet the challenges of rapidly emerging threats and seize the opportunities of the information age.

NETWORK-CENTRIC WARFARE

The concept of EBP is underpinned by the organisational system of network-centric warfare (NCW). The objective of NCW is to create a 'seamless' system of sensors and shooters – sub-surface, surface, air-breathing and space-based – that will exchange relevant information in near real-time, and facilitate the conduct of highly effective operations across the entire network. Yet again, the notion is as old as strategy itself. Commanders have always sought organisational arrangements which best exploit the different but complementary qualities of their various combat capabilities. How, for example, might a medieval captain have assimilated his foot-soldiers, cavalry, and archers? How should they be arraigned, when should each element come into play, how can they communicate, how can the whole be made greater than the sum of its parts? Modern armies invariably have a combined arms studies centre whose task it is to determine ways to integrate armour, infantry, artillery, reconnaissance and aviation, to achieve 'mutually complementary effects'. As the most recent iteration of this process, NCW seeks to utilise powerful modern technologies, especially computers and communications, to achieve a quantum leap in effectiveness.

Dominating the ISTAR (intelligence, surveillance, target acquisition, reconnaissance) domain is the technical key to NCW, because the protagonist who knows more sooner can control competitive decision-making on the battlefield. In an ideal NCW system, the best-located, most suitable sensor will pass real-time targeting information to the best-located, most suitable shooter, which can then prosecute the target with discrimination, from a distance. As far as who does what and where is concerned, none of the environment, or the weapons systems, or the colour of the uniform matters: the only concern is to achieve the desired effect in the quickest, most efficient way.

Because NCW is intended to improve situational awareness and enable the generation of an overwhelming tempo it should, among other things, facilitate the prosecution of fleeting targets and opportunities. This so-called time-sensitive targeting represents yet another stepping stone in the endeavour to generate rapid effects, ideally against high-value targets: that is, to generate strategic paralysis.

Self-synchronisation is another NCW goal. Putting aside the annoying jargon, the concept has merit. Basically, it posits the ability of all of the disparate warfighting elements of a joint force to synchronise their actions in pursuit of a common objective. The ability to self-synchronise will be built on a common understanding of the objective; on a common understanding of the battle through sharing a common operational picture; and on having the necessary training and technology.

Early in 2005 the US Defence Force constructed a prototype NCW architecture which linked a global network of command-and-control and ISTAR capabilities. Numerous systems were integrated to build what amounted to a battlefield Internet, comprising 'hundreds of systems, sensors and warfighters'. The trial demonstrated machine-to-machine connections, security shortcuts, and automated decision aids, and apparently reduced to seconds the time needed to locate and identify targets. Indeed, the network was so fast that the biggest impediment to the rapid prosecution of targets was the time of flight of weapons. Presently the goal is to achieve a standard cycle of ten minutes from identification to strike.

An intriguing possibility some analysts have raised in relation to the EBP/NCW model is the so-called 'strategic corporal'. The prospect is both promising and worrying. The idea is that a solitary soldier who enjoys an overwhelming decision-making advantage through access to superior real-time information, and who is equipped with advanced sensors and long-range precision weapons, may be able to make decisions and take actions that could have a strategic effect. The possibility stands in stark contrast to the tactical actions that in the past have been the individual infantryman's lot. The corollary, of course, is that the same soldier would be capable of making strategic mistakes, with major ramifications. One implication is that the quality of the rank-and-file soldier, as defined by strategic knowledge and decision-making excellence, would require a massive improvement over the historical norm.

No less intriguing in the age of the Internet is the role the ordinary members of a networked force might play in the collection and dissemination of strategic information. Now routinely used by terrorists as their communications system, the Internet has also made possible new information management techniques for national defence forces. Foremost among these has been the use of chat rooms; that is, of world-wide-web pages to which access can be either open or restricted, and on which intelligence, ideas, and information on almost anything else can be posted and exchanged. Among other things, such a system has the potential to challenge the long-standing hierarchical organisation favoured by traditional defence forces. An army-wide chat room to which every soldier has access could enhance both the speed with which information is transmitted and the depth of the information base throughout the organisation, and it could affect who exchanges information with whom. Equally, like every website, chat rooms can be flooded with rubbish, the sheer volume of which can create more problems than it solves. Once again, the answer would seem to lie in the quality of the users; also again, the implied individual skills would seem to be considerably greater than the historic norm. Anyone can buy technology and try to copy ideas, but the development of the right people is a different matter altogether.

The combination of EBP and NCW promises both an unrivalled degree of battle-space awareness and the ability to apply decisive force with discrimination in pursuit of a precisely defined effect. Two major obstacles to realising this prospective war-winning and casualty-minimising capability are how to manage the information, and how to overcome the entrenched single-service cultures of armies, navies, air forces and marines.

Once again, the issue of technology as strategy arises. In this instance, the technology needed to conduct EBP/NCW largely exists: the challenge is to make it work – to employ it efficiently. Telecommunications provides a striking example. During World War II the allies were able to transmit electronic communications at about sixty words per minute. By the time of the US war in Indochina that rate had risen to 100 words per minute; by the 1991 Gulf War to 100 000 words a minute (the equivalent of a modest dictionary); and by the early twenty-first century to three million. Since knowledge is the essence of decision-making in general and of the concept of strategic paralysis in particular, this all sounds encouraging. The difficulty, of course, is turning that information into knowledge, and having enough skilled people to analyse such a vast amount of material. Without the right system and the right people, three million words a minute are nothing more than that. And as demonstrated by the West's ignorance of Vietnamese culture in the 1960s and 1970s, and Middle Eastern culture at the end of the twentieth century, the magnitude of the challenge should not be underestimated.

THE PROBLEM OF MILITARY CULTURE

Turning to military culture, two factors have historically impeded the degree of change implicit in EBP/NCW. First, defence forces have tended to develop through evolution, not revolution. Genuine technological breakthroughs have been few and far between, and even when they have occurred they have not always been recognised or used efficiently. For example, in 1940, the British and French armies grossly misused their relatively new tanks because they insisted on absorbing them into the infantry and cavalry, instead of creating new tank-centred formations, as the Germans had done.

And second, the military mindset is notoriously hard to change. The aphorism that generals prepare for the next war by studying the last one says more about military tradition and single-service cultures than it does about the intellectual capacity of military commanders.

Which leads to an issue that within many defence forces seems almost intractable, namely, the limits imposed on innovative thinking by single-service cultures and attitudes.

A revealing illustration of this emotional and organisational barrier to fostering an holistic and relevant strategic philosophy can be seen in the missions the single services tend to define for themselves. Armies, for example, almost invariably list their mission as being simply to win the land battle. While winning land battles historically has indeed been the main activity of armies, in itself it need not represent a desired effect, and nor does it define the only significant effect we might reasonably expect an advanced land force to deliver. Thus, armies have asserted sea denial (Turkish gun batteries dominating the Dardanelles in March 1915); they have won control of the air (allied troops capturing Luftwaffe airfields in France following the D-Day landings in 1944; Ariel Sharon's armoured columns smashing through the Egyptians' ground-based air defence system along the Suez Canal in 1973); and so on. There are so many other cases that the point should be self-evident, but it is so important that it does need to be emphasised. Navies and air forces similarly tend to couch their missions in strictly environmental terms, which are nebulous within an EBP construct.

The attitudes that this kind of thinking represents constitute a formidable barrier to organisational progress. To extend the line of reasoning, the predilection of armies, navies and air forces to define their capabilities in terms of their particular hardware such as tanks, trucks, frigates, and fast jets, instead of by effects, entirely ignores the often battle-winning roles played by capabilities which notionally belong within an ostensibly different environmental or warfighting model. Furthermore, because organisational arrangements, missions and capabilities are derived predominantly from this 'platforms equal capabilities' definition of what a defence force is and what it might do, both the explicit and implicit effects which flow from that definition are overwhelmingly kinetic. In other words, the singular opportunity to acquire a potent asymmetric advantage that will be open to those defence forces which are able to master the cognitive and informational aspects of EBP/NCW receives no recognition.

The basic problem here is single-service tribalism.

There are good reasons why the evolution of defence forces has traditionally taken place within the distinct environments of land, sea and air. Even now when the influence of information operations and the capacity to act with speed and precision are becoming more evenly balanced across armies, navies and air forces, there are still well-founded specialist and cultural arguments in favour of the long-standing organisational arrangement. Some forty years down the track, Canada's ill-considered decision to peremptorily combine its three services (subsequently rescinded) is still used by guardians of the old order to 'prove' the danger of ignoring history.

It is unquestionably the case that the social compact within a professional, all-volunteer defence force is unique, and that an individual's readiness to risk his or her life can be related to their identification with their service and unit, as well as to their commitment to their comrades. Nevertheless, as J. F. C. Fuller once noted, the fighting power of a defence force lies in the first instance in its organisation.[4] It could be a mistake of the first order if tradition alone were allowed to stand in the way of any reform which promised significantly enhanced performance. If EBP/NCW is to be genuinely embraced it may be intellectually unsustainable for defence forces to retain an operational structure based largely on service-related equipment, as is presently the case. Taking that observation a step further, we might conclude that if we started today with the proverbial clean sheet of paper to shape a defence force for the twenty-first century, we would not end up with an army, a navy and an air force as we now know them. The question then would become one of how to implement change.

That question might be addressed in the first instance by focusing on attitudes rather than by attempting to impose substantial organisational reforms that almost certainly would face counter-productive resistance from the single services. The immediate objective should be to establish a common thread of intent throughout the organisation, an outcome which might be achieved simply by redefining missions and roles in effects-based terms, and by linking existing capabilities, regardless of their service, to one or more of those effects. We might, for example, want our defence forces to be capable of generating one or more of a number of indicative effects, such as shaping, deterrence, and theatre-level dominance; and any rational application of such guidance would lead to distinctive force-structuring conclusions for each required effect and its associated method. The way in which we use words can be a powerful force for change, without immediately threatening vested interests or social compacts.

Whether or not semantics alone would be sufficient to create the kind of organisational shift ultimately implied by strategic paralysis and EBP/NCW is problematic. If it emerged that the key combat elements of a defence force associated with any identified need to generate, say, a deterrent effect, were special forces and strike aircraft, it might become highly desirable to formally bring those elements together organisationally. The almost certain need to have to add cognitive warfare specialists, such as linguists and social and economic analysts, to this particular mix would only increase the prospect that at some stage the case for a major reorganisation would become undeniable.

* * *

In a sense, the concept of strategic paralysis represents strategy as an ideal. The implications of being able to apply overwhelming knowledge superiority and irresistible tempo to the clash of wills that defines strategic competition are obvious. Furthermore, advanced technologies have given the notion more substance than its conceptual predecessors such as the decisive battle and the knock-out blow. In practice, however, no military endeavour is likely entirely to escape the implications of Clausewitz's fog and friction. Additionally, the effects-based thinking and network-centric models that are central to strategic paralysis sit uncomfortably with the platforms-based, single-service dominated organisations favoured by traditional environmentally defined defence forces. Nevertheless, and regardless of its ultimate place in the greater scheme of things, strategic paralysis is representative of the kind of debate strategic analysts must promote if their discipline is to remain dynamic. Perhaps the most salutary observation here is that the main obstacle to such debates within defence forces is neither operational nor technological, but cultural.

7

Contemplating war
Political imperatives and strategic considerations

W AR ALWAYS HAS A purpose. It is an organised group activity undertaken for policy ends, a conscious and rational attempt to use military force to secure a desired end-state that extends beyond victory on the battlefield. The intent may be to repel an aggressor, seize territory or overthrow a regime, weaken the position of a rival power, or compel an adversary to modify their behaviour. Broader objectives may be to achieve greater security, increase stability, or enhance influence and power. In most circumstances governments view the employment of military force against other states as an option of last resort. War is a violent activity that causes death, damage and displacement, and requires a high level of political and economic commitment. The costs of defeat are high, with a whole range of negative outcomes possible: occupation, regime change, territorial dismemberment, dismantling of military capabilities, economic sanctions, and criminal prosecution of national leaders. While major powers defeated in wars against weaker opponents may be spared some of the worst of these consequences, even they are not immune from short- and long-term damage. Their publics may undergo a crisis of confidence, incumbent governments can be vulnerable, and the armed forces may suffer a loss of credibility.

The broader effects of war are unpredictable and by no means guaranteed to be advantageous, even for those who achieve their immediate objectives. Wars can alter the balance of power and rearrange the political landscape, both in the regions in which they occur and globally. The short-term consequence may well be instability and unpredictability, and the longer term may see the rise of new adversaries and of unexpected and unwelcome alignments, and the horizontal and vertical proliferation of weapons technology as other states absorb the lessons of war.*

Wars begin with reasoned decisions by both parties that they can gain more by fighting than by remaining at peace. The organised use of force may not have been planned for, or may be unwelcome, but the historical record shows that wars never begin by accident. Incidents or miscalculations may occur or crises may escalate to a point where unplanned military action seems the only feasible option, but the decision to fight is always deliberate. The case most often cited as an instance of accidental war, the Manchurian Incident of 1931, was in fact deliberate. Japanese military commanders used the pretext of sabotage against a local Japanese-owned railway to attack the Chinese garrison at Mukden without authorisation by the Emperor or the Diet as part of a protracted and ultimately successful struggle to assert the primacy of the military and their values and ambitions. These ambitions included the establishment of Japanese rule over all of Manchuria.

The theory of accidental war gained currency in the Cold War when the advent of nuclear weapons, the instability of superpower relations, and untested command-and-control procedures persuaded many strategic analysts that an accidental launch of a single nuclear weapon was possible and plausible and could precipitate an all-out nuclear war. These fears remain hypothetical because no nuclear weapon has been fired in anger since the end of World War II.

THE DECLINE IN THE INCIDENCE OF WAR

Since the mid-twentieth century the incidence of war between states has declined.[1] Most states no longer use force to settle their disputes and fewer still use force to protect or advance their economic interests or further their political ambitions. This is not to say, of course, that the phenomenon of inter-state war has become extinct. A few disputes

---

* Horizontal proliferation refers to the international diffusion of military technologies while vertical proliferation involves the quantitative and qualitative growth of a particular state or group's arsenal.

over sovereignty, territorial boundaries and access have escalated to war, a few states have invaded smaller neighbours, the United Nations sanctioned the ejection of Iraqi forces from Kuwait in 1991, and the United States twice intervened to overthrow hostile governments. But by the early twenty-first century the ratio of costs to benefits of employing military force to advance national interests was widely perceived by most states as too great. Most governments now found that they could protect or promote their interests without resort to the use of force.

There are a number of reasons for this shift in perceptions, the first of which is that the acquisition of territory is no longer necessary to ensure access to the resources required for economic survival. The end of the age of empire, the globalisation of production, and the freeing-up of international trade mean that those states that can afford to do so can readily and peacefully source their requirements in the global marketplace. Advances in science and technology have ensured thus far that when commodities are short, supply can be increased or substitutes found. Governments expected to deliver rising standards of living for their populations but facing competition in traditional industries can encourage a shift into other sectors, such as services and finances. Companies can move offshore, investing in and utilising the labour of less developed economies.

Land has lost its significance as a defensive buffer with the advent of long-range delivery systems and international suicide bombers, rendering the strategic advantages of distance obsolescent. Nor is it necessary for 'living space'. Populations have stabilised or are decreasing in the most population-stressed areas of the planet and can in any case be adequately sheltered and fed in ever smaller areas, thanks to improved engineering, construction and farming techniques.

Some security analysts argue that the strategic salience of land will increase in the future because it is land that provides access to fresh water. Water is vital to the survival of humans, to agriculture and to industry, but not all states have sole rights to an adequate supply. Some are dependent on rivers that wander through several other countries, making them sensitive to their neighbours' water-usage policies. In situations such as these, including in the Middle East and Southeast Asia, conflict has again been averted thus far by the patient negotiation of regional agreements.

Where land remains a source of tension between states it is because of long-running disputes over sovereignty, either because of vague colonial legacies or some other anomaly of history such as a post-war treaty settlement, or of a population movement. The majority of such disputes have been resolved or are being negotiated by diplomatic means, a process that now often ends with final arbitration by international legal institutions. And that brings us to another reason for the decline in the use of inter-state force.

Since World War II a large body of international laws and regimes governing inter-state behaviour on matters related to international security has been negotiated, agreed and implemented. Advances in international law as it directly relates to armed conflict will be discussed in detail in the following chapter and are the most obvious of these, but an array of regimes, laws and institutions now indirectly ameliorate inter-state tensions. These range from agreements on the free movement of trade that have ended a tradition of naval attacks on rival mercantile shipping, through to law-of-the-sea negotiations formalising and guaranteeing national maritime claims and user-transit rights, to agreements limiting the horizontal and vertical proliferation of weapons systems.

The prospect of having to maintain control over acquired territory is also less attractive than it used to be. Where people were once used to the idea and practice of suzerainty, the development of the state system, the rise of nationalism, decolonisation, and the spread of democracy have all combined to inculcate a global preference for self-determination. Foreign occupation is likely to meet with stubborn resistance unless the local population has been thoroughly exhausted by the preceding war, and the costs of resistance are recognised as dramatically outweighing the benefits.

Both of these conditions applied in the post-war occupations of the twentieth century most often cited as successful, namely, those of Japan and Germany by allied forces after World War II. In both cases the preceding conflict had been long, bloody and draining, and the alternative to accepting allied occupation was probable occupation by the other, more feared, victor of the war, the Soviet Union. The success of the less often cited occupations, by the Nazis of their European neighbours during World War II, and by the Soviet Union of post-war Eastern Europe, can also be explained in part by exhaustion: psychological in the case of those countries which had had their territory fought over and suffered enormous losses in World War I, and literal in the case of the countries which initially had been invaded by Germany.[2] In both categories, the occupiers were able to find local élites who shared their ideology and were willing to collaborate. The means of resistance were in any case limited, with the occupying forces having a monopoly on weaponry and the ability to police and limit the traffic of people and goods. And finally, the occupying forces were more than willing to inflict savage reprisals on resisters.

Neither of the latter two conditions is easy to replicate in the twenty-first century. The very factors that have facilitated the global movement of people and goods have allowed for the easy spread of small arms, undermining the monopoly of violence once held by governments and their armed forces. At the same time, small arms and ammunition have become more affordable, as weapons manufacturers in the West and in the old Soviet states and satellites have retooled to keep themselves afloat, and as used arms have 'cascaded' out of war-settled conflict zones such as Cambodia, into new markets.

Severe reprisals against those resisting occupation are also more problematic. Since World War II, a growing if not yet universal international commitment to individual human rights has combined with a dramatic improvement in communications to make state or group abuse of others both more visible and more likely to attract international censure and punitive action. Where states have been able to escape international condemnation of the ill-treatment of occupied populations, it has only been because the interests of the occupier have been perceived as coincident with those of the major powers and regional states. But interests change, as Indonesia found at the end of the Cold War, when Western silence on repression in East Timor and elsewhere gave way to calls for greater freedom and democracy.

The rising costs and the declining benefits of using force are not the only reasons that states now rarely resort to war. Two other sets of constraints have emerged since the end of World War II. The threat of nuclear retaliation or of escalation to nuclear war induces extra caution, as do the restrictions on the use of force enshrined in the United Nations Charter. The implications of both of these factors for the development and implementation of modern strategy will be discussed in depth in chapter eight.

Wars do, of course, still occur. But for all the reasons discussed, inter-state wars have been rare in occurrence and almost all have been limited rather than total wars. As Clausewitz realised, limited wars are very different in character from total wars, being subject to greater political constraints. Because war is 'an act of force designed to compel an enemy to do our will'[3] and involves a dynamic of action, reaction and escalation, it naturally leads to three extremes: maximum use of force; total disarmament of the enemy; and maximum exertion. The more ambitious the objectives of the groups involved, the more will war follow this natural course and the more 'absolute' it will become. Clausewitz was writing about the Napoleonic wars, which were nothing less than revolutionary in their ambitions and effort compared to the dynastic wars of eighteenth-century Europe, and which seemed to presage a new era of near-absolute war. In fact these 'new' wars were not absolute, because they did not escalate to their abstract potential. Indeed, according to Clausewitz no war ever did, because war is always shaped and constrained by its political purpose, and rationality will always dictate that it stops short of mutual anni-hilation. Nevertheless, the political objectives of Napoleonic warfare were so ambitious that they coincided very closely with the 'military element's tendency to violence', resulting in what has come to be known as total war.

'LIMITED' WARS

The experiences of the two world wars of the twentieth century seemed to confirm a trend towards total warfare, with the antago-nists mobilising their entire populations, converting their economies to war production, and using all available manpower and technology to bring about each other's defeat and surrender. Total war between states has not been repeated since, however, since no two states or groups of states have been as committed to the unconditional defeat of the other, and nor have they exhibited a willingness to use all the means at their disposal. Where war has been total, it has been so only for one side in the conflict. North Vietnam was a case in point, with its leaders in the war to unify the Vietnamese people believing the stakes to be so high that they were willing to commit everything to defeat the technologically superior forces of France between 1946 and 1954 and then the United States between 1962 and 1975. Most wars since World War II, including all of those waged by Western democracies, more closely resemble those of eighteenth-century Europe, having been fought for objectives short of total surrender and subjugation and with less than total commitment. These 'limited' wars may be constrained in their objectives, geographical extent, the means employed, and commitment.

Limited aims might be to coerce or compel a change in state or group behaviour, repel limited threats, punish particular actions, or recover or seize disputed parcels of territory or militarily significant positions. Sometimes the objective is finite, with the parties involved having no further military or political ambitions. The 1982 Falklands War was a good example, with neither Argentina nor the United Kingdom planning to do anything other than assert their sovereign rights to the islands. Or the decision to pursue limited goals may be influenced by concern about the destabilising effects of pursuing more ambitious objectives. The rulers of eighteenth-century Europe confined their military endeavours to the seizure of each other's forts and towns, in part because they realised that more serious attempts to undermine each other's position could open the floodgates to a widespread questioning of the system of monarchical rule on the continent.

The geographical limitation of wars may follow from the assessment of objectives, or it too may be influenced by a desire to minimise the military and political uncertainty that would occur if the war were widened. Not even Hitler would have chosen to fight on two fronts at the same time had he believed that there were other options.

War may also be limited by a reluctance to commit too many resources, a common restraint on the use of force in eighteenth-century Europe. None of the rulers of the time felt they could spare the manpower or resources for all-out conflict because they had been exhausted by the Thirty Years' War and needed a growing population of taxpayers and producers to generate the economic strength that was now their goal.*

Lack of appropriate or sufficient numbers of weapons systems, low levels of technology, and poor transport and supply capabilities may restrict strategic options for some states. Indonesia, for example, had little choice but to confine itself to low-level raids and sabotage during its Crush Malaysia or Confrontation campaign in the 1960s. In such straitened circumstances, there will be an understandable reluctance to risk major escalation, especially when an opponent has the capacity to retaliate.

All states, however sophisticated their arsenals, have to be particularly concerned about escalation in the nuclear age. The way in which strategic choices have been limited by the existence of nuclear weapons is discussed in detail in the next chapter and it is sufficient here to note that these weapons have not only served as a deterrent in times of peace and induced caution in periods of crisis but have limited ambitions and activities in the planning and execution of war.

It is ironic then that the spread of weapons of mass destruction and in particular of nuclear weapons has come to be seen as one of the greatest threats of the twenty-first century and that the prevention of this spread is now a new imperative for war.

As Clausewitz wrote, 'no war should be commenced, if people acted wisely, without first seeking a reply to the question, what is to be attained by and in the same?'[4] This might seem like a statement of the obvious but Clausewitz was making a point that is often forgotten: those in authority need to be clear about the utility of force in achieving their objectives. War is obviously useful in repelling aggressors as it was in the Falklands and in Kuwait in 1991, and force can be used in permissive environments to achieve finite political objectives, such as the kidnapping by a US military expedition in 1989 of the Panamanian dictator, General Manuel Noriega, but in many other circumstances it will prove less than decisive, and may even

---

* Fought between 1618 and 1648, the Thirty Years' War took place primarily in what is now Germany and involved most of Europe's major powers. Religious conflict and dynastic competition were the main causes.

contribute to tension and insecurity. The Iran–Iraq War, the various Indo–Pakistan clashes, and Israel's invasion of the Lebanon in 1982 all fall into this category. The last of these started out with the limited and straightforward objective of halting attacks on Israel by Palestinians in southern Lebanon, but rapidly evolved into an attempt to change the domestic balance of power in Lebanon. After a long and bloody campaign Israel had to withdraw, leaving a legacy of even more embittered relations with the Palestinians.

Many of the expectations of war in the contemporary world are comparable to the invasion of the Lebanon in the breadth of their political ambition and are similarly difficult to meet. Force is now most often used to create the conditions necessary for the political delivery of the objective but its utility in this role may be limited and its use may actually render the political objective impossible.

Since the end of the Cold War in 1989, the few inter-state wars that have occurred have been waged for three types of objectives and have involved two distinct roles for the armed forces. The first, the 1991 Gulf War, was fought with the clear and finite aim of driving an aggressor state out of the country it had invaded. The objective of the US-led United Nations coalition was to expel Iraqi forces from Kuwait and restore that country's sovereignty, a simple and readily achievable military goal given the great disparity of capabilities, the support of neighbouring states, and the open and easily traversable operating environment.

Operation Allied Force in 1999 provided a marked contrast. NATO's aim was to coerce Serbian President Slobodan Milosevic into ceasing the persecution of the Albanian people of Kosovo, and to return to negotiations over the future of the province. NATO demanded Milosevic allow its forces free access to the whole of Serbia, and to agree to independence for Kosovo after a three-year transition period. But these objectives were not easy to achieve by force. Active military coercion is problematic by nature because it goes against the natural grain of war. Instead of involving the massive, concentrated, and continuous effort that is necessary to keep an adversary off-balance, coercion involves limited applications of force interspersed with pauses to allow for enemy compliance and is only gradually escalated in the event of failure. Such a process gives an adversary time to regroup and supplement their forces, harden or disperse their capabilities, and develop and implement counter-strategies. Their resolve is only likely to be stiffened by the reasonable assessment that the limited and measured application of force signals a lack of serious commitment. All these drawbacks were evident in Operation Allied Force, and disagreements about targeting and a difficult operating environment further complicated matters. Political expectations had to be trimmed and new diplomatic manoeuvres initiated to avoid unwelcome escalation from air strikes to a ground war.

The Kosovo intervention was a good illustration of one of the difficulties in achieving wartime objectives, and that is that states often have more than one objective when they go to war. Their stated aim may be to remedy a particular situation but they may have other less obvious objectives, such as reassuring or mobilising their publics, demonstrating resolve or power to other states, meeting popular or international demands for action, burden-sharing, cementing alliance relationships, proving the utility of security organisations, or securing broader interests. In the case of Operation Allied Force, NATO as a whole was not only responding to public humanitarian concern but also was anxious to demonstrate its continuing relevance in a changed European security environment. This secondary requirement complicated efforts to end the displacement of the Albanian Kosovars.

The next inter-state war was the United States' attack on Afghanistan in the wake of September 11. Here the objectives were to decapitate al-Qa'ida and thus neutralise the terrorist organisation, remove their Taliban hosts from power, and pave the way for the development of a democratic and economically viable Afghanistan in which terrorists would no longer be able to find safe haven. Swift retribution would also demonstrate the Bush Administration's resolve to a shaken American public. The use of force, US and local, proved as effective as anticipated in removing the Taliban from power and depriving its leadership of a base. But the wider objective of neutralising al-Qa'ida failed, in part because some of its leaders were able to flee the country, and in part because of a misunderstanding of its nature in the first place. Al-Qa'ida was, and remains, less an organisation than an inspiration, with its leaders providing funds, training and motivation to a scattered population of radicalised Muslims with diverse agendas but a common belief that they can achieve change through violence. The long-term prospects for the democratisation and economic rehabilitation of Afghanistan remain uncertain.

Soon after the attack on Afghanistan, the United States led a small coalition of Western countries in an invasion of Iraq in 2003. Analysts have collated a veritable laundry list of stated US objectives for Operation Iraqi Freedom including, most prominently, the neutralisation of the threat posed by Saddam Hussein's alleged weapons of mass destruction, the overthrow of his brutal regime for humanitarian reasons, and the establishment of a democratic model for the strategically vital and worryingly unstable Middle East. Other governments in the coalition that joined combat appeared to share these objectives but were also motivated by a desire to demonstrate their solidarity with the United States. It was reasonable to assume that military force could achieve the first two of these objectives, given the weakened state of the Iraqi armed forces and the unpopularity of Saddam Hussein among most of his subjects. But creating the conditions conducive to the development of a democratic and quiescent polity should have been recognised as an intrinsically problematic task that could be hindered as much as helped by the use of force.

Planning to use force for regime change requires a great deal of sober thinking. Regime removal might be an option for states that have the necessary military power, but that is only part of the challenge. It is no easy matter to stabilise a disrupted polity and then convert it into a form which is preferable to that of its ousted predecessor. Local administration and services may suffer if the previous regime's loyalists are removed, which in turn can hinder reconstruction efforts and the process of political reform. Indigenous competition for power and influence may well involve violence and the eventual outcome may be the establishment of a polity that is weak, unstable, and even hostile. All of those troublesome characteristics were evident to a greater or lesser degree in post-invasion Iraq in 2003.

STRATEGIC CALCULATIONS

Some wars are undertaken in the expectation that they will have positive effects beyond the immediate theatre. That was certainly the case with Operation Iraqi Freedom, where one of the main objectives was to establish a peaceable democratic regime that would serve as a positive model for the other Muslim countries in the Middle East. The spread of democracy would make a strategically vital region less volatile and simultaneously reduce the political frustration that was believed to be fuelling international terrorism. But all types of wars can have unexpected and even adverse effects on the regions in which they occur, and regime-changing wars are no exception. In this instance, the possible federation of Iraq into Shi'ite, Sunni, and Kurdish regions disturbed Iraq's neighbours with Kurdish minorities, especially Turkey, while the probable political dominance of the Shi'ites worried its Sunni neighbours. These neighbours, along with Iran which is the only predominantly Shi'ite state outside of Iraq, began attempting to influence events, contributing to an unpredictable regional dynamic that did not bode well for regional stability. In the meantime the Iraq War angered many Muslims and provoked more followers to radical violence and governments in the region showed no serious inclination to liberalise.

Before resorting to force, decision-makers should calculate the value of the objective and the chances of success, and consider alternative strategic options and the likely consequences of not fighting.[5] The value of the objective is easy to calculate when a state is faced with a direct and serious threat to its sovereignty, but it is not so simple in other more limited circumstances to decide what price is worth paying in terms of economic resources, casualties, international opprobrium, and potentially negative shifts in the balance of power.

When the alternative to war appears to be national or group annihilation, the probability of success will not feature prominently in planning. Any action will be seen as better than none and operations will be planned in the hope that disaster can be averted until the balance of forces is more favourable. In such extreme and rare situations all other strategic options will have been exhausted or will be impossible to implement. In less dire circumstances the probability of success assumes greater significance. If the objective is extremely limited, if it is achievable by the use of military force alone, and if it is unlikely to provoke a counterattack, success is relatively easy to calculate. Israel's air strike against Iraq's Osirak nuclear reactor in 1981 is one obvious example. But it is far less easy to calculate the probability of success when any or all of those conditions are altered. Being the strongest in terms of deployable manpower, available equipment, and technology is no guarantee of victory, as both the United States in Vietnam and the Soviet Union in Afghanistan learnt the hard way.

Alternatives to war include direct and mediated negotiation over the issues in dispute; military containment; appeasement; the offer of economic or strategic concessions; and a range of deterrent or punitive actions such as the severance of diplomatic ties, pressure in international forums, suspension of aid, or the imposition of arms embargoes or economic sanctions. Governments are likely to attempt most of the alternatives available to them before resorting to force, including the offer of concessions that will not have overly adverse consequences or significantly undermine their own objectives.

Having decided to use force, leaders must then come up with a strategy that will enable them to achieve their military objectives and, by extension, the political purposes or ends of the war. The term 'strategy' is one that is not restricted to the threat or use of force but which can be used to describe any plan of action designed in order to achieve some end. In the realm of security, states or organised groups may have several levels of strategy. They may have a grand strategy, which is a broad scheme for ensuring their survival and promoting their interests and which utilises as many elements of power as are relevant and necessary, including diplomatic, economic and military. They will probably have a defence strategy, which is a plan for defending their territory, population and interests from armed attack. A defence strategy does not have to be wholly defensive, of course, but may include provision for 'forward defence' or dealing with threats before they become too direct. But what we are talking about here is a military strategy, which is a strategy or plan for threatening or using military force against a designated adversary in order to secure certain outcomes. Military strategy is the bridge that links national or group objectives with military operations in times of war.

It may be difficult to develop a sound military strategy in advance of operations because the requirement to act may erupt suddenly, as it did for the United States after Pearl Harbor in 1941; or the response may be required in an unexpected and remote location, as with the case of al-Qa'ida in Afghanistan in 2001; or the decision to take military action may be reactive and incremental, as it was in the Vietnam War. But some kind of strategic framework is important for a number of reasons. Combatants cannot always be there first with the most forces or, for political, social, economic or other reasons, able to engage in endless attrition. They need a plan to maximise the chances of success, minimise the likelihood of defeat, and contain costs and casualties. They also need a plan for calculating force requirements, and for convincing their domestic and international constituencies of their ability to succeed. Without a strategy that links ends, ways, and means, the use of force becomes mindless violence that has no political rationale.

Formulating a sound military strategy may be important but it is not easy. Wartime leaders and military planners are not immune to misperception, prejudice, or preoccupation, and may be prone to illusions of invulnerability, to belief in their own moral or military superiority, or to disdain for the capabilities of their adversary. They may not be open to cautionary advice, and those that they do consult may promote their own agendas or engage in 'group-think', agreeing to what they believe is the consensus view, rather than offering alternative opinions.

As a consequence, calculations of relative strengths may be awry, calculations of the adversary's centre of gravity may be out, or calculations of the probability of domestic or international support may be wrong. History is replete with examples, from Hannibal's miscalculation that the Italian tribes would desert Rome, to the United States' mistaken assumptions that strategic bombing would break the will of the North Vietnamese, or that President Milosevic would buckle after the first air strikes on Serbia, to Saddam Hussein's false hope in the first Gulf War that the coalition against him would fracture under the pressure of popular Muslim protest.

War is moreover a complex activity with many interdependent dimensions that are difficult to harmonise, with planners having to consider a whole range of political, economic, social, logistical, geographical and technological factors and to make judgments about the likely dynamics of the interplay between these factors in wartime.[6]

The level of homefront support for any war is critical. Political support is necessary in many countries for the authorisation of war and in all to ensure continual and sufficient funding to support operations. The refusal of the Carthaginian senate to continue financing Hannibal's campaign against Rome contributed to his defeat on the Italian peninsula in 202 BCE, and to the eventual annihilation of Carthage fifty-six years later. The unqualified support of the armed forces leadership for war is also critical, and although many assume that the military will always advocate the resort to force and continue to support the continuance of war once it is underway, this is not necessarily the case. Both democratic and authoritarian regimes have had to tailor or restrict their operations because of military doubts, as we shall see.

POPULAR SUPPORT

Arguably the most important consideration in shaping decisions about war is the level of popular support and the willingness of political constituencies to tolerate certain costs and possible casualties. Popular support is critical if operations are to be seen through to their objectives, and if governments are to survive the vagaries of war. In liberal democracies governments are answerable to their electorates and many in those electorates have become increasingly uneasy about the resort to force and more likely to question the progress of operations. Even undemocratic leaderships are not always immune from popular discontent over the conduct of war and pressure to end hostilities or change strategic direction, as the Soviet Union discovered when casualties mounted in Afghanistan during its invasion from 1979 to 1989. Authoritarian governments can be just as vulnerable as their democratic counterparts to demands for regime change in the event of a military defeat. The failed attempt of Argentina's junta of generals to seize the Malvinas or Falkland Islands from the United Kingdom was a major factor in their eventual ousting.

Until the mid-twentieth century, governments could often rely on popular support for military action and on that support continuing throughout the war. In many societies war was seen as ennobling and as a routine aspect of international relations. And sometimes no alternative seemed possible, as states had to fight for their very survival. But wars of national survival have occurred only rarely since World War II and where they have, popular support has not been difficult to mobilise.

It is noteworthy that all of the wars in which Western countries have been engaged since the mid-twentieth century can be characterised as wars of choice on their part, rather than as wars of necessity. Policy-makers may believe that the use of force in distant theatres is necessary to prevent the spread of a rival's influence and ensure their state's long-term security, but their unwillingness to commit whole-heartedly to these enterprises suggests otherwise.

In the first decades after World War II, it was relatively easy to convince the citizens of Western countries of the necessity for military action in defence of friends or in partnership with allies. But the US experience in Indochina changed everything. The United States' apparent inability to make any significant progress and a high casualty rate combined to erode domestic support for continued operations, contributing to an undignified withdrawal and a legacy of public unease about foreign military involvement, both in the United States and the wider world.

Many US policy-makers attributed the loss in Vietnam to a failure of will, and governments are now conscious of the need to campaign for popular support in advance of, and throughout, any serious military commitment. Some have developed sophisticated methods of mobilising support based on their experience of shaping public opinion in peacetime. In an era of mass communications and mass political participation, they have developed an appreciation of the most influential mediums and resonant messages. In Australia, for example, the government of Prime Minister John Howard, elected in 1996, understood that it was talk-back radio that reached the widest audience and was aware that many in that audience believed Australia to be particularly vulnerable to threat.

Governments can and do proceed to war against the wishes of the majority of their citizens, as the British and Australian authorities did when joining the United States in the invasion of Iraq in 2003. Whether such a course of action will prove politically damaging depends on a range of factors including voting priorities (most people's political preferences are decided ultimately by economic, social, and other domestic considerations); the progress of the war; casualty levels; and the incidence of reprisals. The government of Prime Minister Tony Blair in the United Kingdom was able to weather widespread popular discontent over the Iraq War because its broader policy agenda held a wider appeal than those put forward by the other parties, but in a subsequent election it lost much of its parliamentary majority. The Howard government in Australia was unaffected by the war, winning the next election handsomely by concentrating on economic policy and exploiting its reputation as a capable manager of security threats. By contrast, the Spanish government, which had supported the war in the face of massive public opposition, and which committed forces to Iraq after the combat operations were concluded, was less fortunate. Following a terrorist attack on a Madrid train in 2004, the government was voted out in favour of a party that had already pledged to withdraw Spanish troops from Iraq.

War planners have to factor assessments of public resolve into their strategies. If domestic support is at all doubtful, planners are unlikely to risk a drawn-out campaign in which there may be only vague indications of progress, and which has the potential for reversals of fortune and escalating levels of commitment. Nor will they want to risk high casualty rates. They will instead want to restrict the duration of war and minimise casualties, and will formulate their strategy around these requirements. Wars of attrition with heavy deployment of vulnerable troops on the ground are out, replaced by the coercive use of air power when the objective is to change the adversary's behaviour and by strategic paralysis when the adversary's defeat is the goal. As the American academic Eliot Cohen once noted of modern air power, it is 'an unusually seductive form of military strength, in part because, like modern courtship, it appears to offer gratification without commitment'.[7]

But sometimes none of these strategies is feasible, and vulnerable ground forces have to be deployed. Where overwhelming force is legitimate and feasible, casualties can be minimised and where it is not, casualty-averse states can try to farm the fighting out to others in what Martin Shaw refers to as 'risk-transfer' warfare.[8] This practice is one that predates the state system, with the Romans employing local tribes to wage their wars on the fringes of empire and medieval princes hiring mercenary forces, but in the late twentieth century it most commonly involved the solicitation of ground force contributions from less casualty-averse states and in the early twenty-first century the support of armed indigenous movements. In Afghanistan, for example, the United States came to rely on the Northern Alliance and its soldiers to oust the Taliban regime that was sheltering al-Qa'ida. This particular type of 'risk-transfer' warfare is another strategic option that will be useful only in certain circumstances. Not every target state will host an organised, hardened and determined resistance movement like the Northern Alliance that can be funded from abroad and supported from the relative safety of the skies. None existed in Iraq in 2003, for example, quashing the brief hope among some that the Afghanistan strategy could simply be transferred to that theatre. But it is yet another option likely to be considered by planners wishing to avoid long and casualty-intensive military engagements.

It is not just domestic casualties that have to be avoided. The spread of mass communications, the development of the electronic media, and the advent of live, visual reportage of war have contributed to an increasing unease about the effects of war on adversary populations. Television images of civilian dead or of the wounded, displaced and traumatised transmit feelings of empathy, guilt and doubt to their audiences. These responses have the potential to undermine support for military operations, especially in those limited wars justified as necessary to rescue, protect or improve the lives of civilian populations.

Since the Falklands War, when the British successfully limited media access to both the theatre and operations, Western planners have placed increasingly stringent restrictions on the press to minimise the likelihood of negative imagery disturbing domestic or international audiences. In the Gulf War most representatives of the media were kept at a distance, with only a select few who were allocated to military units being allowed to cover nominated operations first-hand. But journalists were still able to report from the receiving end in Baghdad, from whence they broadcast images of, for example, dead women and children who had been sheltering in a decommissioned bunker, and from the area around the battlefield. And footage of the massacre of retreating Iraqi personnel on the main Kuwait–Iraq highway was potentially so damaging that it contributed to the decision by the US-led coalition to call a halt to hostilities. An even tighter rein was kept on the media during the invasion of Iraq in 2003. Journalists covering the war had to be either based at one of two headquarters where they were promised constant updates of the action, or 'embedded' with individual forward units. Embedding was primarily designed to achieve two outcomes: to restrict the free movement of media representatives, and to ensure that they developed an empathy with their host units. Both aims were largely met during the combat operations phase of the war.

Saddam Hussein, like all leaders under attack in the age of mass communications, hoped to exploit Western governments' vulnerability to charges of causing civilian suffering. In the 1991 war he sought to fracture the coalition ranged against him by appealing to the sympathy of media audiences, especially those in the Arab world. With an even weaker military capability left to him in the run-up to the 2003 invasion, all he could hope was that his enemy would be drawn into a protracted and bitter fight in population-dense areas. Both times the plan failed because the strategies developed and implemented by his attackers had anticipated his intent.

The appeal to public sentiment will continue to be a major weapon in the arsenal of militarily weaker states and so will continue to influence strategy. As long as governments retain control over their territories they will be able to restrict media access and influence coverage of operations and their effects. President Slobodan Milosevic's actions during Operation Allied Force in 1999 were illustrative.

Aware that public opinion was his adversaries' main vulnerability, Milosevic went to great lengths to manipulate perceptions and shape the media's influence. Foreign media representatives were harassed, detained or expelled from Yugoslavia. The few that were allowed to work were restricted in what they could report and where they could travel outside Belgrade. These restrictions meant that their reports were based largely around the kinds of images and events favourable to the Serb government and damaging to NATO: bomb damage to apparently non-military targets, and civilian death and displacement. Serb allegations of victimisation and NATO brutality were also sent out through a well-organised Internet campaign.

The Serb media campaign was singularly unsuccessful in turning public opinion in the United States against the war, despite the fact that NATO's own media campaign had no appealing imagery to sell and consisted primarily of dull, dry briefings delivered from Brussels. The US public was never very interested in events in the Balkans anyway, and proved largely indifferent to the images of destruction, dislocation and suffering. Significantly, there were no NATO casualties to test the limits of this indifference. European audiences, particularly those who had ethnic or religious affiliations with people suffering in Kosovo or Serbia, were more uncomfortable, and placed some pressure on their governments to restrict targeting.

The imperative to minimise civilian suffering has strongly influenced Western strategic planning since the Vietnam War. Many military options which were acceptable in earlier conflicts are now regarded as too indiscriminate to employ in limited wars, including area bombing and sieges of urban areas. But even precisely targeted forms of warfare, such as the use of coercive air power and strategic paralysis, may have to be fine-tuned to avoid indirectly harming civilians. Infrastructure that is considered a critical target because of its importance to an adversary regime or its armed forces may be dual-use; that is, it may also sustain the civilian population. Power, telecommunications and transport infrastructures all fall into this category.

Discriminate targeting is important for another prudential reason. No sensible war planner wants to alienate an adversary's civilian population. If the objective is to compel a change in regime behaviour, strengthening that regime's domestic support makes poor strategic sense. When the objective is regime change and the installation of a less hostile government, both the short-term requirements of occupation and the long-term objective will be seriously undermined by any ill-treatment of the population.

RESOURCES AND FORCES

Most states embarking on wars as one of the lead combatants are unlikely to be influenced in their strategic choices by considerations of economic affordability. Governments joining wartime coalitions as junior partners are less likely to be as committed to the objective and are therefore more likely to calculate the economic costs. Many will also be faced with limits on the level of manpower they can commit to war. In part this is due to the limited objectives of most campaigns. In such circumstances, all governments will find it difficult to make a case for the mobilisation of more manpower than already exists in their regular armed forces or in their reserves if these are legally allowed to serve overseas. In an era where many states have multiple commitments, to international peacekeeping, stabilisation, and humanitarian missions, and to patrol, policing and garrison duties, even these forces may be stretched.

Populous states with large regular forces and reserve pools might generally expect to meet short commitments without too many difficulties, but as the US experience in Operation Iraqi Freedom in 2003 and the following years showed, governments would be prudent to remember that almost all wars last considerably longer than expected. Thus, as the aftermath to Iraqi Freedom dragged on, the United States had to withdraw troops from other theatres, either by changing its overseas-basing policy as it did in Asia, or by persuading its allies to step into the breach, as it did in Afghanistan. Additional relief for overstretched regular and reserve units was achieved by farming-out security for foreign civilians employed on reconstruction tasks in Iraq to private contractors. But the demands on US ground forces, regular, reserve and National Guard, remained disturbingly high. Units had to be rotated back to Iraq after very short rest periods back in the United States, and regular and reserve personnel whose service contracts or reserve obligations were due to expire, and who may have wished to terminate their service, found themselves ordered to soldier-on when the army enforced a 'stop loss' policy.

It is not just numbers that matter. The right skills must also be available. Modern warfare requires armed forces to do more than fight: the range of essential skills includes, among others, civil engineering, language translation, and psychological warfare. Ensuring that the right mix of specialisations is available for a given mission is difficult, especially for states that dispatch their forces into all kinds of conflict situations all over the globe.

In many countries, such specialists are expensive to employ and are not required by the military in peacetime, and so in time of war are drawn from the reserves. But keeping part-time military personnel away from their civilian occupations for extended periods can cause social, economic, and political problems on the homefront. When Hurricane Katrina hit Louisiana in August 2005, the National Guard's absence from their homestate because of duty in Iraq hampered evacuation and relief efforts, and further undermined the popularity of President George W. Bush. Those kinds of consequences are likely to be much more severe for small states like Singapore, whose defence strategies rely even more heavily on the mobilisation of reserves, and whose economies could therefore be subject to serious disruption in the event of war.

Any armed force preparing for war has to contain appropriately trained personnel. History is littered with instances of poorly prepared troops failing to execute their assignments, bungling operations, retreating precipitately, deserting, and committing atrocities. In the twenty-first century the demands on the armed forces will be more varied than ever before and many personnel will be expected to switch roles over the course of their deployment. They can no longer train only in conventional warfare, or warfighting as it is called in the United States, but must be able to mount counter-insurgency operations, provide peace enforcement, and conduct civil affairs campaigns.

The critical importance of having adaptable forces was brought home by the 2003 Iraq War. A brief period of US interest in peacemaking and nation-building had been all but extinguished by the humiliating failure of the United Nations' humanitarian intervention in Somalia from 1992 to 1995. What were called military operations other than war (MOOTW) were now considered beneath the dignity of the world's only remaining superpower and too messy, inconclusive and casualty-intensive to be worth the risk. Wherever possible they were farmed out to the armed forces of other states and only the Marine Corps recognised the need to continue training for wide-ranging contingencies, preparing its personnel to fight conventional wars, conduct peacekeeping operations, and deliver humanitarian relief in what it called the three-block war. This rump of multi-skilled forces was insufficient to ensure security and stability in the chaos that erupted in the immediate aftermath of the invasion in Iraq.

Nor can a strategy be successful without the means of implementation, as the warring parties on the Western Front during World War I discovered to their great cost. The twenty-first century's equivalent of the massed artillery that finally ended that military stalemate will depend on the objective and the adversary, but many states now as then are likely to have difficulty marshalling a sufficient number of weapons platforms and systems to generate a decisive effect. Cutting-edge military hardware has instead become so expensive that the need for force preservation is already a factor in campaign planning.

The ability to sustain troops in the field is as critical now as it was in the American Civil War, when superior logistics gave the wealthy, industrialised North an immense advantage over the comparatively poor, agrarian-economy South. A different manifestation of the same dynamic was apparent in the Southwest Pacific in World War II, when Japanese forces were left stranded and starving at the distant end of inadequate and easily disrupted lines of communication. In the latter situation, Australian and US forces were able to avoid potentially bloody and time-consuming engagements by simply bypassing isolated pockets of Japanese forces on mainland New Guinea and in their stronghold of Rabaul.

States that are not self-sufficient in matériel production need to ensure an uninterrupted supply from manufacturing countries if they wage a conventional war. Both Iran and Iraq were forced on occasions to suspend operations in their long fight against each other in the 1980s because they ran out of arms and ammunition. Only poor strategic performance prevented one or the other from taking decisive advantage of those pauses. A complicating factor here at the cusp of the twenty-first century is that the major arms-producing countries risk international opprobrium if they transfer weapons to a state at war, unless that war can be demonstrated as being waged in legitimate self-defence or is deemed to be in the interests of the major powers.

MAKING STRATEGY

Most armed forces develop contingency plans for plausible conflict scenarios. But history has shown that every situation is different. An attack may come from an unexpected direction, as it did in Singapore in 1941 when Japanese forces bore down on the island from peninsular Malaya rather than from the sea, as expected, thus rendering plans for a naval defence redundant. Or it may emanate from an unexpected source, as did al-Qa'ida's attacks on the continent of the United States in 2001. In that instance, when the US Administration demanded swift retaliation against al-Qa'ida's leadership and their hosts in Afghanistan, they discovered that their military commanders had no contingency plans.

Although strategic experience can offer important insights, and the doctrines distilled from it can provide a useful framework for planning, history never replicates itself, and doctrine has to be tailored to meet the challenges of each particular operating environment and each particular adversary's strengths and weaknesses.

It is often said that armed forces prepare to fight the next war by studying the last, a cliché that has some basis in fact with the most notable example occurring in France in the 1930s. French strategy in the event of a German attack anticipated a repeat of World War I and had as its centrepiece the fortified Maginot Line along the shared border with Germany, behind which the French Army would have time to mobilise. But German strategists had no intention of repeating their earlier mistakes and this time their forces simply swept around the Maginot Line and through the supposedly impenetrable forests of the Ardennes and newly neutral Belgium.

Given the dramatic pace of contemporary technological development, today's war planners can be subject to a very different kind of miscalculation, namely, expecting their next adversary's capabilities to be more sophisticated than they are. Many of the Western strategic analysts orphaned by the end of the Cold War were so impressed by the conventional technological capabilities of the United States that they attributed a similar or even more advanced level of prowess to potential adversaries. This type of threat inflation was driven in part by the realisation that anyone wishing to fight the United States would have to resort to asymmetric warfare to try to exploit US weaknesses, rather than make an almost certainly futile attempt to defeat the United States on its own terms.

This kind of mindset was also influenced by the common strategic tendency to 'mirror image'. Having concluded that adversarial forces would seek to use non-conventional tactics and weapons, analysts focused their attention on the kinds of threats that actors in a high-technology environment like their own might generate. Thus, a whole literature sprang up on cyber warfare, another on space warfare. Similarly, concerns over the spread of ballistic missile technology and of nuclear, biological and chemical material fuelled fears of 'rogue state' attacks, or of battlefield deployments of weapons of mass destruction.

These kinds of preoccupations led many to ignore the possibility that less conventionally capable actors might opt instead for a low-technology approach, sneaking under the radar rather than attempting to attack it. Al-Qa'ida's September 11 attacks exploited readily attainable civilian skills, routine and easily accessible civilian technology, and willing martyrs to devastating effect. Anthrax was delivered not by ballistic missiles but by the US postal system. No guerilla fighters or terrorists have targeted command-and-control systems or any other critical operating networks by computer hacking, but they have dug homemade bombs into roads, hidden them in animal corpses, and launched them from donkey carts. Al-Qa'ida fighters in Afghanistan did not hide in multi-storied, air-conditioned bunker networks as envisaged but in caves scarcely big enough to shelter a goat. And they were just as likely to contact each other by human messenger, by post, or even by pigeon, as they were to hide encoded instructions on the Internet.

It may make good strategic sense to plan for a worst-case scenario, but planners should have learnt in Vietnam and Afghanistan that worst-cases come in all shapes and sizes.

Good intelligence on an adversary's strengths and weaknesses is vital. Before commanders can formulate their operational plans they need sound assessments of their opponents' military capabilities, force dispositions, level of resolve, and likely responses. Material capabilities and deployments are now easier to gauge, thanks to improvements in surveillance technologies, but resolve and possible responses remain as difficult as ever to calculate.

Some regimes under attack may be able to mobilise widespread and continuing support for war because of popular identification with national goals or because of fear of the alternative. Where this support is strong, aggressors are likely to find that ambitious objectives will be extremely difficult to achieve. But not all governments can rely on popular solidarity in the event of war. If segments of the population have been marginalised or ill-treated or have ambitions for greater autonomy or even independence, they may be reluctant to act in defence of the government and may even welcome war as offering a chance to alter the domestic balance of power. These domestic fissures can be exploited to good effect in wartime, as demonstrated in the Balkans, Greece and India during World War II and more recently in the United States' partnerships with the Northern Alliance in Afghanistan and the Kurds in Iraq in 2003.

Some states plan their defence around regional commands that are expected to exercise considerable autonomy in the event of an armed attack. Indonesia formulated just such a strategy, based on a resort to guerilla activities, to meet the requirements of defending a far-flung archipelagic state on a limited budget. On occasions regional commanders did indeed demonstrate the capacity to act independently of the central government. But given the heavy-handed methods which characterised the administration, some of these commanders might have found it difficult to mobilise their local populations into guerilla forces had a serious external attack eventuated. As the popular uprising in East Timor in the 1990s demonstrated, it is hard to imagine a high level of enthusiasm for the defence of a state whose citizens have been subjected to social and political repression in peacetime.

On the other hand, when authoritarian regimes limit the autonomy of military commanders because of regime security concerns, it can be relatively easy to undermine that regime's ability to conduct effective military campaigns. Saddam Hussein did not trust his commanders any more before the 2003 invasion of Iraq than he had during the Iran–Iraq War some fifteen years previously, and his regional forces consequently were unable to act independently when the US-led coalition disrupted their command-and-control networks.

The resolve of adversary troops is likely to be affected by the experience of previous military encounters. They might have acquired confidence in their ability to defeat their opponents, or at least to survive relatively intact; or they might have learnt the limitations of their competence. Although the latter response might seem to promise an easy military victory for the other side, its implications are more complex. An opponent who realises his conventional military inferiority is likely to develop a range of asymmetric responses, designed in the first instance to avert war, and in the second to negate the advantages of a superior military capability. Such responses are likely to include political tactics aimed at calling into question the legitimacy of military operations, and undermining domestic, regional and international support. Should these tactics fail, they may well resort to guerilla warfare and/or terrorism.

Previous experience of defeat might undermine an opposing military's will to fight, but it is not an unalloyed good to have them desert their posts. Article 3 of the Geneva Convention forbids the killing of combatants who have laid down their arms, and deserters, especially those who are professional soldiers, cannot be guaranteed to remain acquiescent and peaceable. After being on the receiving end of massive US firepower during the 1991 Gulf War, many Iraqi Army soldiers simply abandoned their posts during the 2003 invasion.

Once they had been formally demobilised, many put themselves, their weaponry and their skills to use in attacking the occupying forces.

Strategic choices will be heavily influenced by the geography of the theatre of operations. Open, flat terrain facilitates surveillance, accurate air support, and rapid ground manoeuvre, which is why many army commanders love deserts. Conversely, densely vegetated or hilly terrain makes it difficult to locate enemy positions, complicates targeting, slows down operations, and renders ground forces vulnerable to surprise attack. Climatic conditions also have to be taken into account. Extremes of temperature have contributed to some of the most notable military defeats in history, the onset of monsoonal rains have delayed or complicated operations in some tropical environments, and fog and wind have been known to force changes in strategic direction. Technological evolution might mean that naval forces are no longer in danger of being blown off-course and that bombers will no longer be grounded by low cloud or unable to find targets, but the vagaries of weather will continue to complicate operations.

If the theatre of operations is distant, bases have to be found to support operations. Proximate, easily accessible and secure bases are desirable for the launch of operations, the provision of supply and reinforcements, the security of battlefield surveillance, and the establishment of combat search and rescue facilities. The latter is now considered critical to deny an adversary the ability to use hostage-taking as a political weapon in wartime.

Access is an important determinant in any military strategy, so the more plentiful the available basing options, the greater the strategic flexibility. Negotiating with governments of countries bordering the planned theatre of operations can be a protracted business, slowing response times and limiting strategic choices, as the United States found in Afghanistan in 2001. Denial of access may force a change in strategy, as it did when Turkey withdrew its support for the US invasion of Iraq in 2003 under popular pressure. In response to such problems, the Pentagon has formulated a policy of negotiating military access to as many states as possible. Other states are unable to exercise the same level of leverage but most of their wars will continue to be fought with their neighbours, obviating the need for distant bases.

Military commanders have to be provided with intelligence on the location of potential and desirable targets. Good intelligence on the function of potential targets is critical when targeting errors become ammunition in the accompanying media struggle. Restricted targeting lists are a feature of modern warfare, to minimise both civilian casualties and the prospect of escalation.

Just as important to contemporary strategy-makers is a broad understanding of the political, social and economic dynamics of the country they are planning to attack. The most significant and costly intelligence failure of Operation Iraqi Freedom was not the over-inflation of Saddam's alleged weapons of mass destruction capability, but the over-optimistic assessment of post-invasion social and political developments.

Arriving at such an understanding is not simple. Sometimes a crisis may erupt in an area which hitherto has been considered of limited strategic interest, and little or no expertise may have been developed in the intelligence community or be available in academia. Somalia was a case in point in 1992, when a humanitarian disaster unfolded in a small country remote from the world's centres of power, and in which Cold War interest had died. And sometimes force may be planned against a state whose internal dynamics are obscure, either because that state exercises complete control over its own citizens and restricts foreign access, or because it is considered so hostile that all contacts have been severed, or because of a combination of the above. This has been a particular problem for the United States in recent times. The predilection for labelling states perceived to be adversarial as evil and cutting all ties reduces its ability to garner useful human intelligence on the states it is most likely to engage militarily, and makes it overly dependent on the less than impartial interpretations of defectors, exiles and refugees.

Having garnered all the necessary intelligence and taken all the political, social, logistical, operational and technological factors into account, military planners must devise a plan to compel their adversary to bow to their government's will. They must then determine the types of military operations that are possible and which, within those constraints, are most likely to achieve the desired political results.

The process of strategy formulation for the 2001 attack on Afghanistan is illustrative of the many factors that have to be taken into account. The primary objectives of the attack were to destroy the leadership of al-Qa'ida and remove their Taliban hosts from power, but a secondary objective was to demonstrate to a traumatised American public the US Administration's ability to respond swiftly and surely to the 9/11 attacks. This secondary objective meant there was little time for planning or deployment. The US military had no contingency plans for an attack on Afghanistan because it had not hitherto been viewed as a likely source of threat. The options presented to the Secretary of Defence therefore relied heavily on air power and consisted of a strike with cruise missiles, a strike with cruise missiles and manned bombers, and air strikes supplemented by a troop insertion that would include special forces. The first of these was ruled out because it had not worked in 1998 when the Clinton Administration had launched Operation Infinite Reach in retaliation for the bombings of US embassies in Kenya and Tanzania. Al-Qa'ida and the Taliban were too dispersed and too mobile. Supplementing cruise missile attacks with targeted bombing would not solve this problem; neither organisation had any significant air defences, headquarters, logistical or communications infrastructure to be paralysed. Hitting targets that were available such as Afghanistan's few power plants might well have alienated the civilian population and strengthened support for the Taliban. The air and ground option was ruled out because of the time that it would take to assemble and position the necessary forces and to negotiate their access with neighbouring countries, and because of Afghanistan's forbidding geography, and history of resistance to invaders.

Armed forces commanders were unable to come up with a workable strategy that could be implemented in the required timeframe but the Central Intelligence Agency (CIA), which had a long history of covert involvement in Afghanistan, was able to suggest one that would turn local conditions to advantage and minimise the risks. They proposed that the United States provide support and encouragement to the already extant armed Afghan resistance movement in the north of the country and to tribal leaders opposed to the Taliban and al-Qa'ida in the south. The Northern Alliance had between 10 000 and 30 000 fighters at its disposal but had been prevented from pressing its attacks on the Taliban by a lack of resources and equipment. A massive transfusion of funds was already underway.[9]

The Pentagon was reluctant to cede too much influence and importance to the CIA or to the Northern Alliance which was unpopular with the majority Pashtun population among whom al-Qa'ida would be sheltering and elements of which had shown themselves to be as brutal as the Taliban. While the Northern Alliance's hold over the north of the country would be strengthened, air strikes and military special force insertions would also be undertaken in the Taliban strongholds in the south, in an effort to demoralise and divide their forces and encourage local tribal leaders to rebel.

The United States had already begun negotiations with Afghanistan's neighbour Pakistan which shared long and porous borders and was concerned about the possible effects of any war on its own regional interests and domestic stability. To ensure Pakistan's cooperation, sanctions imposed after its 1998 nuclear tests were lifted, and generous aid and debt relief packages provided. Aid was also offered to Afghanistan's best-situated northern neighbour, Uzbekistan, to secure air-basing.

A campaign to reassure the Afghan population of the United States' benign intent and persuade them of the benefits of political change also swung into gear. Pledges of reconstruction funding were solicited from the international community, and food drops and broadcasting and leafleting campaigns prepared.

The persuasion campaign was successful, partly because many Afghans were ready for a change in government and the Taliban had no means of conducting a counter-effort, having banned most forms of media in the country. But the initial military strategy was a failure. There were few targets to hit, inserted special forces had to be quickly extracted when they ran into stiff resistance, and tribal leaders refused to commit themselves. So the CIA's strategy was implemented instead and the air campaign switched to providing air support for a

Northern Alliance push south. US special forces accompanied the advance, calling in air strikes on the Taliban frontlines that weakened their positions, stiffened the Northern Alliance's resolve and persuaded dithering tribal leaders that the balance of forces was finally shifting.

As the US experience in Afghanistan demonstrated, the formulation of a sound and successful strategy is a difficult proposition in limited wars. Relative technological capabilities are only one factor among many and are unlikely to be the primary determinant; social, political and environmental conditions on the ground, domestic and adversary attitudes to the use of force, and often contradictory political requirements will be just as influential. To have any chance of succeeding, strategy will have to conform to these realities rather than to institutional preferences.

8 | Constraints on war
Strategy, legality, and prudence

GENERATIONS OF PHILOSOPHERS HAVE believed, and national rulers have acted on, the principle that might renders questions of right irrelevant when it comes to warfare. In doing so they have conformed to the position ascribed by Thucydides to the Athenian generals in their dialogue with the Council of the Melians: 'The strong do what they have the power to do and the weak accept what they have to accept'.[1] What the Melians had to accept in that particular situation was immediate surrender or siege and the slaughter or enslavement of almost the entire population. Elsewhere in *The Peloponnesian War*, Thucydides describes a debate over the treatment of the defeated population of Mytilene that makes no reference to the morality of the alternatives but which is argued entirely on the basis of prudential considerations.

The Athenian approach was replicated through the ages with perceptions of political and military necessity dictating the conduct of war. For many rulers and commanders there was no practical difference between enemy combatants and enemy civilians: both were responsible for their state's behaviour and contributed to its capacity to wage war; and both could revolt against occupation if left free when defeated. Nobody could be described as innocent. Where civilians were treated humanely or damage to their environment was limited, it was for prudential rather than ethical reasons. In the fourth century BC, Kautilya, the adviser to the Indian king Chandragupta Maurya and whose book *Arthasastra* made Machiavelli's *The Prince* seem positively idealistic, counselled the king to treat those he conquered well lest they revolt and others became alarmed.[2]

The idea that war should be influenced by considerations of morality and justice is also as old as warfare. It was often derived from religious beliefs, and was common to many of the world's great religions. Ancient Hindu texts, for example, distinguish between 'just' wars and 'unjust' wars, with just wars being those that conform with dharma or divine law. Rulers are exhorted to eschew the use of inhumane weapons, to treat civilians and wounded and captured enemy combatants humanely, to desist from attacking retreating forces, to minimise damage to the environment and civilian infrastructure, and to ensure that battles are fair fights between evenly matched men.[3]

In the Western world, the idea of the just war dates from at least as far back as archaic Rome, when war was legally forbidden unless pronounced just or *bellum iustum* by the college of priests or *fetiales*. To qualify as 'just', a war had to be provoked by the other party's aggression in the form of treaty violations, infringements of territorial rights, or offences committed against allies, and the like; and it had to be preceded by an endeavour to secure satisfaction of the grievance through negotiation. And if all of those initiatives failed, a formal declaration of war was still required.[4]

In both the Indian and Roman cases, the laws of war derived from wider belief systems; and also in both cases, the definition of a 'just' cause tended to be liberally interpreted to suit the ambitions and perceived security requirements of the political authorities. Conduct during and after war was dictated as much by prudential considerations or self-interest as by moral concern. All of these features continued to characterise the slow, fitful, but inexorable evolution of international laws and norms regarding the use of force.

When the Roman Empire formally converted to Christianity in 389 CE, the church had to abandon its pacifism and justify its members' service in defence of the empire and the faith. It was in that context that the philosopher and priest St Augustine revived the 'just' war concept and began a tradition of theological debate by claiming that adversary wrongs necessitated the resort to force. His thirteenth-century intellectual successor, St Thomas Aquinas, summarised the requirements for just war as: princely authorisation, just cause, and right intention. It was just cause that most occupied theologians as they sought first to limit war between Christians, and then tried to export their religion to Muslim lands, in the latter case often by force of arms.

But interest in just war declined as the political geography of Europe gradually changed through the influence of war and inter-marriage. Territory was consolidated in the hands of princes who were independent of superior authority, who could command the obedi-ence of those living in their lands, and who claimed the right to use force when they saw fit. Church scholars and jurists now acknowl-edged the sovereign right of these rulers to defend their states or advance their interests, but were dismayed by the unrestrained and continual war between those rulers over inheritance rights and reli-gious differences, for 'slight reasons, or for no reasons'. For the seven-teenth century Dutch jurist, Hugo Grotius, sovereign rights should instead be considered in light of the requirements of social existence, acknowledging shared values and the necessity of rules regulating inter-state behaviour.

Mercantilism, overseas expansion, and the costs of maintaining standing professional armies contributed more than notions of inter-national society to the relative stability on the continent in the eighteenth century. European states continued to modulate their relationships through bilateral treaties and alliances, and some later attempted to keep the peace – and the status quo – through a con-cert of power. But none of those pacts or balancing mechanisms was able to protect them once the French Revolution of 1789 opened the way to total war, and once Germany had begun to coalesce and the Ottoman Empire to decline, both in about the mid-nineteenth century.

RESTRAINING THE RESORT TO FORCE

The first attempt to legally restrict the use of force came in the Hague Peace Conference of 1899, instigated by Czar Nicholas II of Russia in an effort to halt the costly European arms race. In this and the

Second Hague Peace Conference of 1907, the contracting parties agreed to seek mediation whenever possible before resorting to war, and to refrain from using armed force to recover public debts unless the debtor state refused all alternatives. These limited constraints were not enough to prevent some states from attempting to adjust the balance of power through the use of force or the rise of militaristic nationalism, and the seemingly permanent feature of the European state system and the new combined to produce World War I.

Although the central front in that war remained in Europe, the struggle between the Allies and the Central Powers extended to the Middle East, Africa and the Pacific, and involved peoples from all over the world, including those in the European colonies and dominions and the United States.* By the end of that long and costly slog, the popular appetite for war had been largely exhausted and the leaders of the warring states were willing to consider new approaches to reducing the incidence of war.

During the peace negotiations the US President, Woodrow Wilson, put forward a fourteen-point program for peace. Many of these points related to the reordering of Europe, and some were designed to reduce friction in international affairs, but the last was that 'a general association of nations must be formed under specific covenants for the purpose of affording mutual guarantees of political independence and territorial integrity to great and small nations alike'. The establishment of the world's first collective security organisation was one of the fourteen points agreed to at the Paris Peace Conference of 1919.

The constitution of the new League of Nations bound contracting parties not to resort to war, and established international law as the code for relations between them. Any war or threat of war was declared a matter of concern to all the member-states and the League would take any action considered 'wise and effectual' to safeguard peace. Member-states resorting to war would be deemed to have committed an act of war against all the others and would be immediately subjected to economic sanctions.

* The alliance's major members were France, Russia, the United Kingdom, Italy, and the United States; while the central powers included Germany, Austria–Hungary, the Ottoman Empire, and Bulgaria.

The US Congress refused to authorise America's entry into the League of Nations because it was concerned that the collective security obligations could draw the country into another European war. Instead the United States became an initiating party to the 1928 Kellogg–Briand Pact with France and sixty-one other parties. Otherwise known as the General Treaty for Renunciation of War as an Instrument of National Policy, this pact committed member-states to settle their disputes by pacific means.

Neither the League of Nations nor the Kellogg–Briand Pact was able to prevent the recurrence of war. Although the League did manage to avert a few conflicts, it was weakened by the absence of the United States, by its inability to penalise infractions, and by a lack of commitment on the part of signatory states who simply ignored it when it suited them, or resigned. The Kellogg–Briand Pact allowed too many vague exemptions to its prohibitions on the use of force and contained no provision at all for the punishment of transgressions. Both initiatives proved unequal to the rise of militaristic nationalism in Italy, Germany, and Japan.

REGULATING WAR AFTER 1945

After World War II, the imperative of avoiding a repetition saw a much greater commitment to the idea of securing the peace through collective security. The United Nations was founded in 1945 with the objective of saving 'succeeding generations from the scourge of war, which twice in our lifetime has brought untold sorrow to mankind'. Article 2 (4) of the Charter committed member-states to 'refrain in their international relations from the threat or use of force against the territorial integrity or political independence of any state, or in any manner inconsistent with the purposes of the United Nations'. In only two circumstances could the prohibition on inter-state war be waived: states retained the right to use force in the event of an armed attack against them, and the United Nations itself could authorise military action.

Unlike all previous attempts to limit the use of force in international affairs, the UN Charter backed its laws with provisions and institutions for their enforcement. A Security Council consisting of five permanent major power members and six elected members (later increased to ten) from the rest of the international community was empowered to deal forcefully with any 'threat to the peace, breach of the peace or act of aggression'.* States committing these offences would be subject to a collective response by the other UN members, who would contribute armed forces as and when needed for this purpose.

The Cold War revealed a serious flaw in this system of enforcement. The five major powers had each been given veto rights and both sides in the struggle for ideological dominance exercised these rights whenever it suited their interests. The Security Council was effectively paralysed for the duration, able to authorise and implement only one collective security action. This occurred in 1950 when the Soviet Union was boycotting the council in protest at the Republic of China's (Taiwan) continued possession of China's council seat. The absence of the Soviet Union and the exclusion of the People's Republic of China allowed the other Security Council members to authorise a military response to the North Korean invasion of South Korea in June of that year.

The agreed and successful UN campaign to oust Iraqi forces from Kuwait in 1991 fuelled hopes that the enforcement of international law would become routine and breaches less likely. UN-mandated peacekeeping missions became more common and the organisation even began to sanction interventions to protect civilian populations in times of humanitarian crisis. However, the evolution of norms qualifying the sovereign rights of states and the practical difficulties encountered in multilateral humanitarian operations contributed to the erosion of the sovereignty principle and undermined international enforcement mechanisms. Both the legal and practical problems of humanitarian operations are discussed in depth in the following chapters, and it is sufficient to note here that by 2003 the United States was willing to ignore the United Nations and proceed to war against Iraq alone or with what it called a 'coalition of the willing'. The justification for doing so was the alleged existence of an imminent threat from weapons of mass destruction but the real

---

* The permanent members are France, the United Kingdom, China, Russia, and the United States.

reason was to force regime change in order to achieve wider and longer-term security objectives.

Inducing regime change is, of course, a strategic tool as old as mankind and had been commonplace in the Cold War, when nuclear deterrence inverted Clausewitz's dictum that war is the continuation of politics by other means. Both the Soviet Union and the United States and their respective client states provided support to resistance movements and insurgent groups of their particular political stripe and assistance was provided for the overthrow of unfriendly rulers in Iran, the Congo, Chile, and Indonesia, among other places. But the idea of intervening directly to force regime change is a threat to the sovereignty of states and the stability of the international system, and it is doubtful whether the humanitarian impulse of voters in democratic states would extend to such a potentially costly commitment. Consequently, as chapter four discussed, the 2003 invasion of Iraq was portrayed by the US Administration as a necessary pre-emptive strike.

The right to self-defence in the case of an actual attack is recognised as conferring the right to pre-empt, particularly if the threatened state will be at a serious disadvantage if it waits for that attack to begin. The pre-emptive Israeli strike on Egyptian forces in the Six Day War of 1967 was legitimate because Israel could reasonably claim fear of imminent attack and concern about the costs of military delay. Tensions had been growing between Israel and its Arab neighbours, peaking in May when Egyptian President Gamal Nasser mobilised his troops, reached military agreements with Jordan, Syria, and Iraq, ordered the UN Emergency Force deployed as peacekeepers in the Sinai to leave, announced a blockade of Israel's vital maritime access through the Strait of Tiran, and publicly stated that his goal in any war with Israel would be the destruction of the Jewish state. Israel was small, vulnerable to dismemberment, and faced serious economic problems if its reservists had to be called up for a long defensive war. Nasser's grand strategy made pre-emption Israel's only rational military strategy.

A similar argument might be made by Singapore, among others, should it ever be threatened. With even less strategic depth than Israel and also dependent on the mobilisation of its civilian workforce as reserves, Singapore could reasonably make a case for a pre-emptive strike against any hostile adversary that was obviously preparing to attack.

The invasion of Iraq was not a pre-emptive attack. No evidence existed of an imminent threat to the United States, its allies or interests or to any other state. Rather it was a preventive strike, namely an attack designed to prevent the eventuality of a threat. The Bush Administration argued the necessity and legitimacy of this military action on the grounds that the strategic environment had changed dramatically. The September 11 attacks had demonstrated that a threat could become reality without warning, and that states of all shapes and sizes were at a strategic disadvantage in an era of ballistic missiles and the proliferation of weapons of mass destruction, and international terrorism. Aggressive intent would no longer be signalled by the visible mobilisation of armies, navies and air forces, and an attack could eventuate from far outside a country's borders.

When it became evident that the UN Security Council would not authorise an invasion of Iraq, the United States argued its legality on the principle of continuance: Saddam Hussein had not complied with previous Security Council resolutions which had warned him that consequences would ensue in the event of non-compliance. The argument was also made that the use of force had been just, that it had conformed to the just war principles of right authority, right intent, and right outcome. Right authority derived from the United States' sovereign right to self-defence and the legitimacy of its actions. Legitimate actions are those that are believed to be right and proper, with legitimacy differing from legality in that it is widely perceived to derive from approval and consent rather than law. What is considered right and proper will depend on judgments about authority, intent and outcome and will differ according to audience and circumstance and over time. In this instance it was argued that the United States' actions were legitimate because the invasion had the active support of the US population and a number of states and the tacit consent of many Iraqis and because the exercise of US power was generally accepted as necessary to the maintenance of global order and the greater good.

Claiming legitimacy does not conjure it into reality. As already noted, many in the international community were not persuaded of the United States' right to act unilaterally, had doubts about its real intent, and were unconvinced about the outcome. The Iraqi population was similarly divided. Moreover, legitimacy is not fixed but is subject to the vagaries of time and changes in circumstance. As conditions worsened in Iraq, the legitimacy of the invasion was brought ever more into question, in the international community, in Iraq, and even among Americans.

The revival of the just war argument is as problematic when divorced from the restraints of international law as it was in the era of European conquest and colonisation. Theologians and political leaders from different faiths or cultures can proclaim the justice of all sorts of otherwise unacceptable causes and actions. Al-Qa'ida justified its terror activities on the grounds that jihad was a religious obligation and that targeted civilians supported the oppressive activities of their governments or were insufficiently pious. States that are similarly difficult to deter may also attempt to impose their notions of order and justice on an unwilling world.

The inability of the Security Council to prevent the US invasion was a reminder of the problems caused by the special position accorded in international law to its five permanent members. The veto power strengthens their inherent ability to resist international sanction in the event of illegal behaviour. States without a committed great-power patron are vulnerable to a range of punitive actions: economic sanctions, arms embargoes, prosecution for war crimes, and military strikes, as Libya and Iraq have discovered. But while the permanent members of the Security Council may be immune from legal action, they cannot entirely escape negative consequences for their actions. Other states are likely to attempt to balance against great powers perceived to be threatening the status quo, and they can and do withhold support that may be critical to the achievement of strategic objectives.

UNILATERALISM HAS COSTS

With the end of the Cold War, international relations analysts and theorists had turned their attention to the implications of the new world order. Some thought the new international structure would be multipolar and debated the likely outcomes of the dispersion of power and the ways in which it could best be managed. Others saw a unipolar world in which the United States was the predominant power and here much of the argument revolved around the likely responses of other states, particularly the second-order powers. While some thought the United States' actions would trigger historically common balancing behaviour, others pointed to the singular conditions attending its dominance. The United States had an incontestable military advantage over its potential rivals, was geographically isolated, and was viewed by the vast majority of governments as benign and preferable as a global leader to any other power. In these circumstances, other states could not – and would not want to – engage in balancing behaviour.

This belief in the immunity of the United States to the operations of the balance of power, and the existence of widespread enthusiasm for US predominance, was not confined to the realm of theory. Many in the upper echelons of the second Bush Administration were similarly convinced, and these assumptions informed their official security doctrines for the new millennium and influenced foreign policy and decisions regarding the use of force.

The refusal of most states, including all the other major powers bar the United Kingdom, to sanction the invasion of Iraq, together with increasing cooperation between Russia and China and calls by some European governments for greater foreign policy independence, led to renewed academic debate on the concept of the balance of power. Few argued that 'hard' balancing or an effort to develop a military counterweight to the United States was occurring, but some analysts detected a trend towards 'soft' balancing or the development of new relationships. Perceptions that the United States was a benign power and the primary brake on balancing, they argued, had been altered by its insistence on invading Iraq.[5]

The counter-argument that other governments were not balancing but were acting out of short-term interest, and were motivated by economic, domestic and strategic concerns that had nothing to do with perceptions of excessive US power, rested on an analysis that was partial in both senses of the word. Embedded in a foreign policy culture that views international law and international institutions as weak and largely irrelevant to the maintenance of global order, these arguments ignored the possibility that other states were seriously concerned about the long-term legal and practical implications of a preventive attack on Iraq.

Preventive war is a troubling concept and a problematic endeavour. If states are accorded the right to attack any state or group without obvious signs of imminent aggression, post-World War II restraints will be seriously jeopardised. States could argue the necessity for attacking each other on all sorts of pretexts, threatening the sovereign rights and security of all and undermining predictability and stability in the international system. Moreover, preventive strikes may not even be successful in their objectives.

Governments wishing to avert a long-term threat by military means have to decide whether to destroy the incipient capability or remove the regime that is attempting to develop that capability. There are several problems with strikes on sites believed to be involved in the production of biological, chemical and nuclear weapons. The window of opportunity will close as soon as development has advanced to the point where a strike would result in dispersal, capabilities can be reconstituted, and efforts to acquire such capabilities may actually be redoubled because the targeted regime feels even more threatened or determined. Tensions will not be reduced and retaliation is a serious possibility. Preventive regime change would surmount all of these difficulties in theory but may not in practice. Replacement regimes may be neither friendly nor durable, and even if they are, their policies and actions may give rise to other security concerns. Moreover, the transition period is likely to be fraught with difficulty.

International concern about the second invasion of Iraq cost the United States dearly. After the UN-authorised Gulf War, the United States had been able to recoup most of the considerable costs it had incurred as the largest contributor to the military coalition. By contrast, it could not argue the legitimacy of financial burden-sharing following the 2003 invasion. Moreover, the United States had to do without the benefit of the United Nations' institutional experience in post-conflict nation-building and without active assistance from many of the member-states most practised in peace enforcement.

LAW, PRUDENCE, AND THE CONDUCT OF WAR

International laws regulating the actual conduct of war also have ancient moral and prudential origins, and their implementation has had a fitful but inexorable history. Some of the religious proscriptions on the practice of warfare were widely adhered to for long periods, including the Hindu prohibition on harm to farmers and their crops, while others were abandoned as interfering with the pursuit of power and the requirements of security. In early medieval Europe, war was endemic and its intensity and reach were restricted only by the limitations of technology. Neither the church nor the defenceless were safe.

Tenth-century church canons prohibited violence against church officials and property, and also against pilgrims, peasants and townspeople going about their usual business, and people travelling through war zones. These prohibitions obviously had some basis in self-interest as the church itself suffered when deprived of the income from pilgrims, and from food and manufactures. Later exemptions of women, children, the elderly, the infirm and the mentally impaired derived in part from the codes of knightly conduct. Religious proscriptions on the use of particular weapons, such as the crossbow and its variants, were probably motivated by both humanitarian and strategic considerations, the crossbow being a particularly lethal weapon but its use, like that of the longbow, threatened the élite monopoly of arms.

Church efforts to limit the damage and instability caused by war in Europe had little effect, with the changing requirements of political, economic and military necessity being more important determinants of popular safety. The supposedly innocent lost their immunity when they were sheltering in castles under siege and whole populations were starved and harassed by mercenaries who had to supply themselves during and between campaigns. By the latter half of the eighteenth century, the development of state power and organisation, and of wealth and enlightenment, seemed to herald a new era of limited war in which professional and disciplined armies would fight their battles and leave everybody else to go safely about their business.

But the transformation in the nature of sovereignty sparked by the French Revolution, the increasing identification of populations with state goals, and mass mobilisation all combined to undermine the notion of civilian immunity. Wars were now seen as being waged between peoples, not just between the armed supporters of lords, princes, and kings.

The first agreed code of wartime conduct between the new nation-states of Europe was aimed at protecting soldiers rather than civilians, with the Geneva Convention in 1864 binding its signatories to facilitate the care of the wounded and treat prisoners of war humanely. The signatories to the first Hague Peace Conference in 1899 forswore the bombing of undefended cities, towns and villages but once aircraft had been introduced into war, states were reluctant to deny themselves the perceived strategic advantage of being able to so easily terrorise adversary populations. Draft Rules of Aerial Warfare drawn up in 1923 were never formally adopted and the League of Nations' prohibitions on the intentional bombing of civilian populations were ignored.

During the Spanish Civil War and World War II civilians were considered legitimate targets because they supported and enabled their nations' war efforts. Population centres were deliberately subjected to area bombing in the hope it would undermine morale and fatally weaken their leaders' ability to continue fighting. When the massive conventional bombardment of Japan's cities failed to secure its unconditional surrender, the United States dropped on two of them the first atomic bombs.

The horrors of Hiroshima and Nagasaki did not prevent states from wishing to acquire their own nuclear devices, but as the technology spread and capabilities became ever more lethal their limitations as weapons of war became apparent. Nuclear weapons can inflict appallingly high levels of immediate casualties, serious infrastructural and environmental damage, and long-term human suffering. Their use might hasten a military victory but they may not prove so useful against an enemy less exhausted than the Japanese, and could well invite retaliation in kind by nuclear-capable adversaries or allies of non-nuclear adversaries, rendering any military advantage a pyrrhic victory. The potentially catastrophic consequences of nuclear war restricted the utility of nuclear weapons to deterrence, an effect which at least induced an additional degree of caution among those contemplating the use of force.

The possibility that peacetime crises or conventional wars could escalate to a nuclear exchange exercised the imaginations of political leaders, strategic analysts and military contingency planners throughout the Cold War. This is not to say that the existence of nuclear weapons acted as a universal or complete deterrent. Some non-nuclear states were not deterred from using conventional armed force to advance their interests in disputes against nuclear states, their governments calculating, correctly, that the issues in dispute were too minor and their objectives too obviously limited for their adversaries to risk the use of nuclear weapons. Two cases in point were the Egyptian and Syrian assaults on Israeli positions in the Sinai and the Golan Heights in the 1973 Yom Kippur War, and the Argentinean invasion of the Falklands.*6 But even here, evaluations of risk were evidently undertaken.

We cannot know how often states have refrained from using force altogether out of concern for nuclear retaliation, partly because of information limitations imposed by state secrecy provisions, and partly because of the difficulties in determining the procedural origin of any such caution. Governments may attempt to manage crises in such a way as to minimise the potential for escalation or they may already have factored the requirement to avoid a nuclear response into the fundamentals of their defence postures and foreign policy. We do however know that no non-nuclear state has used armed force to threaten the survival of a nuclear state, and that no two nuclear states have fought a conventional war.

It is difficult to tell exactly what role nuclear deterrence played in 'the long peace' between the world's first two nuclear powers. Most of the literature on the Cold War assumes a defensive attitude on the part of the Western powers and the successful nuclear deterrence of direct Soviet aggression but there is as yet no evidence to suggest that this deterrence was actually necessary. Soviet leaders were willing

---

* Israel probably had about twelve atomic bombs by the time of the Yom Kippur War; while the United Kingdom had become a nuclear power in 1953.

to use any measure, including nuclear attack, in the event of the Western aggression that they feared, but they do not appear to have had any ambitions for the overt conquest of Western Europe or the military defeat of the United States. But we do know that the nuclear states were careful to minimise direct military confrontation with each other during times of crisis and to avoid escalation when applying force to reinforce diplomatic pressure. The Cuban missile crisis grew out of fears of nuclear war and was eventually resolved because of those same fears. And although China was willing to attack disputed Soviet positions on the Ussuri River and along their shared Central Asian border in 1969, mutual concerns about the potential for escalation appear to have limited the intensity and scale of the exchanges and contributed to the diplomatic resolution of the crisis.

During the Cold War, nuclear states in conflicts with non-nuclear states also had to exercise restraint because of perceptions that the excessive use of force might draw their nuclear rivals into the fray. Fears of war widening and the unpredictable and unwelcome escalation it would entail certainly limited the strategic choices for the United States during the Vietnam War. Although the United States was prepared to take extreme measures to prevent South Vietnam from falling to communism, an invasion of North Vietnam and air strikes on southern China were ruled out because they might have drawn China and the Soviet Union directly into the confrontation.

Concerns about escalation to nuclear confrontation also affected conventional doctrine and research and development into military technology. The potentially devastating strategic effect of tactical actions saw the introduction of rules of engagement (ROE), while the need to match the Soviet conventional capability without resorting to a nuclear response provided impetus to the pursuit of a technological edge. The acquisition of standoff, precision-strike capabilities in turn influenced doctrine and expectations of war.

The Cold War might be over, but strategists still have to calculate the probability of nuclear retaliation, either by an adversary or by a nuclear-armed ally of that adversary. Such retaliation may be targeted at forces in theatre, at allied states, or at one's own territory. In other words, battlefield options are still going to be limited by the requirement to avoid escalation.

Strategic flexibility is also being undermined from another quarter where morality and prudence coincide, with the conventional use of force in circumstances where civilians are present becoming ever more problematic.

Despite the expectations of many, the deliberate targeting of civilians did not contribute to the achievement of strategic goals during World War II. Nazi Germany's policies of mass murder, collective reprisals, and subjugation, and Japan's widespread atrocities failed to win them their overall objectives; while the allied bombing of German cities was not essential to their victory. Only in the case of Japan's surrender could the targeting of civilians be said to have clearly weighed on the scales.

The industrial-scale death and damage coupled with what seemed to be the inutility of civilian suffering finally convinced governments that the axiom *inter arma silent leges* – 'in times of war, the laws are silent' – could no longer hold. Some wartime activities were now deemed criminal, giving rise to the Nuremberg trials of German war leaders and military officers and to the widespread ratification of the 1949 Geneva Convention for the Protection of Civilian Persons in Time of War. The concept of civilian immunity was given added potency by the 1968 United Nations declaration on human rights and a large number of protocols and conventions codifying these rights.

When warring states ignored these new norms (to their strategic cost), renewed efforts were made to stiffen international law and restrict the reach of war. In the aftermath of the Vietnam War, for example, a protocol was added to the 1949 Geneva Convention granting further protection to civilians, and the signatories to a United Nations Convention on Certain Conventional Weapons agreed to restrict the use of landmines, fragmenting munitions, and incendiary weapons such as napalm.

Even states reluctant to cede sovereignty and military leaders who argued the primacy of political and military necessity came to acknowledge the general illegitimacy of indiscriminate warfare, a recognition that has influenced doctrine, strategy, the use of weapons systems and munitions, targeting plans, and command-and-control procedures. Governments and military leaders now feel bound to justify civilian casualties as the unfortunate products of 'collateral damage', and legal specialists such as representatives of the judge advocate general have become commonplace in the deployed armed forces of Western states.

Quantum improvements in surveillance and targeting capabilities and the development of munitions designed to neutralise capabilities rather than kill them seem to promise advanced states the ability to destroy their adversaries' ability to resist without harming the general population. But thus far, advances in technology and the doctrines they enable have proved useful only in certain circumstances. Opposing conventional forces could be more easily defeated, as they were in the Gulf War, but the issue of civilian immunity would complicate the achievement of strategic objectives in other instances in ways that might have been predicted but were not.

The US-led coalition took great care to minimise harm to civilians during the 2003 invasion of Iraq, but after its rapid battlefield victory the coalition was soon facing guerilla attacks from groups determined to draw it into doing just that.

Lacking the military capabilities to engage an adversary's armed forces in direct confrontation, guerilla fighters launch small-scale attacks against their opponent's dispersed assets and personnel with the objective of gradually undermining their will to fight. Guerillas use stealth and strike quickly at their target before the defender can respond, and avoid detection between attacks by using physical cover provided by the terrain or vegetation or simply by blending into the civilian population. Popular support in their area of operations is critical to their success; even if they are not hiding among civilians, guerilla fighters depend on the local population to supply intelligence, logistical support and replacements.

This dependence on popular support confers on guerilla fighters some measure of legitimacy at the international level, though this has been qualified by perceptions of the rightness and justice of their cause, and is greatly undermined when they resort to terrorism, as they sometimes do. Guerilla fighters have rights that are enshrined in the international laws of war, most notably the 1977 Geneva Protocol.

But it is not those rights that make guerillas so difficult to combat, nor is it the detection of unidentified combatants. The real problem lies in the legitimacy of guerilla war at the local level and the military necessity of depriving fighters of this critical popular support. Any use of punitive measures against civilians or imposition of controls on their freedom of movement or association is likely to increase rather than decrease civilian support for guerilla movements. Moreover, it is a fundamental characteristic of guerilla operations that the guerillas themselves will not give up the battle for hearts and minds but will do whatever they can to tempt their adversary into indiscriminate and inhumane behaviour and to undermine efforts to provide security, deliver services and improve living standards.

In some conflicts it has been possible to defeat insurgent movements using guerilla tactics because their constituencies were finite and efforts to deprive them of even this limited support were carefully crafted to address the real grievances of the population. The Malayan Emergency from 1948 to 1960 provides a good example. But in many cases guerilla movements have been able to win widespread support through a combination of popular mobilisation and adversary overreaction, which in combination has enabled the insurgents to wear down their opponents over time and eventually achieve their goals.

In Iraq in 2003, the United States' efforts to stabilise the country and secure the establishment of a friendly democratic polity were greatly hampered by the support of the minority Sunni population for groups using guerilla tactics against the coalition's armed forces. Although these groups had a finite constituency within Iraq they were able to draw support from the wider Sunni community, and even without it would have been able to obstruct, delay and complicate the process of political and economic reform. The extended deployment of forces, rising costs, and slow but inexorable drumbeat of casualties eroded support for the war in the United States and the Administration's commitment to its original objectives.

The difficulties encountered by the United States in Iraq will have been noted by other states. Although a strategy that rests on guerilla defence is problematic because it cannot be implemented until an adversary has already gained a territorial foothold, states disheartened by the technology gap first revealed in the Gulf War will be able to develop deterrent and defence postures that go a good way towards compensating for their military disadvantage. Iran has already modified its defence strategy, force structure and training to allow for a guerilla defence, and states like China and Indonesia are likely to evidence a renewed interest in their traditional models of people's war. The balance of military advantage has shifted back to the defence.

Although technological advancements might have promised ever more sophisticated and advantageous ways of waging war, strategic flexibility has in some cases been eroded by some of those advances and by changing patterns of social expectation and political organisation. As Michael Howard has pointed out, the new restraints that they have engendered 'can no longer be regarded as an intrusion from the moral into the military sphere. They belong to the category of those purely military constraints . . . in the absence of which war becomes mere indiscriminate and inconclusive violence.'[7]

9

Controlling war
Soldiers, civilians, and the optimum use of force

THE CHALLENGES POSED BY what General Rupert Smith calls 'wars among the people' have been recognised by military leaders since the Vietnam War, but the lessons drawn and responses made have often been skewed by institutional defensiveness and traditional preferences.[1] The wrong turn made by the US military, which has been the most actively engaged in inter-state war since 1945 and which has insisted on leadership in the multinational operations in which it has been involved since the end of the Cold War, has in turn further undermined the United States' own ability and the ability of the coalitions it leads to achieve the objectives set for them.

The political authorities who are the ultimate decision-makers in matters of war and determine these objectives, generally agreed with military priorities during the Cold War when both parties were most concerned with the potential for inter-bloc conventional war in Europe. They too had an interest in avoiding a repetition of Vietnam and allowed their armed forces to concentrate on what they saw as their core business: conventional warfighting. But the end of the Cold War and the rash of civil wars that spread over the new strategic landscape altered perceptions of national interest and forced a re-examination of military priorities. This re-examination resurrected an old debate about the proper relationship between civilian and military leaders and opened a new one about the proper relationship between states cooperating to use force in the changed international environment. Neither of these debates was confined to the realm of ideas but each was to have a significant impact on the conduct – and incidence – of inter-state war.

The US Vietnam experience had a profound impact. Whereas the North Vietnamese achieved their objective of unification with the South, US forces suffered high levels of casualties, inflicted a great deal of suffering to no avail, and returned home to a country that wanted to forget the whole episode. Humiliated and angry, many in the military blamed the political leadership for their defeat. Claims were made that the campaign had been fatally hindered by numerous political failings: unclear objectives, restrictions on the conduct of the war, civilian micromanagement of operations, and failure to ensure continuing domestic support.

The proper relationship between civilian authorities and military commanders in times of war has been a matter of debate since the Punic Wars. Because war is waged to achieve political purposes, the ultimate decision-making authority should rest with the leadership of the state, or with the political or international grouping involved. It is the political leadership, acting in the interests of their community, that determines the national interest, and that decides the policies to enact and the actions to take in pursuit of that interest. As Lawrence Freedman has pointed out, the management of war 'is political through and through, not only in setting objectives but also in handling allies, isolating enemies, tapping national resources, and setting conditions for peace. It is a political responsibility to assess the burdens a society can accept and the harm it can legitimately impose on others, and where necessary to lead the people up to these limits or away from them.'[2]

Most military leaders concede that the right to determine when and where to use force or to threaten the use of force, and the responsibility for rallying support and allocating resources, both properly lie with the political authorities. A source of recurring dispute has, however, been the balance of influence in deciding the type of military strategy to be pursued and the actual conduct of operations. A view popular with military commanders was asserted by the nineteenth-century Prussian field marshal, Helmuth von Moltke, namely, that 'strategy serves politics best by working for its aim, but by retaining maximum independence in the achievement of this aim. Politics should not interfere in operations.'

But Moltke's belief makes neither political nor strategic sense. As Freedman noted, war's fundamentally political character requires constant political oversight and even intervention. An example from Moltke's own experience explains why. Following the Prussian victory over the Austrians at the battle of Konnigratz in 1866, Moltke wanted to advance to Vienna and annihilate the enemy. But Prussian Chancellor Otto von Bismarck did not want to humiliate the Austrians because they might then oppose Prussia in any war against France, and when Napoleon III himself offered to mediate, Bismarck felt he could not refuse without antagonising the French Emperor. Moltke's military objective was incompatible with Prussia's broader interests, which, as Bismarck pointed out, recognised that 'we don't live alone in Europe but with three other Powers who hate and envy us'.[3]

A similar disconnection between military and political objectives occurred in Korea in 1950, when US President Harry Truman took the advice of the United Nations' commanding general, Douglas MacArthur, and allowed UN forces under US command to cross the thirty-eighth parallel that divided North and South Korea and advance towards the Yalu River on the Chinese border. When Chinese forces entered the war and drove the UN forces back down to the southern tip of the Korean peninsula as quickly as they had previously advanced, MacArthur advocated escalating the conflict still further by attacking China with nuclear weapons. Truman refused to authorise such a disproportionate and strategically dangerous move and began cease-fire negotiations, which MacArthur attempted to stall.

The US Joint Chiefs of Staff were as alarmed as was Truman by MacArthur's inappropriate behaviour because they did not want to be drawn into a direct confrontation with either China or, possibly, the nuclear-armed Soviet Union. The upshot was that Truman sacked MacArthur, and the Joint Chiefs endorsed an alternative and much more politically rational strategy.

But this has not always been the case. Some military commanders have been reluctant to act, believing the military objective unattainable, and others have been unable to achieve the objectives set or have failed to proffer alternative strategic ideas when these have been needed. They have also disagreed among themselves on the best course of action as they did in Korea and Kosovo or become drunk with success as did both Moltke and MacArthur. Given these potentially disastrous possibilities it would be a dereliction of duty for the political leadership to allow military commanders complete independence in waging war; on the contrary as Eliot Cohen argues, they should prod, restrain, mediate or otherwise intervene to maximise the chances of success and to ensure the continual alignment of military actions and political requirements.[4]

Cohen disputes the conventional wisdom of the US military establishment that the Vietnam War was lost because of political meddling. He acknowledges that American objectives in Indochina were unclear, and that the war was badly directed by civilians who were unsure of how to proceed and who failed to solicit useful advice from their generals. But he also points out that those generals neither suggested nor implemented strategies that might have turned things around. The problem was that the war was probably unwinnable. The Vietnamese people had endured centuries of occupation, colonialism and division, an experience that conferred a great deal of local legitimacy on the North's vision of a unified and independent country. The United States was propping up a corrupt and unpopular government and what little legitimacy it might have enjoyed as protector of the South Vietnamese from communism was progressively undermined by its insistence on using massive and indiscriminate military force. In the battle of wills, the balance shifted inexorably in favour in the North Vietnamese.

Some 140 years earlier, Clausewitz had explained the importance of understanding the character of every war, but during the Vietnam disaster, US politicians and civilian and military officials were so busy blaming each other for their defeat that, at the time, none of them recognised the real reasons for their failure. A more reflective appraisal might have alerted them to a critical shift in the character of war that henceforth would seriously complicate efforts at military intervention. From Vietnam onwards, the success or otherwise of most uses of armed force has been critically shaped by domestic, adversary and international perceptions of the legitimacy of both the actor and his actions. Military interventions in which legitimacy, or its absence, has been a central strategic consideration include: the US deployments to Beirut, the Soviet occupation of Afghanistan,

Iraq's invasion of Kuwait and the response of the UN coalition, the interventions in Somalia, Bosnia, Kosovo, and East Timor, and the US-led invasions of Afghanistan and Iraq.

As it was, the US experience in Vietnam firmed military opposition to active engagement in conflicts on the Asian mainland and resulted in President Nixon's 1969 enunciation of what was to become known as the Guam Doctrine, setting limits on US military involvement in Asia. Henceforth the United States would continue to deter major threats in that region and to provide technical and training assistance to its allies but it would expect them to take primary responsibility for their own defence. At home in the United States, moves were made to restructure the armed forces to foster greater civilian support for future wars elsewhere while ensuring an adequate supply of troops. The draft was ended and in 1973 the 'Total Force' was created, integrating regular and reserve units. As volunteers, the reserves would be willing participants in war and their mobilisation and deployment supported by their communities. The Total Force concept was also seen as a potential brake on any ill-considered military ventures, because the potential for social and economic disruption would force the Congress to take more interest in the Executive's decisions relating to war.

After Vietnam, the United States focused its attention on the major Cold War front in Europe, and on the strategically vital Middle East, home to most of the world's oil production, an important American ally, Israel, and a vital shipping route. It was to help resolve a crisis involving Israel that the United States deployed forces to the Lebanon twice between 1982 and 1984. On the first occasion the United States joined France and Italy in facilitating the evacuation of the Palestine Liberation Organisation from Beirut where it had been under siege by Israeli forces. This mission had the support of the Arab states, some of whom agreed to accept the PLO; of the PLO itself, whose militia were willing to withdraw as long as the families they left behind were protected; and of the Israelis, who were seriously overstretched and glad to have someone else remove their adversaries. The objective was quickly and easily achieved, but only days later the Christian Lebanese Prime Minister Bashir Gemayel was assassinated.

Concerned that this would disturb the newly established balance of power in the Lebanon, Israel joined with the forces of Gemayel's brother to push into Muslim West Beirut, where they allowed them to massacre a thousand Palestinians. US President Ronald Reagan immediately ordered the redeployment of US marines 'to establish a presence' and attempted to negotiate a halt to the fighting. When Jordan and the PLO rejected Reagan's initiative, the marines came under increasing attack from Lebanese factions who viewed them as vulnerable symbols of US support for the government and Israel. By mid-1983 the United States' strategic objective had changed from stabilisation to the expulsion of foreign forces, namely, the Syrians, who were sponsoring most of the factions opposed to the United States. The marines were ordered to participate in joint patrols with Lebanese Armed Forces, which escalated tensions between them and the opposition militias, and which undermined their ostensible neutrality. On 23 October 1983 a suicide bomber drove a truck into the marine barracks in Beirut, killing 241 troops.

President Reagan resisted calls for a withdrawal, arguing that the marines' continued presence was necessary to prevent a Soviet takeover of the Lebanon and the wider Middle East. Instead he ordered additional forces deployed, increased military assistance to the Lebanese Armed Forces, and signed a new defence cooperation agreement with Israel. But the rout of the Lebanese Armed Forces after an attack by Shi'ite militia on Beirut in January 1984, and Gemayel's rapprochement with the Syrians, finally brought home the futility of the continued presence.

The debacle of the second Beirut deployment had an immediate and far-reaching impact. No sooner had the marines been withdrawn than the US Secretary of Defence, Caspar Weinberger, announced a new set of guidelines for the use of force. From now on, Weinberger said, the United States should not commit forces to combat overseas unless the mission was deemed vital to US national interests or those of its allies. If the government decided it was necessary to put combat troops into a given situation, it should do so wholeheartedly and with the clear intention of winning, and if it was unwilling to commit the forces or resources necessary to achieve its objectives it should not commit them at all. When committing forces to combat overseas, it should have clearly defined political and military objectives, and a clear understanding of how its forces could achieve those objectives. It should have set a schedule to achieve those objectives and sent the forces needed to do just that. The relationship between US objectives and the forces committed – their size, composition, and disposition – must be constantly reassessed and adjusted if necessary. Before the United States committed combat forces abroad, there must be some reasonable assurance that the mission had the support of the American people and their elected representatives in Congress. And finally, the commitment of the armed forces to combat should be a last resort.

All of the services except the marines supported what came to be known as the Weinberger Doctrine unreservedly, and in 1989 one of the doctrine's strongest proponents, the army general Colin Powell, became chairman of the Joint Chiefs of Staff. Powell had been military adviser to Weinberger and although he acknowledged that the end of the Cold War made the vital national interest more difficult to quantify, he still believed that force should be a last resort and then used wholeheartedly. In fact, as noted in chapter four, Powell took the argument further than Weinberger by insisting that the United States should always act with overwhelming force.

These attitudes shaped Powell's response to the Iraqi invasion of Kuwait in 1990. He was reluctant to use force, but once persuaded of the need for military action insisted on having a massive capability and a free hand. As it happened, military requirements meshed with political preferences, because President George H. Bush was anxious to avoid a repetition of Vietnam and had drawn much the same conclusions regarding the reasons for the United States' defeat in that war.

The application of overwhelming force by the UN-endorsed, US-led coalition was successful in driving Saddam Hussein's forces out of Kuwait at very low cost. Coalition politicians and generals agreed that this marked the 'culminating point of victory', the stage in an offensive operation where the capability of the attacker no longer significantly exceeds that of the defender, and beyond which continued offensive operations risk overextension, counterattack, and defeat. It is often difficult for political and military leaders to gauge the moment at which such a stage has been reached: success in battle can tempt them to push their advantage, as MacArthur had done in Korea. But in the Gulf War, the culminating point was obvious. Had the United States decided to advance on Baghdad to overthrow Saddam Hussein's regime, it would have proceeded beyond the bounds of the UN mandate and may have lost key coalition support. Furthermore, ousting Saddam had the potential to destabilise the region by raising the aspirations of the Kurdish minorities in Syria, Turkey and Iran and thus threatening those states' territorial integrity. It might also have resulted in the establishment of a Shi'ite-dominated state in uncomfortably close proximity to the Sunni Gulf states. And finally and perhaps most importantly, an invasion of Iraq might have drawn the United States into a long war among a hostile population.

KEEPING BOOTS OFF THE GROUND

The Gulf War was hailed as demonstrating the power of recently developed surveillance, command-and-control, targeting and delivery technologies, the efficacy of US warfighting doctrine, and the appropriateness of military autonomy in wartime. But none of the international crises that followed it was of the same character. The conflicts in the disintegrating Yugoslavia and in the Horn of Africa were essentially civil wars in which the Bush Administration and the military were not disposed to become involved. Criticism of the military's reluctance and calls by Congress and the media for a reduction in military spending and a peace dividend prompted General Powell to defend its record and assert the importance of force in US foreign policy in 1992.[5] He cited recent military successes such as the Gulf War, the abduction of Manuel Noriega from Panama in 1989, and the evacuation of US Embassy personnel and others from Liberia through the autumn and winter of 1990. He also pointed to US contributions to humanitarian relief operations such as Bosnia and Somalia. What he did not mention was that the US military contribution in the Balkans had thus far been limited to air drops of food to the beleaguered Muslims of Srebrenica and that they had only agreed to go to Somalia to head off demands for greater involvement in Bosnia.

The humanitarian crisis in Somalia seemed easier to resolve. Drought and the depredations of civil war had effectively wiped out food production in even the richest farming regions in that country, resulting in famine and the displacement of about a third of the population through war or hunger. The United Nations had negotiated a cease-fire between the warring factions, begun delivering humanitarian relief and deployed two small contingents, first to monitor the cease-fire and then to protect aid workers and prevent looting.

The situation in Somalia continued to deteriorate to the point where television stations throughout the world were broadcasting images of thousands of starving Somalis. In his presidential campaign, Democrat candidate Bill Clinton was pointing to the disaster in Somalia as evidence of Bush's inept foreign policy. Bush responded by announcing a unilateral decision to airlift emergency food supplies into Mogadishu but the looting and extortion continued and even intensified. The 500 UN peacekeepers sent to Mogadishu in September 1992 remained under virtual siege at the airport, so in November Bush requested from General Powell options for a more robust intervention.

The military surprised everyone by saying it was willing to send as many as two divisions. Powell believed that Somali lives could be saved, that the military could protect themselves, and that if the mission were limited and clearly defined, it could then be turned over to the United Nations, enabling the United States to get out quickly.

The mission decided on was to open the locked warehouses of Mogadishu and to clear south-central Somalia's principal roads for the delivery of humanitarian food shipments. US troops were supposed to achieve this quickly and to return home by January 1993, to be replaced by a UN force. In other words they had a clear exit strategy in mind. An exit strategy is a plan for the extraction of military forces developed in advance of deployment or during operations. There are two types: end-date and end-state, the former being self-explanatory and the latter being determined by the achievement of particular objectives. The US mission in Somalia had both of these: the objective was to facilitate the delivery of humanitarian aid and the time allowed to achieve this was set at a month.

Twenty-one countries agreed to join the US-led UNITAF (Unified Task Force) and 37 000 personnel were eventually deployed to central Somalia but it took time and given the limited port and airfield facilities in Mogadishu, only the two US infantry divisions and their support elements were in place by January 1993. Once they were on the ground they made arrangements with the faction leaders Mohammed Aideed and Ali Mahdi to leave them in charge of their respective areas of control in Mogadishu in return for their agreement to store their weapons and avoid confrontations with UNITAF.

UNITAF achieved most of its limited military objectives within two weeks and US commanders were anxious to get out so certain mission objectives, such as minimal restoration of roads and bridges outside the capital, were set aside as being too time-consuming. The navy wanted to take its engineers to do this job but could not get permission and had to leave without ever getting their equipment out of port. But the rush to leave and the very limited objectives set and achieved had more serious consequences.

In March 1993 the incoming Clinton Administration succeeded in persuading the Security Council to pass resolution 814 establishing UNOSOM II (United Nations Operation in Somalia) with a broad mandate to tackle Somalia's underlying social, political and economic problems and to help the country get back on its feet. Joint Chiefs of Staff planners drafted the relevant Security Council resolutions as they had for the UNITAF deployment. UNOSOM II's initial military tasks were to monitor the cessation of hostilities, prevent any resumption of violence, maintain control of heavy weapons pending their transfer to a national army, seize small arms from unauthorised groups, maintain the security of all transport infrastructure for the delivery of relief aid, protect aid personnel, continue mine-clearing, and assist in the repatriation of refugees.

The UN Secretary-General had been reluctant to take on a peace enforcement role in Somalia and had insisted to no avail that the United States widen its mandate during UNITAF to create a secure environment that would lay the groundwork for the UNOSOM deployment.

In May 1993 US commanders turned over their headquarters to the incoming UNOSOM command. By then most UNITAF forces had left and the UN inherited a small and incoherent force to implement the daunting task of nation-building in a hostile environment. Neither Aideed nor Mahdi had given his consent to the expanded operation and neither was ready for peace or to see his power eroded by the restoration of the state. Neither would cooperate with the weaker UNOSOM force.

The United States wanted a robust mission and attached to UNO-SOM II a Quick Reaction Force (QRF) but this was part of the regular US chain of command. It was not permitted to undertake regular UNOSOM II operations but was supposed to be an emergency back-up force that had combat capabilities that UNOSOM II lacked.

In June 1993 Aideed's forces attacked and killed twenty-four Pakistani peacekeepers and the United Nations issued resolution 837 calling for the apprehension of the Somalis responsible. The QRF began to play a much more aggressive role against Aideed and were joined in August by a ranger task force from the joint operations special command under the operational control of Central Command. In October a US assault on Aideed's headquarters resulted in the death of eighteen Americans and hundreds of Somalis. Television images of American corpses being dragged through the streets of Mogadishu were enough to panic the Clinton Administration into the withdrawal of US forces and UNOSOM II was not long in following.

Years after the withdrawal of UNOSOM II Somalia remained a failed state, desperately poor and riven by violence. The United Nations and particularly the United States were so wary of repeating the experience that they did not act to prevent or halt the genocide in Rwanda. The Clinton Administration disingenuously blamed the United Nations for Somalia and the US military blamed both the Clinton Administration and the United Nations for what they termed 'mission creep'. Mission creep describes the expansion of the original, limited military mission under pressure of unfolding events to encompass new and more difficult tasks, especially those not traditionally in the realm of military operations. It is a negative term for what might otherwise be described as mission change and it is important to note that this negative attitude is not shared by all armed forces. British military doctrine takes a directly opposed approach that acknowledges the dynamism of conflict, encourages mission development, and allows for the exercise of initiative at all levels as long as the operation stays within policy guidelines and the force commander's operational intent. Implicit in this approach is a rejection of the utility of pre-planned exit strategies and a recognition that commitment, credibility and flexibility are necessary to the achievement of strategic objectives.

US responses to the continuing conflict in the Balkans had been heavily influenced by the military's reluctance to become involved in what it thought was a complicated and insoluble conflict that could cost American lives and result in an escalating commitment. Clinton's Secretary of State, Madeleine Albright, had been so incensed by General Powell's intransigence on the matter in 1993 that she had asked him what the point was in having a military when it could not be used. Powell's successor as Commander of Joint Chiefs of Staff, General Shalikashvili, was more sympathetic to the coercive use of force and to military operations other than war more generally and agreed to air strikes against Serb forces in Bosnia in 1995. But many in the armed forces maintained their reservations and Clinton was so anxious to avoid a repetition of Somalia and to mollify his military and congressional critics, that he himself placed constraints on US involvement in the Kosovo crisis.

When fighting broke out between Albanian and Serbian forces in the Serb province of Kosovo and the international community tried to mediate, Serbia claimed that the situation was an internal affair and nobody else's business. In March 1998 the UN Security Council imposed an arms embargo and economic and diplomatic sanctions on Serbia and called for dialogue between the disputing parties. As the fighting escalated NATO stepped up its military presence in neighbouring Macedonia and Albania and started to threaten Milosevic with air strikes. In September 1998 the UN Security Council issued resolution 1199 calling for an immediate cease-fire, the withdrawal of military and paramilitary forces from Kosovo, complete access for humanitarian groups (by this time there were about 200 000 refugees from the fighting), and cooperation in the investigation of war crimes. In October, Milosevic and US Special Envoy

Richard Holbrooke agreed on a partial withdrawal of Serb forces and the deployment of a verification mission of 2000 unarmed personnel from the Organisation for Security and Cooperation in Europe. By January 1999 the cease-fire had broken down so the Contact Group, comprised of representatives from the United States, the United Kingdom, France, Germany, Italy, Russia, the European Union presidency and the European Commission, summoned the Serb and Kosovo Albanian parties to negotiations at Rambouillet, France. The negotiations were to define the terms of an agreement that would provide for a cease-fire, an interim peace settlement and system of self-government for Kosovo, and the deployment of an international force to Kosovo to uphold that settlement.

NATO warned both the Serbs and the Kosovo Albanians that if they failed to attend the Rambouillet negotiations, halt the fighting and comply with the October agreement, NATO would take whatever measures were necessary to avert a humanitarian catastrophe. The Serbs sent a low-level delegation and refused to sign anything. NATO then decided it would have to use military force to compel Milosevic to agree to its terms.

The United States and the West Europeans decided to cooperate under the auspices of NATO because they had good reason to believe that Russia would use its position on the Security Council to block any action by the United Nations. Russia was a long-time ally of Serbia but also wanted to avoid a precedent being set for intervention in the affairs of the former socialist countries of Eastern Europe. NATO seemed an ideal alternative because it was composed largely of European states who could argue a legitimate interest in the resolution of the Kosovo crisis and who were keen to demonstrate the organisation's continuing relevance.

NATO had been formed in 1949 as a defensive alliance against the threat of the Soviet Union and to stabilise and limit German power. When the Cold War was winding down, the allies persuaded the Soviet Union to agree to the unification of Germany by promising to recast NATO's mission so that it was not geared to military confrontation with the Soviet Union but would continue to restrain Germany by playing the dominant role in European security and keeping the US military connected to Europe. NATO's 1991

Strategic Concept redefined the threats to European security: some of these were seen as emanating from the instability resulting from serious economic, social and political difficulties, including ethnic rivalries and territorial disputes, faced by many countries in Central and Eastern Europe. Although the Strategic Concept defined NATO's core mission as collective defence, by 1999 it had added the new mission of crisis management, including crisis response.

NATO's military options in the Kosovo crisis were heavily influenced by the reluctance of the Pentagon to become involved in what they believed should be a European affair, President Clinton's veto on the deployment of US ground forces, and the US Air Force's desire to settle the Gulf War debate on the utility of air power in its favour.

Lieutenant General Short, the air-component commander, believed NATO should target the head of the snake and subject the Milosevic regime to an intense and sustained attack but strategic paralysis was not a politically attractive option. NATO was resorting to bombing only reluctantly and was convinced that a minimum amount of force would persuade Milosevic to settle. After all, twelve days of NATO air strikes had seemed sufficient in Bosnia in 1995. Moreover NATO was anxious to avoid inflicting harm on Serbian civilians, partly out of humanitarian concern and partly because this would allow Milosevic to question the operation's legitimacy. The strategy would therefore be one of coercion rather than paralysis.

Operation Allied Force began on 24 March 1999 with attacks on Serbian early warning and air defence systems, airfields, military communications and electronic intelligence sites, missile storage facilities and army and police headquarters. Phase II targeted Serb military positions in Kosovo. There were four measures of merit in the selection of targets: to avoid the loss of NATO aircraft, to disable Serb forces on the ground, to minimise collateral damage, and to maintain alliance cohesion. These requirements were not compatible with each other or with the objective of halting the displacement of the Kosovo Albanians. The need for force protection dictated that aircraft fly at altitude and speed while the need to avoid collateral damage dictated that targets could not be hit unless they were clearly visible. The weather was poor, cloudy and foggy, the terrain rugged and well forested and the Serb forces were deployed in small units, their heavy weapons, ammunition depots and forward headquarters dispersed and camouflaged. Not surprisingly, air strikes were unsuccessful in preventing the forced displacement of Kosovo Albanians. In fact, the ethnic cleansing campaign intensified to the point where the vast majority of the Kosovo population was heading for the borders of neighbouring countries. Far from acceding to NATO demands, Milosevic attempted to undermine NATO unity and Western domestic support by playing up collateral damage and pointing to the worsening position in Kosovo.

In late April air attacks were redirected to targets in Serbia in an effort to undermine popular and élite support for Milosevic. Command-and-control infrastructure, fuel stocks, bridges, media facilities, and electricity were all targeted but it took a further five weeks for Milosevic to capitulate. NATO had not taken into account a critical difference in the circumstances of the 1995 air strikes and those in 1999. In 1995 the tide had already turned against the Bosnian Serbs and Milosevic had been looking for a way out; the air strikes had been successful in exploiting what William Zartman describes as a 'ripe moment' in the conflict. In early 1999 by contrast, Milosevic was still firmly wedded to the objective of maintaining Serbian sovereignty over Kosovo and believed, quite rightly, that he had sufficient domestic support to withstand NATO's limited application of pressure. His sudden agreement on 3 June to the withdrawal of Serb forces from Kosovo came only when NATO moderated its demands and agreed to involve Russia as a mediator and peacekeeper. The withdrawal of Russia's support for continued resistance and its promise to provide a presence alongside NATO forces in Kosovo were unarguably the key factors in Milosevic's change of heart. And it was the belated recognition of Russia's status as a major power and its interests in an inclusive architecture of European security that had persuaded its leaders to assist in ending the conflict.

The recriminations over the failure of the air campaign to change Serb behaviour began long before the operation was over. The air force blamed the Supreme Allied Commander Europe (SACEUR), General Clark, for failing to implement a strategy of paralysis, the US military blamed the civilian leadership for intervening in a crisis that was not of vital national interest and with less than wholehearted commitment, and almost everybody in US defence policy circles blamed their NATO allies for placing too many constraints on the delivery of force.

The Kosovo campaign had brought into stark focus the difficulty of conducting alliance operations in situations short of total war. Organisations like NATO have no independent strategy-making capability and in times of crisis must cobble together a strategy that suits the interests and meets the concerns of alliance members. Stronger and more militarily capable powers will attempt to dictate terms and conditions, and may resent having to consult their allies on strategy and operations. Smaller powers may disagree with proposed plans, diplomatic manoeuvres, and military actions but not be in a position to compel change or implement alternatives. If a strategy does not have the firm commitment of all from the outset or if its implementation does not achieve immediate positive results, the process of negotiation between allies on where to go next is likely to be as time-consuming and difficult as that of negotiating with the adversary. For all these reasons, the Kosovo experience left the United States and some of its NATO allies with serious reservations about working together in the future.

RUMSFELD'S REACTION

To sum up, the period between the end of the Vietnam War and the end of the twentieth century was characterised by increasing political assertiveness on the part of the US military which sought to maintain its credibility and prestige by determining the conditions under which it would fight. This trend reached its apogee in the years of the Bush and Clinton presidencies when their administrations were turning to the United Nations and alliance partners for assistance in negotiating the changed strategic landscape. The new century would witness an inevitable counter-reaction to the military's assertiveness and a somewhat less predictable assertion of unilateralism.

When President George W. Bush came to power in 2001, his Administration dusted off plans for the forceful assertion of US primacy first suggested by Paul Wolfowitz at the end of Cold War. To enable this vision Defence Secretary Donald Rumsfeld moved to reassert civilian control over the military. His primary aim was to transform the somewhat reluctant armed forces into a leaner and more agile instrument of state power but it was also obvious that the United States could not fully exploit that power unless it had a military that was willing to do what the government asked of them. The alternative might otherwise be delay or paralysis, undermining the credibility of threats to use force, undermining the utility of force itself, undermining foreign policy objectives, and ultimately undermining state power.

As noted in the previous chapter the new Administration also had a low opinion of international law and collective security. It repudiated the Kyoto Protocol on global warming, the Biological Weapons Convention and the International Criminal Court; hampered agreement on limiting the international transfer of small arms; refused to sign the anti-personnel mine ban treaty and announced that it would abrogate the Anti-Ballistic Missile Treaty with Russia and proceed with the development of missile defence systems. Drawing on its interpretation of the lessons of Somalia and Kosovo, it argued that collective security responses were slow and unwieldy, with the need for consensus hindering the effective application of force. Henceforth, instead of the coalition determining the mission, the mission should determine the coalition.

Accordingly, when the United States attacked Afghanistan in response to the September 11 terrorist strikes, it did not attempt to mobilise support through the United Nations or to call upon its formal alliance partners for contributions. What it sought instead was a 'coalition of the willing'. The existence of such a coalition would confer legitimacy on the campaign while its voluntary composition would allow the United States to dictate the timing and direction of the war without compromising its goals or jeopardising its command structure.

The rout of the Taliban was taken as evidence of this policy's success and the Bush Administration proceeded with plans to invade Iraq with a similar coalition of supportive countries. What it failed to realise was that the Afghanistan success owed more to local conditions than to the advantages of unilateralism, and that it was these circumstances combined with a general international consensus on the justness of this particular US military action that had actually provided legitimacy. As noted in the previous chapter, local and international attitudes would be very different in the case of Iraq and success much more difficult to achieve as a result.

The ousting of Saddam Hussein had been a long-time goal for many in the new Administration who believed that the decision to end hostilities after the Gulf War had been a strategic mistake. Twelve years on Saddam was still in power, international commitment to maintaining economic sanctions on his regime was eroding, and the extent to which the UN weapons-of-mass-destruction disarmament program had worked remained unclear. Risk evaluations had also changed since 1991; civilian officials in the Pentagon now saw no likelihood of resistance or civil strife, arguing on the contrary that the United States would be greeted as liberators by a secular and united population that would move swiftly towards the establishment of a democratic and friendly polity. Both the Administration and the military therefore assumed that Saddam's regime was the centre of gravity and that the war would essentially be a conventional one. It would finally be a textbook case of strategic paralysis.

When strategic paralysis gave way to anarchy and insurgency the opening shots in the blame game were predictably fired between the military and the civilian leadership. Many in the armed forces held Rumsfeld responsible for ignoring the advice of army commanders and insisting that 100 000 US troops would be sufficient. As usual, this attribution of blame overlooked more fundamental flaws in the strategy. Strategic paralysis targets the will and capabilities of the political leadership and armed forces and is a useful way to limit the duration and costs of conventional conflict. But the objective in Iraq was never simply to remove Saddam Hussein from power or neutralise his armed forces. Had it been, President Bush could have withdrawn his forces at the end of the 'combat operations phase'. The objective had always been a political one, namely to turn Iraq into a democratic state and consequently the real centre of gravity had not really been the Ba'ath Party or the Republican Guard but the Iraqi population. As noted in chapter five the strategy of strategic paralysis had allowed many Iraqi officers and soldiers to slip back into the population, where they formed the nucleus of resistance to the occupation. But strategic paralysis had two other unexpected consequences. The targeting of dual-use infrastructure worsened living conditions for many Iraqis, particularly in the capital Baghdad. And the speed with which the ousting of Saddam was achieved led to a vacuum of power that allowed widespread looting and further damage to institutions and facilities providing essential services. Instead of alleviating the economic hardship under which Iraqis had been labouring for years, the war had made things worse. For most of the majority Shi'ite, religious and political freedom and the prospect of parliamentary dominance were sufficient compensation, but for the now powerless Sunni minority it added insult to injury.

Although a larger deployment might have helped to curb some of the looting, the failure to stem the subsequent Sunni-dominated insurgency owed less to numerical insufficiency than to the inflexibility of US military attitudes to war. This inflexibility stemmed from years of aversion to and avoidance of missions other than conventional warfighting and was encouraged in Iraq by the Bush Administration's refusal to acknowledge the character of the conflict in which it had become embroiled. Attempting to maintain its domestic legitimacy in the face of rising casualties and strife, it labelled all those who resisted as terrorists or insurgents. In doing so, the Administration was encouraging a military response that only contributed to the spiral of violence and instability.

It was three years into the war before the military acknowledged the need to reduce military operations and devote more effort to winning hearts and minds, but even then combat operations continued alongside the oil spot strategy suggested by Andrew Krepinevich.[6] In any case 'victory' had by then become extremely unlikely. The insurgency and the democratic process had undermined secularism and entrenched sectarian politics and the polity that the coalition would leave behind looked set to be fractious, and the new authorities less than liberal. In the meantime the hoped-for process of political reform in the wider Middle East had produced the reassertion of Islamic nationalism in Iran and the victory of the radical Hamas in the Palestinian elections.

The United States could not simply withdraw its forces from Iraq despite evidence that its presence was increasingly unwelcome and in some ways strategically counter-productive. Rising domestic pressure for the enunciation and implementation of an exit strategy had to be resisted because of the damage that a withdrawal from an unstable and violent Iraq would inflict on US credibility.

The 2006 Quadrennial Defence Review failed to address these serious complications in the United States' recent experience of using force. Its authors talked of asymmetric warfare, violent extremism, new and elusive foes and multiple complex challenges, obfuscatory language that allowed for a less than rigorous re-evaluation of defence posture, force structure, and acquisitions. But US responses to other international crises suggested a more sober appreciation of the limitations of force. When North Korea attempted to secure more aid for its starving population by using its only leverage, the threat of nuclear proliferation, the United States agreed to negotiate and to involve the regional powers, China, Japan, and Korea, in the process. And when Iran announced plans to develop nuclear power, the United States turned to the offices of the European Union, the International Atomic Energy Agency and the United Nations Security Council to halt this potentially dangerous process. Ongoing operations in Afghanistan were handed over to NATO.

It is impossible to know how the next chapter in the American debate over the use of force will play out, because the lessons of history have a way of being lost in the fusillade of recriminations or of simply being misinterpreted. Only two predictions can be safely made. The first is that attitudes in relation to war and wars themselves have evolved in a dialectic fashion and that process will continue to unfold. And the second is that the changing character of conflict demands ever more caution and care from those involved in the formulation of strategy and the prosecution of war. Both political authorities and military commanders will have to develop a wider and more nuanced appreciation of the relationship between military force and political objectives and work together on bridging the gap between them.

10 | Peacemaking
Intervening to protect and repair

C ARE AND CAUTION MIGHT make eminent good sense when formulating strategies for international conflicts but there is an increasingly common category of force employment where a rapid response appears critical. This is in the event of a humanitarian disaster. At the end of the Cold War the thawing of the strategic landscape seemed to presage a wave of state collapses, civil wars, and humanitarian crises, a phenomenon that coincided with a revival of enthusiasm for peacekeeping and collective security. Neither of these trends was to maintain its momentum into the twenty-first century, but military intervention and stabilisation of post-conflict environments remain the most likely tasks that most armed forces will be called on to undertake. Recent experience suggests that these missions will pose a range of serious challenges.

Civil wars can be defined as sustained internal conflicts involving large sections of the population and causing a significant number of deaths. They are not new phenomena, having troubled political communities for millennia and many states since the formation of the state system. Essentially they are armed disputes about the distribution of power within political societies, occurring when communities or élites disagree over the nature, structure or extent of political authority or over the polity's allocation of resources, and fail to resolve their disagreements through peaceful means. Civil wars have been fought over the legitimacy of particular rulers, over the governing principles of political organisations, and over community rights.

Because civil wars are conflicts for power within finite territories, the combatant parties have nowhere to retreat. If they lose they must either accede to political arrangements that they find intolerable or abandon their homelands to become exiles or refugees. This unattractive set of options fuels the determination to force or resist change and can lead to conflicts of great duration and intensity. The casualty levels in some of the civil wars of the past two centuries have been staggering. During the Taiping Rebellion in the nineteenth century in China about thirty million people are estimated to have died. Over half a million died during the American Civil War, some eight million in the Russian Civil War, and over 300 000 in the Spanish Civil War.

As more and more states came into being in the wave of decolonisation after World War II, communal disagreements became an increasingly common feature of the international landscape. Sometimes these took place soon after independence, resulting in a hasty and traumatic partitioning of the new state as it did in India. More often states resisted secessionist impulses and managed either through their own resources or with the help of the colonial powers, the superpowers or United Nations forces to quell rebellions. Some low-level insurgencies would rumble on for years and others would escalate to civil war, involving whole communities and causing widespread dislocation and suffering.

INTERVENTION IN CIVIL CONFLICTS

External powers or parties have had a long tradition of intervening directly or interfering in civil conflicts, but until the end of the Cold War they did so because they had an interest in supporting the cause of one or other of the combatant groups rather than out of humanitarian concern. During the years of superpower confrontation, both the United States and the Soviet Union provided support to insurgent groups of their particular ideological bent all over the globe, and actively intervened in Vietnam and Afghanistan respectively. South Africa and Cuba provided active support to the different warring sides in Angola and Israel and Syria intervened directly in the Lebanese Civil War. The competing superpowers and their proxies justified these interventions on the grounds that their assistance had been sought by the legitimate authorities in the states concerned. The Security Council was prevented from condemning their actions by the existence of the veto mechanism, but the General Assembly regularly issued condemnations of intervention and interference.

The United Nations only undertook to ameliorate two civil crises during the Cold War and did so in both instances at the behest of national governments under threat from internal and external forces. In both cases the superpowers supported multinational intervention, though for very different reasons.

The first instance came in 1961 when Patrice Lumumba, Prime Minister of the newly independent Congo, requested UN assistance. The writ of his new government was being undermined by the machinations of its former colonial power, Belgium, and by the secessionist aspirations of provincial leaders. The Congolese armed forces themselves were embroiled in fighting against their Belgian officers. Both the United States and the Soviet Union had an interest in seeing the situation stabilised under UN auspices because each feared that the other might otherwise exploit the turmoil and each hoped that a UN intervention might influence events in their favour.

The Security Council authorised the dispatch of ONUC (Operation des Nations Unies au Congo) with an initial mandate to ensure the withdrawal of Belgian forces, assist the government in maintaining law and order and provide technical assistance. UN forces did manage to replace Belgian troops and restore some semblance of peace in the capital and the towns along the Congo River but they were not mandated to move against the secessionist southeastern province of Katanga or authorised to use force when fighting broke out in the central southern Kasai province. Lumumba therefore turned to the Soviet Union who transported his forces into Kasai and demanded that the UN act against Katanga. This was a step too far for the United States which feared the establishment of a pro-Soviet regime in such a large and central African state, and for Belgium which maintained a strong presence and interest in mineral-rich Katanga. Lumumba was arrested by the army Chief of Staff, Mobutu Sese Seko, and after twice escaping was killed in suspicious circumstances.

The United Nations had responded to Lumumba's arrest and the emergence of rival contestants for power by expanding ONUC's mandate to allow all appropriate measures to prevent the occurrence of civil war – including the use of force. When all of these groups except those from Katanga agreed to elect a new Congolese government, yet another mandate authorised the apprehension, detention or deportation of the mercenaries who were stiffening the province's resistance to central government forces.

The Congo intervention had mixed results. Some semblance of order was restored, foreign forces were removed and Katanga was incorporated into the state. But the Prime Minister had been killed and the government was soon to be ousted by the West-leaning Mobutu who introduced one-party rule and was able to plunder his mineral-rich and strategically important country undisturbed for over thirty years. Many members of the United Nations were unhappy that the organisation had been used to further the interests of the superpowers while the mission had cost the lives of dozens of peacekeepers and of the Secretary-General himself, when his plane had crashed on a mediation mission. It had also been such a drain on resources that the United Nations would be unable to adequately finance peacekeeping operations for years to come.

In 1964 the United Nations responded to a request from the government of Cyprus to intervene when a Joint Truce Force of British, Greek and Turkish troops failed to restore peace to the island. It was hoped that a UN force would carry more legitimacy with the warring Greek and Turkish communities and would therefore be able to mediate a solution to the political crisis and stave off direct intervention by Greece or Turkey. The United States' primary interest was in preventing the crisis from escalating to an all-out confrontation between two of its NATO allies, while the Soviet Union wanted the Cypriot government to survive because of its commitment to non-alignment. Neither exercised its veto power because both had an interest in seeing tensions on the island alleviated.

UNFICYP (United Nations Force in Cyprus) was successful in tamping down the violence but was unable to resolve the political stalemate or prevent Greece and Turkey from interfering. When Turkey invaded the island in 1974, the UN peacekeeping role simply changed to policing the line that now divided the Greek and Turkish halves of the island. UNFICYP would remain in Cyprus for more than forty years, it proving impossible in all that time to find a political solution acceptable to all parties. Some have argued that the very presence of peacekeepers has contributed to the stalemate by removing any incentive for committed negotiation.

Superpower competition undeniably entrenched and complicated some civil conflicts and here the end of the Cold War introduced push and pull factors for resolution. The decline in political interest and the withdrawal of financial and material support to warring parties was coupled with a new commitment on the part of the international community to assist in the resolution of civil conflicts. Thus the United Nations was able to mediate an end to civil wars in Namibia in 1989, Cambodia in 1991, and Mozambique and El Salvador in 1992.

But all trends have multiple effects and in Europe the end of ideology actually contributed to the eruption of new civil wars. At the end of the Cold War the loosening grip of communist regimes saw the Soviet Union, Czechoslovakia and Yugoslavia break down into states loosely based on nations, and there were demands for greater autonomy made by other groups. In Czechoslovakia, the Slovak and Czech peoples agreed fairly amicably to form separate states. The Soviet leadership could not prevent the secession of the Central Asian republics, the tiny Baltic states, and the various republics along its southern European borders, but fought all attempts at secession by peoples living within the borders of Russia itself. And in Yugoslavia the final collapse of the federation was accompanied by bitter and many-sided conflict between the weakened centre, republics and provinces seeking independence, and ethnic groups within those areas resisting change. Ideology no longer had any utility as a tool for popular mobilisation in these conflicts and élites appealed instead to ethnic and religious nationalism. President Josip Tito had originally established a federal system in Yugoslavia to assuage the concerns of other communities about Serbian domination and had hoped that shared socialist values would transcend community differences, an outcome he attempted to ensure by punishing any signs of narrow nationalist sentiment or mobilisation. But uneven development and the measures taken to introduce greater equity in economic capacity had a contrary effect, entrenching grievances and contributing to communal identification. The federation tottered on after Tito's death but it could not survive the economic crisis of the 1980s and the end of the Cold War.

The momentum towards disintegration gathered steam as federal politicians revived communal grievances that in some cases dated back to the days of the Ottoman Empire. Their appeal to ethnic and religious sentiment was of course exclusive, provocative, and zero-sum. It had no universal reach, so people of other backgrounds or faiths could not be persuaded of its benefits. The only alternative in contested areas was to remove them physically and this was carried out in campaigns of 'ethnic cleansing', either by forced dislocation or mass murder. Once this process began, communal grievances and identification deepened, leading to escalating and increasingly bitter conflict.

European governments' declarations of sympathy for the nationalist aspirations of the different communities in the Balkans had inadvertently contributed to the slide towards war, but they were deeply concerned by the consequences. The displaced populations added refugees to the influx of post-Cold War economic migrants into Western Europe and the conflict had the potential to widen to involve other parts of the former Yugoslavia and adjacent states and even to invite intervention by traditional allies. Moreover, there was growing public concern about the scale of human suffering.

Humanitarian disasters were also unfolding in Africa where some states were similarly imploding at the end of the Cold War. The withdrawal of superpower patronage proved the death-knell for some regimes which had only been able to cling to power by dint of foreign aid and arms. The government of Mohamed Siad Barre in Somalia was an early casualty, disintegrating under the twin pressures of its own economic mismanagement and armed opposition. Somalia dissolved into civil war, not between different ethnic groups, but between factions led by men who mobilised support from within the Somali clans. It was one of the first examples of what has become known as a failed state.

FAILED STATES

Failed states are those in which the government no longer has the capacity to provide opportunities or security for its citizens. The government cannot collect the taxes necessary to provide services, does not have the capacity to deliver services anyway, cannot control public disorder or exercise control over its borders. Authority is fatally undermined by armed challenges from sub-state groups and the population must fend for themselves as best they can. Poverty, violence, crime, hunger and disease are rife.

State failure was also a source of unease for Western governments. Again the humanitarian impulse was joined by prudential concern; failing states generated huge numbers of refugees, threatened the stability of neighbouring states, invited foreign exploitation and interference, and provided a haven for trans-national criminal groups like narcotics suppliers who needed bases outside the reach of law. Later in the 1990s, some would provide a refuge for terrorist organisations.

Despite the resolution of some long-standing conflicts on its soil, Africa remained host to some ongoing civil wars and was the locus of several new ones, most often in failing or failed states, that seemed to evidence a new type of conflict: civil war motivated by greed rather than grievance. A good number of African states have rich mineral resources and some of these are of the easily portable and disposable kind, such as gold and diamonds. Competition over access to resource-rich areas, and the funding secured by any period of control, fuelled conflict between governments and sub-state groups and between different sub-state groups. Interestingly, the first insurgent group to turn to resource exploitation in a serious way was Angola's UNITA (National Union for Total Independence of Angola) which was looking for alternative funding after the withdrawal of US and South African assistance.

The wars in these states were as brutal as those in the Balkans. Without any realistic and attractive policies to persuade populations to their cause or the means to provide more immediate incentives for cooperation, rebel groups recruited the young and morally unformed to engage in rival campaigns of terror. Civilians were killed, raped and tortured, and given no choice but to submit or flee.

The horrors of all of these post-Cold War civil conflicts were transmitted to a global audience. Demands for action were met with an increased willingness to intervene on the part of a more unified UN Security Council. Without ideological axes to grind and flush with the recent international successes in the Gulf War and peacekeeping missions, the major powers believed they should and could act to ameliorate the new wave of civil conflicts.

Traditionally military intervention had been seen as a breach of sovereignty, violating the cardinal principle of international order. The norm of non-intervention and its political corollary non-interference in the affairs of other states are enshrined in Article 2 (7) of the UN Charter and in the founding documents of a host of regional agreements from the Association of Southeast Asian Nations to the Organisation of African Unity. The UN Charter prohibits the organisation itself from intervening in matters which are 'essentially within the domestic jurisdiction of any state'.

HUMANITARIAN INTERVENTIONS

Although civil wars and failing states would be the primary source of concern after the Cold War and would provide much of the impetus for a new humanitarian activism, the first such intervention in a domestic crisis occurred in the wake of a conventional inter-state war. Encouraged by US broadcasts to rise up against Saddam Hussein after the defeat of his forces in the 1991 Gulf War, the Kurdish and Shi'ite populations of Iraq attempted a rebellion in the north and south of the country respectively. Concrete US support never materialised and Saddam's response was swift and predictable. His remaining security forces quelled the uprisings with such ferocity that in the north thousands of Kurds fled through the mountains towards Iran and Turkey.

The UN Security Council condemned Saddam's persecution as constituting a threat to international peace and security and demanded that he cease the oppression. Resolution 688 was a ground-breaking breach in the walls of sovereignty and although it was not backed up by provisions for enforcement, it called for member-states to assist the Kurds and provide relief. Operation Provide Comfort involved the deployment of US, British, French and Dutch military forces to northern Iraq where they created safe havens for the Kurdish refugees. Ground forces built refugee camps, distributed supplies, ensured order and protected the refugees from pursuing Iraqi forces. Air units provided air cover for the ground forces, dropped supplies into the more inaccessible areas, and enforced a no-fly zone above the 36th parallel that prevented Saddam's forces from attacking the refugees or defending their own positions from the air.

In the Iraq case, the use of military action without the consent of the host government had been opposed by many UN member-states because they saw it as setting a revolutionary and danger-ous precedent. The organisation itself had not therefore actively intervened. In the Somalia crisis that followed soon afterwards, the United Nations was not as constrained because there was no gov-ernment in that state to undertake the sovereign responsibilities of providing security and services to the population or to exercise the sovereign rights of requesting assistance or rejecting intervention. There was general international agreement that in such circumstances of state failure, concerns about the abrogation of sovereignty were irrelevant.

The Security Council authorised military intervention under Chapter VII, declaring that 'the magnitude of the human tragedy caused by the conflict in Somalia, further exacerbated by the obstacles being created to the distribution of humanitarian assistance, consti-tutes a threat to international peace and security'. Chapter VII of the UN Charter is the only mechanism that allows the Security Council to over-ride the general prohibition on the abrogation of sovereignty and contains provisions for enforcement. Even the Convention on the Prevention and Punishment of the Crime of Genocide, which came into force in 1951 and declares genocide to be a crime under international law which UN members undertake to prevent and pun-ish, contains no provisions for collective intervention. If the Security Council wishes to sanction intervention it must describe an internal crisis as a threat to international peace and security as it had in the Congo and Cyprus interventions during the Cold War.

The Somalia intervention had been preceded by one in the Balkans earlier in 1992, and in this case the Security Council had first gained the agreement of the Croatian President, Franjo Tudjman, for the establishment of UN-protected areas in the Serb enclaves of

Eastern Slavonia, Western Slavonia and Krajina. The mandate was soon extended to provide for the security and monitoring of access, some border control and the demilitarisation of the Prevlaka Peninsula. By June the United Nations Protection Force had also been drawn into the unfolding three-way drama in Bosnia-Herzegovina. Here its role was originally to facilitate the delivery of humanitarian relief, but while it had the formal consent of the Serbian government to undertake this mission it did not have its real commitment. It had no consent at all from the Bosnian Serbs.

In both Somalia and Bosnia the highest priority for the contributing member-states was force protection. As noted in the previous chapter, UNITAF's mission had been limited in time and scope by the lead country's unwillingness to risk a more active approach to the conflict. In Bosnia, the mission was also limited in its ambitions, the mandate being to ameliorate the situation rather than to restore the peace. UNPROFOR (United Nations Protection Force) was therefore instructed to remain impartial and to use force only in self-defence. But because even the delivery of humanitarian aid and the protection of civilians can alter the dynamics of a civil conflict, the impartial and unassertive UN contingents were soon under considerable political and military pressure. They were used by the warring parties as both hostages and shields.[1]

Serb forces attacked humanitarian relief convoys destined for beleaguered Bosnian Muslim enclaves, while the Bosnian forces attempted to pressure the United Nations into intervening more actively by making provocative attacks on Serb positions that undermined the security of aid deliveries to their own people. The Serbs attacked UN-protected safe havens because they knew the United Nations would not use force to protect those inside, while efforts to evacuate Muslim civilians were resisted by the Bosnian government because it did not want to cede territorial rights or lose bases for future operations.

Dispersed in small national contingents and prevented from taking the initiative by the requirements of impartiality and force protection, UNPROFOR was unable to bring any concerted pressure to bear on those committing human rights abuses. All of its actions were reactive and tactical and some of them inadvertently contributed to the escalation of the conflict. The worsening plight of civilians was publicised by the international media, leading to pressures for more action and an accretion of mandates, none of which UNPROFOR was better prepared to enforce. The objectives of the diplomatic effort to halt the fighting and the objectives of UNPROFOR were not synchronised and the UN efforts to contain and protect were at odds with the United States' preference for coercion and deterrence. In other words, the Bosnian intervention lacked a strategy.[2]

THE ABSENCE OF STRATEGY

Many interventions in civil conflicts, failing states, and humanitarian crises have been characterised by, and consequently suffered from, an absence of strategy. They have been conceived in haste, incremental, reactive, and influenced as much by the preferences of the interveners as by the exigencies of the situation on the ground. The requirements for legitimacy, consensus, impartiality, and commitment have also contributed to the establishment of vague mandates rather than the formulation of strategies for success.

The Somalia intervention was another notable example. The original two insertions of UN peacekeepers were made in response to the difficulties being faced by humanitarian agencies attempting to deliver food aid to the starving. The United Nations called for and sanctioned the third and much more ambitious deployment but as usual was not in a position to draw up a strategy or demand its implementation. The organisation lacks the institutional capacity and the expertise to plan for operations involving military force and participating states would, in any case, be unwilling to cede it the right to do so, particularly those that are playing a lead role.

The third force insertion was led by the United States but consisted of twenty-two national contingents. As was observed in an earlier chapter, the United States was acting reluctantly and was more focused on the end-date of its deployment than the end-state of the mission. Its task was simply to alleviate the suffering caused by the famine and then to hand back responsibility to another UN force, so ease of access and force protection over-rode strategic considerations.

Because Mogadishu had an airport and seaport that were militarily and logistically useful, US commanders rejected advice that they bypass Mogadishu and deliver aid straight to the starving outlying regions. Choosing Mogadishu as the base for operations made the capital more valuable to the rapacious Somali factions, increased their power and escalated competition and conflict between them. The United States' concern to minimise casualties and to exit quickly meant that they resisted undertaking activities they considered marginal to their 'core mission'. The Mogadishu fighters were not permanently disarmed, no attempts were made to rebuild the Somali police, and the northern part of the country, which might have proved a fruitful area for a reconstruction of national institutions, was ignored.

The replacement UNOSOM II mission suffered from its weaker force composition, the vagueness of its original mandate which was consequently interpreted in different ways by several of the bigger national contingents, and by the reactive accretion of mandates and the responses to these. It too lacked a strategy, but it is hard to see how it could have had a successful one, given the conditions it had been bequeathed by UNITAF and the faction leaders' determination to resist any serious challenge to their power.

The initial strategic error of failing to establish realistic and meaningful political goals for the Somalia interventions led to a series of operational errors and aggravated tensions between the United States and the United Nations, between the faction leaders, and between regions of Somalia. It failed to restore the peace, disarm the factions, bring any lasting reconciliation or build sustainable local institutions. Instead it fostered the conditions for lasting conflict by consolidating the clan-based factions.

The Clinton Administration did attempt to make constructive use of its Somalia experience, and in 1997 issued a directive on what it called 'Complex Contingency Operations', calling on foreign affairs agencies to approach similar situations in a more systematic and strategic manner and to undertake them in the context of a political–military implementation plan. But Clinton's Administration was under pressure from his Republican opponents and from all services of the armed forces, except the Marines, to minimise

United States involvement in risky peace operations, especially those involving the United Nations. During the 2000 election campaign, his rival George W. Bush promised that the US military would not be called on to do nation-building but would be allowed to focus on what it did best – fighting and winning. Once he was in office, the only US military institute devoted to instruction in peace operations was closed down.

The United States had in the meantime ignored the Rwandan genocide, contributed only coercive air power to NATO operations against Serb forces in Bosnia and the Serbian government in the dispute over Kosovo, and resisted direct involvement in UN operations in East Timor.

The former Portuguese colony of East Timor had been forcibly integrated into Indonesia in 1975 and much of its increasingly Catholic population remained unreconciled to Jakarta's rule and its local manifestation in the repressive activities of the Indonesian military. After the fall of long-time Indonesian president Suharto in 1998, his successor President Habibie responded to local and international demands for democratic reform and announced that a referendum would be held in East Timor on the issue of its continuing integration into Indonesia. In 1999 he negotiated agreements with the United Nations and Portugal and in June the UN established UNAMET (United Nations Mission in East Timor), to organise and conduct an August referendum. The referendum would only ask the East Timorese whether they wanted special autonomy within Indonesia but Habibie stated publicly that a vote against autonomy would be interpreted by Indonesia as a vote for independence.

The Indonesian military was opposed to the referendum and to the prospect of East Timorese secession. As self-appointed guardian of state unity it had worked long and hard at quelling resistance in the province and it was reluctant to see all its efforts nullified. And it was also concerned about the effect on other areas of discontent in Indonesia, especially the provinces of Aceh and West Papua which also had long histories of resistance against the central government based on the particularity of their circumstances. The military's response was to try to influence the outcome of the referendum through a campaign of persuasion and intimidation. Anxious not to further alienate its domestic and international critics it did not undertake this campaign itself but sponsored locally recruited militia.

These militia took their responsibilities very seriously but they did not deter 78.5 per cent of the eligible East Timorese population from voting against autonomy. President Habibie announced that he would accept the outcome and when the militia went on a rampage, torching whole towns, looting and killing, he ordered the Indonesian armed forces to restore order. When the declaration of martial law failed to halt the violence, the Indonesian government agreed to accept international assistance in restoring law and order and implementing results of the referendum. The UN Security Council authorised a Chapter VII deployment which Australia, as a neighbour capable and experienced in peacekeeping, was persuaded by the United States to lead. Under pressure from the United States, the international community and Australia, and after assurances from Australia that it had no ambitions to dismember Indonesia, the Indonesian armed forces agreed to cooperate with the incoming multinational force and INTERFET (International Force for East Timor) began deploying on 20 September 1999. Four days later Indonesia lifted martial law and withdrew its forces. Most of the militia soon followed.

INTERFET's success in East Timor owed something to its clear mandate, its lead state's understanding of local political dynamics and security challenges and Indonesian sensitivities, centralised and uncontested command-and-control arrangements, and a sound strategy that involved laying the groundwork for transition to independence. But the principal reason for the mission's success was that it had the active consent of the vast majority of the East Timorese population, the official consent of the Indonesian government and the grudging consent of the Indonesian armed forces. There was only one exchange of fire between the Indonesian Army and UN forces in an area where border demarcation was unclear and only a handful of skirmishes with militia remnants were reported.

PEACE SUPPORT OPERATIONS

The problem of consent or legitimacy was addressed directly by the British Army when it began to formulate a doctrine that would be

appropriate to military intervention in humanitarian crises. Originally the British distinguished between interventions agreed to by
the warring parties and those where consent was not given or was
later withdrawn, and concluded that peacekeeping should not be
attempted if it was going to cross what had become known as 'the
Mogadishu line'. By the late 1990s it was evident that this approach
would cripple their ability to respond usefully to humanitarian crises
and the doctrine was carefully revised to allow for deployment into
contested environments. Local consent was no longer seen as a fundamental requirement but where it did not exist, creating and then
maintaining it was to be a key task for intervening forces. In the
meantime, they would need to be combat-capable and ready and
willing to enforce the peace, not so much to produce military results
as to ensure credibility and improve their ability to deter attacks on
their own positions, protect civilians and coerce the combatants into
modifying their behaviour.

Peace Support Operations, or PSO as they are termed in the United
Kingdom, are not designed to achieve a military victory but rather to
create the conditions in which civilian agencies and the indigenous
population and authorities can build a self-sustaining peace. They are
impartial at the strategic level because there is no designated enemy.
Instead, actions are taken in support of or against any party for its
degree of compliance with the operation's mandate and international
law. A menu of options is available so that no matter what the nature
of the challenge, an appropriate response can be made, and intervening forces are ordered to prepare for whatever mission changes might
be necessary to achieve the objective. PSOs are planned strategically,
with the military effort tailored to the political objective, but retain a
flexibility that recognises the inherent dynamism and unpredictability of conflict.

The British approach contrasted with that of the United States in
several significant ways. The most obvious were its willingness to send
ground forces into contested and risky environments and its commitment to staying the course rather than insisting on pre-planned
exit strategies. But another key difference was the British decision
to make PSOs part of core military business. This had three important outcomes. It meant that the British government had a military
willing and able to conduct PSOs, that peace support doctrine was

given almost as much thought and attention as regular warfighting doctrine, and that the lessons of each were incorporated into the other. This allowed British forces to plan their 2003 deployment to Iraq with the long view in mind and to switch easily between combat operations and peace support.

The United Kingdom's PSO doctrine has shaped its own missions and influenced practice for NATO and the United Nations. British forces targeted rebels in support of UNAMSIL in Sierra Leone and UNOMOC personnel began seeking out those responsible for human rights abuses in the eastern Democratic Republic of Congo in 2005. But this willingness to be assertive was dependent on the attitudes of contributing states and their armed forces and was still far from being the norm in the international community. Although UN officials, many human rights advocates, and some politicians and scholars believed that it was in the interests of all states that the United Nations act forcefully to protect civilian populations, many governments remained concerned about the implications of abandoning the long-held principle of impartiality and the practice of force protection. Few states are willing to put their armed forces in harm's way. While the UN member-states might claim that humanitarian crises pose threats to international peace and security, most believe that the threat to their own national interests in these situations is low. It is therefore hard for them to justify military casualties to their domestic constituents or to their armed forces.

Any change to the international laws and norms of humanitarian intervention would force governments and their armed forces and populations to fundamentally reassess notions of security and its attendant responsibilities. Some states would feel less secure if they had to worry about active intervention in their domestic crises while others would have to re-evaluate a whole range of assumptions about sovereignty, state primacy in international relations, the national interest, and the use of force.

ENFORCEMENT AND IMPARTIALITY

Assertive peace enforcement can also be problematic. While the British approach to punishing infractions is supposed to be even-handed and impartial, there remains a danger that the actions of intervening forces may deliberately or inadvertently favour one or other side in a conflict. Deliberate partiality contradicts the central tenets of international law, namely the rights of peoples to determine their own destinies and the responsibility of states to refrain from interfering to their own advantage in the domestic affairs of other states. Impartiality has been a cornerstone of peacekeeping practice ever since the United Nations' Congo experience, when both super-powers attempted to use the organisation's intervention to further their own interests.

Partiality might produce an outcome desirable to the interven-ers, but if it is exercised on the part of the stronger, it may involve support for the group committing the most widespread or egregious human rights abuses and if used to support the weaker may pro-voke the stronger to escalate the fighting, prolong the conflict and lead to unsustainable solutions. It is also dangerous for peacekeep-ers themselves to be seen to be taking sides as the United States found in Somalia. In doing so, the US forces effectively become combatants in the conflict, to be treated as legitimate and necessary targets.

Some of these problems were in evidence in the humanitarian interventions in the West African civil wars of the 1990s. The difficul-ties faced by the United Nations in mobilising international support for intervention in these crises persuaded the Economic Community of West African States to organise a regional response. ECOWAS mediated a cease-fire between weakened government forces and Charles Taylor's National Patriotic Front and dispatched a moni-toring group entitled ECOMOG (ECOWAS Monitoring Group) to Liberia. Some 3000 West African troops were deployed in 1990, most of them from the biggest regional state, Nigeria, and nego-tiations produced a new interim government by the end of 1991. But the cease-fire broke down in August 1992 and Taylor's forces attacked the capital, Monrovia, and the ECOMOG forces stationed there. ECOMOG returned fire, pursued them, and recaptured some of the territory over which Taylor had established control. Not all the West African states believed this was a good idea, complaining that Nigeria was partisan and using its dominant position to further its own ambitions for regional leadership. Some of them consequently provided military assistance to Taylor.

These differences meant that although ECOMOG was supposed to answer to an ECOWAS Defence Council and the force commander had nominal operational control, the swelling number of contingents took their orders from the commands in their home countries for much of the nine years of deployment.

Funding for the mission was inadequate, many of the contingents lacked proper equipment, and troops went unpaid for long periods. Some battened on the population and their venality and brutality cost the force important local legitimacy. Although additional funding, a new commander, and the rotation out of the most ill-disciplined improved the situation in Liberia, the spectre of corruption would return to undermine ECOMOG's subsequent efforts in neighbouring Sierra Leone. That country's unpoliced diamond diggings proved an irresistible temptation that muted the enthusiasm of some in the force for peace enforcement and for efforts to reach a political settlement.

Despite the problems in Liberia and Sierra Leone, the United Nations' continuing difficulties in securing international support for African intervention and a recognition that ECOMOG's interventions had, on balance, been useful, meant that regional organisations continued to play a prominent role in peacekeeping and peace enforcement on the continent. ECOMOG deployed to Guinea-Bissau in 1999 and the African Union dispatched about 7000 peacekeepers to the southern Darfur province of Sudan to monitor the 2004 cease-fire between the government and rebels. In the latter case the peacekeepers' ability to enforce the peace and protect civilians was seriously hampered by a lack of funding, equipment, and logistical support. They barely had enough ammunition to protect themselves and without vehicles or fuel could not often venture out of camp.

Some regional organisations remain reluctant however, to undermine their own rules of non-intervention in each other's affairs. Most members of the Association of South East Asian Nations continue to believe in the importance of this rule because they are aware of the potential for mutual meddling in the region. Only reluctantly did they agree to contribute to, and confer additional legitimacy to, the United Nations' intervention in East Timor in 1999 and it is difficult to envisage them organising and leading a regional humanitarian intervention.

NATO has no such compunction and since intervening in Bosnia and Kosovo has taken responsibility for peacekeeping in Afghanistan. Its right to act in Afghanistan, which can hardly be described as regional, has thus far not been questioned but the tacit consent of the Afghan population will have to be carefully maintained. This may prove difficult if troops are used to secure outcomes deemed important to some of the lead states but which threaten the political power or economic wellbeing of sections of the community. A potentially explosive example is the eradication of the opium poppy trade, on which an increasing number of impoverished Afghan farmers have come to rely.

HUMANITARIAN INTERVENTION IN 21ST-CENTURY CIVIL WARS

The incidence of civil wars began to decline in the mid-1990s. The Balkans' conflicts had been frozen by peacekeeping and economic reconstruction efforts and a number of those in Africa disrupted by intervention and mediation and the restoration of democracy. Some persisted, including those in Somalia, Chad and Sudan, and a new, bloody and dynamic one erupted in the Democratic Republic of the Congo as challenges to the weakened centre and local rivalries were complicated by the manoeuvrings of self-exiled Hutu militia from neighbouring Rwanda and the Rwandan government, and by the interference of armed forces from other African states.

Civil wars remain difficult for outside parties to resolve because they have complex causes and dynamics and the interests of the warring parties are often irreconcilable. They are unlikely to cooperate with mediators until they have reached a stalemate that they cannot afford to prolong. If they still think they can bear the costs and win, they are likely to resist efforts to end conflict. Even in these instances it will not be easy to persuade the combatants to disarm because doing so will deprive them of leverage and could confer an advantage on a less scrupulous adversary. The alternative to war must also offer promise. Proposed political arrangements will have to accommodate the interests of all parties and formulating such arrangements is bound to be problematic when the issues of power distribution and the nature of the state were the causes of war in the first place. It may be difficult to locate impartial and acceptable local advisers and planners because the non-partisan have either fled or been killed. And finally, diaspora populations and their host governments may act as spoilers in the process of negotiation. Refugee camps in neighbouring countries sometimes provide safe breeding grounds for determined resistance, as they have in Pakistan, the Middle East and the Congo, while exiles and economic migrants sometimes resist accommodation and lobby their new governments to insist on their preferred solutions.

The only alternatives to a negotiated agreement on new political arrangements are partition or a long-term peacekeeping presence. Partition is not a solution that most states would endorse; the states which are directly involved want to maintain their territorial integrity and their ability to protect the rights of their population, and the international community is unlikely to endorse partition because the norm of territorial dismemberment is not one that it wishes to see entrenched. Besides, partition may result in the internationalisation and escalation of community tensions, as it has to an alarming degree in South Asia. Peacekeeping is a preferred option despite the fact that it is very costly and requires a long-term commitment from the international community. But it is far from ideal, keeping tensions in a state of suspended animation, as the Cyprus, Bosnia, and Kosovo experiences have demonstrated. It has to be accompanied by concerted efforts to rebuild confidence and trust between the parties and to provide the material improvement in economic circumstances that is necessary to undermine identification with sectarian or nationalist goals.

Although civil wars were at least temporarily on the wane by the early twenty-first century the incidence of state failure looked set to increase. According to Britain's Department for International Development, some forty-six states were in danger of imploding at the turn of the century with the ten most at risk being the Ivory Coast, the Democratic Republic of the Congo, Sudan, Iraq, Somalia, Sierra Leone, Chad, Yemen, Liberia, and Haiti.

Rebuilding failed states is doubly demanding. Restoring security through military intervention, disarmament and the creation of capable and uncompromised indigenous instruments of law and order is challenging enough but it is also insufficient for durable nation-building. Training and assistance have to be provided for the re-establishment of other state institutions and services, civil society has to be strengthened, and strategies for economic recovery have to be formulated and implemented. The last of these requirements is fundamental but very problematic. States are unlikely to remain stable for long without a functioning economy, as Haiti's recent history demonstrates, but many failing states have very limited opportunities for growth.

At the beginning of the twenty-first century the United Nations attempted to strengthen its capacity to intervene in humanitarian crises in a timely, efficient and sustainable manner but several fundamental problems remained. It remained difficult for the organisation to intervene at all because of the international legal restrictions. Despite calls for a shift in emphasis from the rights of states to the responsibilities of states, concerns relating to the abrogation of sovereignty were still likely to slow, or even render impossible, international action. States want to ensure that interventions are legitimate expressions of humanitarian concern and not partisan attempts to shape domestic crises to the advantage of any particular state or group of states. The need for consensus on the Security Council is consequently difficult to reach in the requisite timeframe, complicating attempts to draw up all but the most broadly defined and practically circumscribed of mandates. Although the UN Secretary-General, Kofi Annan, has argued for the formulation of more concrete mandates, mission goals may have to be left vague and ambiguous to encourage participation by member-states who might feel uncomfortable with particular roles or specific objectives. Establishing a norm of robust intervention may also prove difficult, given state concerns about the potential for casualties and the erosion of the impartiality principle. Many of them will remain reluctant to make anything other than a token contribution to humanitarian interventions because these are low on their list of military priorities, or to place their forces under foreign command and control.

It would be a pity if these problems were to cripple the United Nations' ability to intervene in humanitarian crises. The organisation's international character means that when it does act, it does so with altruistic and impartial intent, and this endows most of its actions with a legitimacy that individual states or groups of states have to actively manufacture. And other organisations are likely to pick and choose their interventions according to their interests and resources, leaving a great many of the world's most intractable conflicts unresolved and many communities suffering.

11 War in the twenty-first century
The end of strategy?

THE THREAT AND USE of force in the twenty-first century is likely to be characterised by some features that are enduring and by others that are unique to this particular stage of world history. Force will continue to be wielded by some states to further their political objectives, and for many it will constitute an important tool in their efforts to shape the strategic environment, deter armed attack, and change adversary behaviour.

As a component of grand strategy, the threat and use of force has always been viewed as an important shaping mechanism. States have used force to induce others to submit to their rule, to cooperate, and to abstain from particular actions or modes of behaviour. They have used it to extend their influence and access to resources and labour, to impose their preferred ideologies or models of governance, to deter rivals, and to punish infractions of international law or local agreements. Military force is also used to gain respect, instil caution, and ensure that diplomatic pressure is credible.

The defence strategies of states will continue to incorporate elements of deterrence and response as they seek to dissuade real or potential military adversaries from contemplating aggression, and try to retain the ability to prevail should deterrence fail. Plainly nuclear deterrence still has an important role to play at the level of inter-state competition. Evidence for this exists in the relative stability of the relationship between India and Pakistan since both became nuclear-capable, and in the clandestine efforts of other states such as Iran and North Korea to acquire nuclear weapons as a means of generating general deterrence against Israel and the United States for Iran, and the United States, Japan and South Korea for North Korea. Conventional deterrence is likely to continue to contribute to caution among nation-states.

Military strategies in times of war will continue to be informed by the fundamental and time-tested operational principles of armed combat that have endured since the times of Sun Tzu and Thucydides. Regardless of how state and non-state actors decide to approach their need for security in the twenty-first century, their strategists must clearly understand what it is they wish to achieve. They must know what they mean by 'winning', and their desired end-state must be complemented by its associated ways and means.

Defence force commanders will continue to need good intelligence, an excellent understanding of the physical environment in which they operate, an awareness of their adversary's likely responses, and an informed appreciation of both the enemy's and their own centres of gravity. When formulating their plans they will still need to appreciate the advantages conferred by surprise, speed and mass, noting that the characteristics of the latter have changed in recent decades. They must appreciate the importance of striking the right balance between manoeuvre and the application of force, and of supporting their operations with sound logistical procedures. They will have to prepare, as did their forebears, for longer than expected campaigns, for changes of mission, and for asymmetric responses. And above all else, they must have a nuanced appreciation of the strategic effects generated by the dynamics of war.

Commanders from developed states will have at their disposal a range of platforms and technologies that facilitate manoeuvre and the application of force. Air and space platforms have evolved to provide an unprecedented degree of visibility, mobility, speed and surprise, while other technological advances have facilitated better and more comprehensive surveillance, improved command and control, the precise delivery of munitions, and greater force protection. These kinds of capabilities confer on their owners a great advantage when fighting conventional wars against the militaries of less advanced states, though it is necessary to note that technology is never sufficient in itself.

As both the most technologically advanced state and one of the most reluctant to engage in long and casualty-intensive wars, the United States has been at the forefront of doctrinal development. US military theorists have formulated strategic concepts that exploit new capabilities and avoid the need for costly attrition by concentrating sustained and massive force on an adversary's centres of gravity, and by pursuing strategic effects through knowledge superiority, a high operational tempo, and precision targeting. Many in the US armed forces and some of their colleagues abroad believe that strategic paralysis and effects-based operations will provide the intellectual template for future operations.

But neither the international environment nor battlefield conditions will remain unaltered in the twenty-first century, for as Colin Gray observed, 'just when we found the answer, they changed the question'.[1] Several critical shifts have been overlooked by most strategic theorists and analysts, partly because they, like everyone else, have been transfixed by another and more spectacular transformation in the use of force.

THE WAR ON TERROR

The September 11 terrorist attacks on New York and Washington in 2001 seemed to confirm the fears of analysts who had pointed to the weaknesses of traditional nuclear deterrence and of the proposed ballistic missile defence system. Small non-state groups cannot be dissuaded or prevented from acting against the United States, or anywhere else for that matter, by postures or systems that are unable to detect their whereabouts or halt low-technology attacks. Traditional deterrence – nuclear weapons or powerful conventional forces – are unusable against small, fleeting targets. Furthermore, as noted previously in relation to mutual assured destruction, if the concept of deterrence is to work, the protagonists must have a common definition of rationality. And by definition, an individual who welcomes death as a means to martyrdom is undeterrable.

September 11 represented the high noon of deterrence, at least as it had been applied for over half a century. Despite owning the most powerful army, navy, air force, marines, and space force in the history of human existence, the United States was unable either to deter or prevent some twenty individuals from making unopposed attacks on its national capital and its most iconic city in broad daylight.

The terrorist attacks on the United States also suggested that its threat perceptions had been misplaced. The United States was attacked not by a rival power but by a loose trans-national grouping of extremists who drew their inspiration from Osama bin Laden, a wealthy Saudi Arabian hiding in the failed state of Afghanistan. Analysts and officials had been properly concerned that the United States' overwhelming conventional military preponderance would force others to resort to asymmetric warfare, but they had been excessively focused on the threats posed by the spread of ballistic missile technology and nuclear, biological and chemical material, and the potential for cyber attacks on military and civilian command, control, and communications systems. Terrorists had already attacked US forces and facilities overseas and at a couple of sites in the United States, but the damage, casualty levels and psychological effect had not seemed to the new Bush Administration in early 2001 to warrant major concern.

The Administration's response to September 11 was to declare a major transformation in the global strategic environment and a correspondingly radical shift in US grand strategy. In what was called the post-9/11 world, the United States would conduct a war on terror, in which it reserved the right to act as it saw fit to eradicate the threat of terrorism. Other states had only one choice: they could cooperate or they would be considered adversaries. It seemed to many that a new era had arrived in which terrorism posed the most serious threat to international stability and the security of states, and in which the United States' new assertiveness would determine the incidence and dictate the character of war. But both of these assumptions were questionable.

Sporadic international terrorist attacks can cause a temporary disruption of economies and services, but for Western governments the primary concern is that terrorism increases the insecurity of civilians, whose protection is a state's most important function. Even attacks against hazardous sites, such as nuclear power stations, are feared more for their probable psychological impact on the population than for the physical damage they might cause. Governments that are unable to secure their populations from terrorism may be vulnerable to popular pressure for their replacement.

But terrorism is likely to lead to stronger identification with the state and governments will be allowed a greater ability to punish domestic sympathisers and to curb their activities. They will only be seriously troubled by terrorism when the tactic is used routinely as an expression of repressed popular will and where it is a symptom of a much deeper political problem. Only then will it pose a threat to the integrity or sovereignty of developed states. The use of terror can undermine weak states, as has already been the case in parts of Africa, but in such instances state failure is already in train.

COUNTER-TERRORISM AND THE UTILITY OF FORCE

There is a limit to the utility of international force in dealing with terrorism. Only in Afghanistan in 2001 and 2002 was it possible to over-ride national sovereignty and intervene to seek and destroy a terrorist group. Afghanistan's Taliban regime was not recognised by much of the international community as either legitimate or able to exercise real sovereignty. The Taliban presided over what was essentially a failed state, were unpopular with much of the population because of their draconian rule, and were being contested militarily over wide sections of the country. In those circumstances intervention was perceived as legitimate and was relatively easy to achieve.

But even in that permissive political environment it proved difficult to locate and destroy terrorist targets. Terrorists operate in small groups, are indistinguishable from the rest of the population, and are extremely mobile. In Afghanistan, those that did not stand and fight alongside the Taliban were able to slip away and hide among their sympathisers in the inaccessible regions on both sides of the Afghan–Pakistan border. Attempts to target suspected hideouts from the air were not notably successful. Aerial surveillance cannot accurately distinguish between terrorists and innocents and human intelligence is often problematic, either because it is dated or because sources are unreliable.

A good number of terrorists have been captured since 2001, primarily because of careful intelligence gathering and cooperation between domestic and international civilian agencies. Arrests have usually been made by the police rather than the military because it is they who have the best intelligence and are trained to act with care in domestic operations. It is the police and intelligence agencies who have tracked down terrorists in Spain, the United Kingdom, Indonesia and Pakistan.

Few states would be willing to allow foreign military forces to intervene in their countries in pursuit of terrorists. Most have the capability to take primary responsibility for such tasks themselves and even if they did not would resist and protest any such direct abrogation of their sovereignty. Governments allowing foreign forces to operate in their territory on such politically sensitive missions risk incurring the displeasure of their populations, as Pakistan found.

In the days when terrorists used hostage-taking as their main political weapon, it was much easier to use military force, even across international boundaries. There was undisputable physical evidence of terrorist activity, the perpetrators were highly visible and largely static targets, and governments had the legal right to rescue their own nationals. Israeli Defence Force commandos were therefore able to storm Uganda's Entebbe airport in a hostage-rescue mission in 1976, and Indonesian special forces did the same at Bangkok airport in 1981.

Terrorists conducting hit-and-run or suicide-bombing operations are not as visible or static, so pre-emption, protection, or prevention have become the preferred ways of halting their attacks. Pre-emption is difficult because of the opaque nature of terrorist organisations and their plans. Protection of likely targets and critical vulnerabilities is a more realistic option and many concerned governments have moved to buttress important sites and harden and protect public transport systems. But because it is impossible to completely deny terrorists access to populations that they wish to attack, prevention has become a major feature of the global campaign against their activities.

Prevention has taken many forms. Governments have moved to restrict extremist groups' access to funding, introduced measures to tighten traveller access and improve their ability to identify potential terrorists, and clamped down on the dissemination of material that encourages or enables terrorist attacks. They have strengthened their powers of surveillance, arrest and detention, as much to deter potential terrorists as to deal with those who are already suspected.

Counter-terrorism has also become enmeshed in the grand strategies of some governments, most notably that of the United States, where the George W. Bush Administration developed a multi-faceted global campaign of prevention. The first strand consisted of warning states of the consequences of harbouring terrorist groups, and of acting against those that did not comply. In Afghanistan the consequence was war, but against stronger states it involved diplomatic pressure or the threat of economic sanctions. The second strand acknowledged anti-US sentiment in much of the Muslim world as a factor in terrorist recruitment, and resulted in a campaign of public diplomacy to improve perceptions and change attitudes. A third strand, arrived at somewhat reluctantly, involved nudging Israel towards some kind of accommodation with its Palestinian population, again in an effort to reduce Muslim suspicion and antipathy. A fourth strand promoted international cooperation and provided counter-terrorism assistance to foreign governments, and a fifth involved a complicated strategy for the democratisation of the Middle East, to be achieved by force and by diplomatic and economic pressure.

Some of these measures were successful. Al-Qa'ida was deprived of a base in Afghanistan, the Israeli government was persuaded to offer some concessions to the Palestinians, and many states cooperated in restricting the activities of extremist groups. Public diplomacy was less successful because the US message appeared to many Muslims to be contradicted by its deeds. The US attack on Iraq, the extra-legal detention of suspected terrorists, prisoner abuse, and pressure on Iran, Syria and the Palestinians, instead further undermined the United States' legitimacy in the Muslim street and provided extremists and terrorist groups with a ready supply of recruits.

Most states and peoples were originally sympathetic towards the United States' desire to eradicate al-Qa'ida and many supported the invasion of Afghanistan. Governments throughout Asia, the Middle East and Europe were willing to cooperate in monitoring and restricting the activities of suspicious groups and arresting and detaining suspected terrorists. As it happened, it suited many of them to do so. Some were thereby able to demonstrate their strategic relevance to the United States, to clamp down on domestic political opposition, or to renew otherwise controversial military relationships. But US actions subsequent to the attack on Afghanistan troubled many governments and not just those in the Muslim world. Most, including Russia, China, Germany and France, opposed the invasion of Iraq because they were not convinced of the imminence of threat and were concerned about the dangerous precedent it would set for the unilateral abrogation of sovereignty. UN officials and many of the organisation's member-states were concerned about the erosion of international norms regarding the use of force and the Bush Administration's evident disdain for international institutions and laws, while Middle Eastern regimes were concerned by the United States' new-found commitment to the democratisation of their region.

Even the strongest power will not be able to shape the strategic environment in its own image if that image is not attractive to other states or peoples. The strategic environment is not one state's enclosure but a global commons, and other states and communities will have their own interests in its character and direction and in turning it to their advantage. All states will find their grand strategies affected by those of others and by the consequent shifts in the balance and nature of power.

STRATEGIC TRENDS

At the beginning of the twenty-first century, no state had the ability to challenge the United States militarily but some were already manoeuvring to assert their own influence, using soft power. China became a keen proponent of the United Nations and moved to strengthen ties with Russia and the Central and Southeast Asian states. Russia took a similar stance but also began to involve itself actively in Middle

Eastern security issues and to use energy diplomacy as a means of reasserting its influence in Eastern Europe.

Colin Gray's argument that major war is enjoying an off-season because of US dominance attributes too much weight to this phenomenon. The reasons for the decline in the incidence of inter-state wars are more complex than that, with a whole range of mitigating factors having coincided in the late twentieth century. These include the integration of the states in one of the world's most historically war-prone regions, Europe; the spread of democracy and free trade; the rising costs and declining utility of force; the development of nuclear weaponry; and the formulation and widespread acceptance of ameliorating laws and norms. By the year 2000 most governments believed that they could gain more by remaining at peace than by resorting to war.

For a brief period between the end of the Cold War and the invasion of Iraq in 2003, it appeared to some Western analysts that patterns in the use of force were being transformed by changes in the nature of the state. Philip Bobbitt's research into the evolution of the state system led him to conclude that nation-states – as defined by geographic boundaries, shared community values and interests, and state responsibility for citizens' welfare – were being transformed into market-states where the primary role of government is instead to 'maximise the [economic] opportunities for all members of society'.[2] Bobbitt believed that this process was already in train, was inexorable and would transform the global security environment. Like nation-states before them market-states would take different forms: they might be mercantile like Japan, managerial like Germany, or market-mitigating like the United States. Each model would have different attitudes to the utility of force, with the mercantile being defensive and alliance-reliant, the managerial being cooperative and inclined towards peacemaking, and the market-mitigating selectively interventionist but focused on threats to its own interests.

Bobbitt reached these conclusions before 9/11, after which he revised his thesis somewhat to allow for the likelihood of 'epochal war' with what he described as the new virtual-state of al-Qa'ida. This view conformed with the US tendency to look for big threats.

Robert Cooper by contrast divided the world into pre-modern, modern and post-modern states. Most Western European states were now post-modern, secure from conventional attack and cooperative in their relations, most non-Western powers such as India, China and Russia were modern and still preoccupied with traditional inter-state threats and national interests, and much of the rest of the world remained pre-modern, simply struggling to exist. For Cooper, the central problem of world order was the disorder emanating from the pre-modern world. This very European view was informed by Europe's proximity and vulnerability to the problems of the pre-modern world and by its welfarist culture. Cooper's analysis was more prescriptive than Bobbitt's and argued for a new form of imperialism to restore order in the pre-modern world. His commentary was written before the onset of the war on terror and the war in Iraq, but it seems likely that he would view both of these as evidence of a struggle between the pre-modern and the modern world to which he saw the United States as still belonging.[3]

These ruminations on the changing nature of the state system overlooked the fact that the forces of globalisation had already fuelled a rise of nationalism in most parts of the world, including the developed West. Many working people in the United States, Western Europe and Australia felt vulnerable as productive facilities moved offshore to lower labour-cost countries and cheap imports flowed in. They feared the arrival of refugees and economic migrants, who are one of the physical embodiments of globalisation, and they worried about the dilution of their cultures through immigration. Criticism of demands for government action was often dismissed as élitist and only increased community defensiveness and nationalist sentiment. Governments responded to majority concerns and some were compelled to slow or reverse their plans for greater economic liberalisation and to assuage community apprehensions by appearing to clamp down on immigration.

In other parts of the world there was dissatisfaction with the uneven spoils of globalisation and the inequity of free trade, and concern about the erosion of local cultures by encroaching Western, and particularly US, influence. In some states this has resulted in the election of governments committed to developing robustly indigenous models of governance or regional communities of interest; in others, governments that have been unable to deliver prosperity continue to mobilise popular support through appeals to ethnic or religious solidarity. China and Japan have engaged in nationalist posturing in an effort to undermine each other's international and regional influence. The Iranian and Venezuelan governments have used US pressure to mobilise nationalist sentiment.

As history has demonstrated, the rise of nationalism is a dangerous phenomenon, nationalism being exclusive and often antagonistic. Nationalism raises the stakes when issues are in dispute, making accommodation more problematic and increasing the pressure for military action or the determination to resist. Its assertion in the uncertain world of the twenty-first century only underlines the continued need for international regulations on the use of force. The detractors of international law often overlook its prudential impetus and its strategic utility. For example, international law prohibiting attacks on merchant shipping in peacetime had its genesis in the objections of trading countries like the Dutch Republic and the United States to the attacks and blockades that were hindering their economic growth in the seventeenth and eighteenth centuries.[4] Although naval powers like Great Britain and France resisted the notion of restraint on naval operations in wartime, a growing appreciation of the economic benefits of free trade (and the strategic calculations of land powers like Prussia) resulted in agreement to allow unimpeded maritime traffic in times of peace. This agreement has had two incalculable strategic benefits. The unfettered movement of trade allows states to access food and resources peaceably, greatly reducing the motives for territorial acquisition, and the security of merchant shipping has removed a common cause of tension and warfare.

Another argument for adherence to laws restricting the use of force is that nationalism makes war itself a more problematic endeavour. It was the intensity of nationalist sentiment that doomed the US intervention in Vietnam and the Soviet invasion of Afghanistan and made the Balkans wars of the 1990s so brutal, persistent and difficult to mediate. It was also a complicating and complex factor in the Iraq War, with contending religious nationalisms deepening divisions between the country's Arab communities, Sunni nationalism driving the insurgency, and Kurdish nationalism obstructing the establishment of a unified state.

The Iraq experience should have driven home the fact that wars can no longer be conceived of as combats between military forces or even between regimes. They will have to be fought among the people, virtually in the courts of public and international opinion, and physically in most conflict situations other than engagements at sea.[5] Unless brief military actions are sufficient to deliver the desired political effect – and they rarely are – armed forces may well find themselves caught up in a long and costly fight against resistant populations or at least against adversary forces using those populations for camouflage and support. And this does not just apply, as many thought, only to civil wars. Guerilla responses to inter-state attacks can take place during or after a military intervention and completely negate any conventional advantage.

The revival of guerilla war poses serious challenges for states wishing to use their armed forces against others. It is not just a simple matter of reconfiguring those forces to fight in environments populated by civilians, improving intelligence and surveillance capabilities, acquiring superior weapons, or developing better ways to protect personnel from attack. The problem is that the real target of counter-insurgency operations must be the civilian population from which the guerillas derive their strength.

The expectation that civilians should be protected from the depredations of war because they have special rights as non-combatants has evolved slowly over time and has become enshrined in international law. But there is an important prudential reason for treating civilian populations well that was recognised long before the establishment of the nation-state system. The assent of the bulk of the population is necessary for the imposition or introduction of any major political changes unless states are willing to engage in long-term repression. Conversely, a protagonist who enjoys popular legitimacy is very difficult to defeat. Even overwhelming conventional force is unlikely to deliver peace and security if its proprietor lacks legitimacy.

Although the Western powers, including the United States, can point to earlier experiences of successful 'small wars', the Vietnam

War showed that resistance movements are not as readily suppressed or populations as easily cowed as they once were. Force is unlikely to produce a rapid or lasting result, and military pacification is unlikely to be either acceptable or useful. Governments may be able to contain or wear down their armed domestic adversaries but outside forces typically lack the patience, the right, or the resources to implement the long-term strategy of pressure, inducement and amelioration that is necessary for the creation of a durable peace.

The past may be a prologue but it cannot be relied upon to predict the future. War cannot be separated from its political, economic and social contexts and these will continue to evolve in a non-linear fashion at the national and international levels. But the experiences of warfare in the late twentieth and early twenty-first centuries offer several suggestions for future strategists. Planning for the threat or use of force will continue to be affected by a range of 'traditional' military and political considerations but will also have to rest on the less easily constructed foundations of credibility, commitment, and legitimacy. It no longer makes strategic sense to conceive of operations as either conventional or non-conventional or to plan in discrete and differentiated packages. Conflict might well place simultaneous and potentially contradictory demands on armed forces, and actions taken to prevail in one sphere might undermine efforts in another. Tactical and operational effects may have unwelcome strategic effects, and strategic effects themselves are unpredictable and uncertain. And finally, the threat or use of force can no longer be planned or implemented without a view to the long-term consequences or without accompanying efforts to deliver material improvement and political reassurance. Strategies for a better peace will have to rest as much on negotiated notions of justice as on order.

Notes

INTRODUCTION

1 Martin van Creveld, 'The End of Strategy', in Hugh Smith (ed.), *The Strategists* (Canberra: Australian Defence Studies Centre, 2001).

2 'War and Peace in the 21st Century', in *Human Security Report 2005* (Vancouver: The University of British Columbia, 2005), pp. 1–2.

3 Rupert Smith, *The Utility of Force* (London: Allen Lane, 2005), esp. pp. 371–404.

1 HOW TO WIN

1 Carl von Clausewitz, *On War* (Harmondsworth: Penguin Books, 1982), p. 389.

2 STOVE-PIPED STRATEGY

1 Thucydides, *The Peloponnesian War* (Harmondsworth: Penguin Books, 1975).

2 B. H. Liddell Hart, *Strategy* (New York: Frederick A. Praeger, 1954), esp. chapter 10.

3 Arrian, *Annabasis Alexandri*, Vol. 1 (Cambridge: Harvard University Press, 1989), pp. 57–67; Plutarch, *The Age of Alexander* (Harmondsworth: Penguin Books, 1977), pp. 268–9.

4 Antoine-Henri de Jomini, *The Art of War* (London: Greenhill Books, 1996).

5 Giulio Douhet, *The Command of the Air* (Washington DC: Office of Air Force History, 1983).

6 Bernard Brodie, *Strategy in the Missile Age* (Princeton: Princeton University Press, 1991), p. 73.

7 See Desmond Ball, 'Can Nuclear War be Controlled?', in *Adelphi Papers*, No. 169 (London: International Institute for Strategic Studies, 1981); and Martin van Creveld, *The Transformation of War* (New York: The Free Press, 1991), pp. 1–32.

8 Sun Tzu, *The Art of War* (Oxford: The Clarendon Press, 1963).

9 Clausewitz, *On War*.

10 Niccolo Machiavelli, *The Prince* (New York: Bantam Classic, 2003).

11 Machiavelli, *The Prince*, p. 67.

3 TRADITIONAL WARFIGHTING CONCEPTS AND PRACTICES

1 Clausewitz, *On War*, p. 342.
2 Michael Howard, *The Franco–Prussian War* (London: Routledge, 2001), p. x.
3 Richard Overy, *The Battle* (London: Penguin Books, 2001).
4 Thucydides, *The Peloponnesian War*, pp. 400–8.
5 Haywood S. Hansell, Jr, *The Air Plan that Defeated Hitler* (New York: Arno Press, 1980); *The Strategic Air War Against Germany, 1939–1945: Report of the British Bombing Survey Unit* (London: Frank Cass, 1998).
6 Brodie, *Strategy in the Missile Age*, p. 73.
7 Thomas C. Schelling, *Arms and Influence* (New Haven: Yale University Press, 1966), p. 3.
8 See Robert S. McNamara, *In Retrospect* (New York: Random House, 1995, p. 32); Neil Sheehan, *A Bright Shining Lie* (London: Jonathan Cape, 1989); Stanley Karnow, *Vietnam* (New York: Penguin, 1991); and David Halberstam, *The Best and the Brightest* (New York: Ballantine Books, 1993).
9 Robert L. Scales, 'Checkmate by Operational Maneuver', in *Armed Forces Journal International* (October 2001).
10 Sun Tzu, *The Art of War*, pp. 77, 84.
11 George H. Quester, *Deterrence Before Hiroshima* (New Brunswick: Transaction Books, 1986).
12 Clausewitz, *On War*, p. 389.
13 William S. Lind, *Maneuver Warfare Handbook* (Boulder: Westview Press, 1985), pp. 17–18.
14 B. H. Liddell Hart, *History of the Second World War* (London: Pan Books, 1973), p. 636.

4 MANOEUVRE AND THE APPLICATION OF FORCE

1 Liddell Hart, *Strategy*, esp. pp. 39–42, and chapter 10.
2 Arrian, *Annabasis Alexandri* Vol. 1, pp. 57–67; Plutarch, *The Age of Alexander*, pp. 268–9.
3 Quoted in Douglas Southall Freeman, *Lee* (New York: Touchstone Books, 1997), p. 423.
4 Shelby Foote, *The Civil War: A Narrative, Fredericksburg to Meridian*, Volume II (New York: Vintage Books, 1986), p. 963.
5 Douhet, *The Command of the Air*.
6 Clausewitz, *On War*, pp. 113–14, 130–4.
7 See Joan V. Bondurant, *Conquest of Violence: The Gandhian Philosophy of Conflict* (Berkeley and Los Angeles: University of California Press, 1965), esp. pp. 8, 11–12, 17, 19.

5 SHAPING THE STRATEGIC ENVIRONMENT

1 George Kennan ('X'), 'The Sources of Soviet Conflict', in *Foreign Affairs* (July 1947).
2 Joseph S. Nye, Jr, *Soft Power: The Means to Success in World Politics* (New York: Public Affairs, 2004), pp. 33–4.

3   Paul Lashmar, *Spy Flights of the Cold War* (Phoenix Mill: Sutton Publishing, 1996), pp. 211–18.

6   STRATEGIC PARALYSIS

1   John A. Warden III, *The Air Campaign* (Washington: Brassey's, 1989). Warden elaborated on the ideas presented in this book in a number of journal articles.
2   Boyd never published a substantive work on strategy. His thinking was formalised in several large slide shows, built up over years, and which could take two or more days to present. The most important of these was the presentation 'Discourse on Winning and Losing'. For more on Boyd, see http://www.d-n-i.net/second˙level/boyd˙military.htm.
3   Gary L. Crowder, 'Targeting for Effects' in *Jointness*, Proceedings of the 11th International Air Strategy Symposium (Daejeon: Republic of Korea Air Force, 2005), pp. 195–219.
4   J. F. C. Fuller, *The Conduct of War 1789–1961* (London: Methuen & Co., 1977).

7   CONTEMPLATING WAR

1   'War and Peace in the 21st Century', in *Human Security Report 2005* (Vancouver: The University of British Columbia, 2005), pp. 1–2.
2   David M. Edelstein, 'Occupational Hazards: Why Military Occupations Succeed or Fail', *International Security*, 29:1, Summer 2004.
3   Clausewitz, *On War*, p. 101.
4   Ibid., p. 367.
5   Richard Betts, 'The Trouble with Strategy: Bridging Policy and Operations', *Joint Forces Quarterly*, Autumn/Winter, 2001.
6   Colin S. Gray, *Modern Strategy* (Oxford: Oxford University Press, 1999).
7   Eliot A. Cohen, 'The Mystique of US Air Power', *Foreign Affairs*, January/February 1994.
8   Martin Shaw, *The New Western Way of War: Risk-Transfer War and its Crisis in Iraq* (Cambridge: Polity Press, 2005).
9   This account of the process of strategy formulation for Operation Enduring Freedom in Afghanistan is drawn from Bob Woodward, *Bush at War*, Simon & Schuster, New York, 2002.

8   CONSTRAINTS ON WAR

1   Thucydides, *The Peloponnesian War*, p. 402.
2   Roger Boesche, 'Kautilya's *Arthasastra* on War and Diplomacy in Ancient India', *Journal of Military History*, January 2003.
3   Surya P. Subedi, 'The Concept in Hinduism of Just War', *Journal of Conflict & Security Law*, 8:2, 2003.
4   Yoram Dinstein, *War, Aggression and Self-Defence* (Cambridge: Cambridge University Press, 2001).
5   Robert A. Pape, 'Soft Balancing Against the United States', *International Security*, 30:1, 2005.

6   T. V. Paul, 'Nuclear Taboo and War Initiation in Regional Conflicts', *Journal of Conflict Resolution*, 39:4, December 1995.

7   Michael Howard (ed.), *Restraints on War: Studies in the Limitation of Armed Conflict* (Oxford: Oxford University Press, 1979) p. 12.

9   CONTROLLING WAR

1   Rupert Smith, *The Utility of Force*.

2   Lawrence Freedman, 'Calling the Shots: Should Politicians or Generals Run Our Wars?', *Foreign Affairs*, September/October 2002.

3   Gordon A. Craig, *The Politics of the Prussian Army: 1640–1945* (Oxford: Oxford University Press, 1955), pp. 199–200.

4   Eliot A. Cohen, *Supreme Command* (New York: The Free Press, 2002).

5   Colin Powell, 'US Forces: The Challenges Ahead', *Foreign Affairs*, Winter 1992.

6   Andrew F. Krepinevich, 'How to Win in Iraq', *Foreign Affairs*, September/October 2005.

10   PEACEMAKING

1   Rupert Smith, *The Utility of Force*.

2   Rupert Smith, *The Utility of Force*.

11   WAR IN THE TWENTY-FIRST CENTURY

1   Colin S. Gray, 'How has War Changed Since the End of the Cold War?', *Parameters: US Army War College Quarterly*, Spring 2005.

2   Philip Bobbitt, *The Shield of Achilles: War, Peace, and the Course of History* (New York: Anchor Books, 2003).

3   Robert Cooper, *The Breaking of Nations: Order and Chaos in the Twenty-First Century* (London: Atlantic Press, 1989).

4   Bryan Ranft, 'Restraints on War at Sea before 1945', in Michael Howard (ed.), *Restraints on War* (Oxford: Oxford University Press, 1979).

5   Rupert Smith, *The Utility of Force*.

Select bibliography

BOOKS

Arrian, *Annabasis Alexandri* (trans. P. A. Brunt) (2 Volumes) (Cambridge: Harvard University Press, 1989)

Bellamy, Alex J., Paul Williams and Stuart Griffin, *Understanding Peacekeeping* (Cambridge: Polity Press, 2004)

Bobbitt, Philip, *The Shield of Achilles: War, Peace and the Course of History* (New York: Anchor Books, 2003)

Bondurant, Joan V., *Conquest of Violence: The Gandhian Philosophy of Conflict* (Berkeley and Los Angeles: University of California Press, 1965)

Brodie, Bernard, *Strategy in the Missile Age* (Princeton: Princeton University Press, 1991)

Byman, Daniel and Matthew Waxman, *The Dynamics of Coercion: American Foreign Policy and the Limits of Military Might* (New York: Cambridge University Press, 2002)

Chang, Jung and John Halliday, *Mao: The Unknown Story* (London: Jonathan Cape, 2005)

Clark, Wesley, *Waging Modern War: Bosnia, Kosovo and the Future of Combat* (New York: Public Affairs, 2002)

Clausewitz, Carl von, *On War* (Harmondsworth: Penguin Books, 1982)

Cohen, Eliot A., *Supreme Command: Soldiers, Statesmen, and Leadership in Wartime* (New York: The Free Press, 2002)

Douhet, Giulio, *The Command of the Air* (trans. Dino Ferrari) (Washington DC: Office of Air Force History, 1983)

Foote, Shelby, *The Civil War* (3 Volumes) (New York: Vintage Books, 1986)

Freeman, Douglas Southall, *Lee* (abridged by Richard Harwell) (New York: Touchstone Books, 1997)

Fuller, J. F. C., *Armament & History* (New York: Da Capo Press, 1998)

Fuller, J. F. C., *The Conduct of War 1789–1961* (London: Methuen, 1977)

Garthoff, Raymond L., *Soviet Military Doctrine* (Glencoe: The Free Press, 1953)

Halberstam, David, *War in a Time of Peace: Bush, Clinton, and the Generals* (New York: Simon & Schuster, 2002)

Howard, Michael (ed.), *Restraints on War* (Oxford: Oxford University Press, 1979)

Howard, Michael, *The Franco–Prussian War* (London: Routledge, 2001)

Howard, Michael, *The Invention of Peace and the Reinvention of War* (London: Profile Books, 2002)

Howard, Michael, *War in European History* (Oxford: Oxford University Press, 2001)

Huntington, Samuel P., 'The Clash of Civilisations?', in *America and the World: Debating the New Shape of International Politics* (New York: A Council on Foreign Relations Book, 2002)

Jomini, Antoine-Henri de, *The Art of War* (London: Greenhill Books, 1996)

Liddell Hart, B. H., *Strategy: The Indirect Approach* (New York: Frederick A. Praeger, 1954)

Lind, William S., *Maneuver Warfare Handbook* (Boulder: Westview Press, 1985)

Luttwak, Edward N., *Strategy: The Logic of War and Peace* (Cambridge: The Belknap Press, 2001)

Machiavelli, Niccolo, *The Prince* (trans. Daniel Donno) (New York: Bantam Classic, 2003)

Mahan, A. T., *The Influence of Sea Power Upon History* (Boston: Little, Brown, & Company, 1898)

Montefiore, Simon Sebag, *Stalin: The Court of the Red Tsar* (London: Phoenix, 2004)

Mueller, John E., *The Remnants of War* (Ithaca: Cornell University Press, 2004)

Nasution, Abdul Haris, *Fundamentals of Guerilla Warfare* (Djakarta: Indonesian Army Information Service, 1953)

Nye, Joseph S., Jr, *Soft Power: The Means to Success in World Politics* (New York: Public Affairs, 2004)

Paret, Peter (ed.), *Makers of Modern Strategy* (Princeton: Princeton University Press, 1986)

Prior, Robin and Trevor Wilson, *The First World War* (Washington: Smithsonian Books, 2005)

Quester, George H., *Deterrence Before Hiroshima* (New Brunswick: Transaction Books, 1986)

Record, Jeffrey, *Dark Victory: America's Second War against Iraq* (Annapolis: Naval Institute Press, 2004)

Schelling, Thomas C., *Arms and Influence* (New Haven: Yale University Press, 1966)

Shaw, Martin, *The New Western Way of War: Risk-Transfer War and its Crisis in Iraq* (Cambridge: Polity Press, 2005)

Smith, Hugh (ed.), *The Strategists* (Canberra: Australian Defence Studies Centre, 2001)

Smith, Rupert, *The Utility of Force* (London: Allen Lane, 2005)

Sun Tzu, *The Art of War* (trans. Samuel B. Griffith) (Oxford: The Clarendon Press, 1963)

Thucydides, *The Peloponnesian War* (trans. Rex Warner) (Harmondsworth: Penguin Books, 1975)

Väyrynen, Raimo (ed.), *The Waning of Major War* (London: Routledge, 2006)

Warden, John A. III, *The Air Campaign* (Washington: Brassey's, 1989)

Woodward, Bob, *Bush at War* (New York: Simon & Schuster, 2002)

ARTICLES

Gray, Colin S., 'How has War Changed Since the End of the Cold War?', in *Parameters*, (Spring, 2005)

'War and Peace in the 21st Century', in *Human Security Report 2005* (Vancouver: The University of British Columbia, 2005)

Zartman, William, 'The Timing of Peace Initiatives: Hurting Stalemates and Ripe Moments', in *The Global Review of Ethnopolitics* (Vol. 1, No. 1, September 2001)

Index

Cuba
  guerilla tactics in 24
  missile crisis 113, 211
  regime change in 90
culminating point of victory 223
cultural imperialism 111, 268
culture, need to understand 141, 151
Cyprus, UN intervention 240

Darius, defeat by Alexander 39
data links 157
'decapitation', see assassination strategy
decentralisation 131
deception 30, 31, 74
decisive engagements 36
deep battle doctrine 42
defence strategies 80–7, 178
delivery systems, nuclear weapons 63
democracies, see heads of state; liberal
  democracies
Democratic Republic of the Congo, see
  Congo
Desert Storm, see Operation Desert Storm
desertion, mixed results of 192
determinism 20–2, 47
deterrence
  as Cold War strategy 11
  coercive use of 36
  force structuring for 124
  reliance on rationality 261–3
  risk and 57–64
  strategic effect 6
  with nuclear weapons 22, 211, 259
  within conflict 64
dictators 180, 192, see also heads of state
Dien Bien Phu 83
diplomacy 101, 130
discontinuities, search for 87–94
discriminate targeting 185
dispersed battlefields 55
doctrinal development 261
domestic support, see homefront support
  for war
Douhet, Giulio 20–2, 86
dual-use infrastructure targeting 185, 235

East Germany, see Germany (1945–)
East Timor
  deterrence of Indonesian opposition 6
  independence movement 191, 249
  intervention in 6, 155, 250
  uncertainty about Indonesian reaction 155
Eastern Europe
  East German weapons stockpiles 131
  post-Soviet collapse 241
  Soviet occupation of 169
EBP 147, 148–55, 156

ECOMOG 253
Economic Community of West African States
  253
economic issues, sphere of influence and 110
effects-based planning 147, 148–55, 156
effects of war 166
Egypt, Six Day War 121, 204
Eisenhower, Dwight D 62–4, 117
El Salvador, UN involvement 241
élite units 91
embedding of journalists 184
emotional prejudices 129
end-date exit strategy 225
ends, ways and means 8–13
  centres of gravity and 67
  effects-based planning 156
enemy, morale of 192
enforcement of peace 252–5
Enola Gay 98
Entebbe raid 264
epochal war 267
espionage, see intelligence gathering
ethical issues 98–100, 198, 206
ethnic cleansing 231, 242, see also genocide
euphemisms, for nuclear attacks 23
Europe, see also Balkans; Eastern Europe;
  Operation Overlord
  as post-modern state 268
  economic overtures to Iran 110
  European Economic Community 105
  focus on land warfare 89
  legality of war in 200, 209
  limited wars in 171
  Marshall Plan 105
evolution of strategic paralysis 145–8
exit strategies, Somalian crisis 225
experts 187
exultation of the offensive 28

F-15C fighters 71
F-86 Sabre 143
failed states 190, 243, 256, see also Afghanistan;
  Somalia
Falklands War 35
  as limited war 172
  intelligence gathering 118
  media coverage 183
firepower, see also force
  and manoeuvre 15
  application of 16
  decisive 69, 70
  in WW1 75
flanking campaigns 42, 51
  prior to WW1 55
  US flies B-29s to Britain 72, 73
fleet-in-being 20
flexible response, with nuclear weapons 22

Printed in Great Britain
by Amazon